Introduction to Radio~

Production and Programming

Introduction to Radio~

Production and Programming

MICHAEL H. ADAMS

San Jose State University

KIMBERLY K. MASSEY, Ph.D.

San Jose State University

WCB Brown & Benchmark
PUBLISHERS

Madison, Wisconsin • Dubuque, Iowa

Book Team

Executive Editor *Stan Stoga*
Developmental Editor *Mary E. Rossa*
Production Editor *Jayne Klein*
Photo Editor *Shirley M. Lanners*
Visuals/Design Developmental Consultant *Marilyn A. Phelps*
Visuals/Design Freelance Specialist *Mary L. Christianson*
Marketing Manager *Pamela S. Cooper*
Advertising Coordinator *Susan J. Butler*

Brown & Benchmark

A Division of Wm. C. Brown Communications, Inc.

Executive Vice President/General Manager *Thomas E. Doran*
Vice President/Editor in Chief *Edgar J. Laube*
Vice President of Marketing and Sales Systems *Eric Ziegler*
Director of Production *Vickie Putman Caughron*
Director of Custom and Electronic Publishing *Chris Rogers*

Wm. C. Brown Communications, Inc.

President and Chief Executive Officer *G. Franklin Lewis*
Corporate Senior Vice President and Chief Financial Officer *Robert Chesterman*
Corporate Senior Vice President and President of Manufacturing *Roger Meyer*

Cover and interior designs by Tara Bazata

Cover photo courtesy of Michael Adams

Copyedited by Marilyn Frey

A Times Mirror Company

Library of Congress Catalog Card Number: 93–79350

ISBN 0–697–15354–1

Printed in the United States of America by Wm. C. Brown Communications, Inc., 2460 Kerper Boulevard, Dubuque, IA 52001

10 9 8 7 6 5 4 3 2 1

CONTENTS

S E C T I O N   T H R E E

The Techniques of Production

▼

S E C T I O N   F O U R

Turning Radio Programming into Production

PREFACE

▼

We have written *Introduction to Radio: Production and Programming* for several reasons. First and most important, we want you to look beyond the *how* of the technology of radio production, beyond the process of creating a short announcement or half hour program or news story, and to understand the *why* of production. We want you to know how programming decisions have a direct effect on the production performed in a radio studio. We believe that this approach makes the study and practice of production more meaningful, more real. We have worked in commercial and educational radio for many years, and we have observed its people and its programming. We have used our experiences to write this book.

As a production text, most of what follows is certainly about the basics of audio production for radio: what is sound and what is audio; how to identify, select, and operate production studio and on-air control room equipment; how to prepare and organize for a production. We have included chapters on how to produce a short news story; how to produce a radio documentary; how to make commercials, public service, and promotional announcements; how to be a disc jockey/air personality; how to work with comedy and drama. Integrated into each presentation of a production technique is an explanation of why a station's particular music or information format, or the needs of an advertiser or community organization has led to the production that you will be expected to do at that station. In many instances, we have put a current programming genre or production technology and process into both a historical context and a future prediction. We have given radio production and programming a past and a future. We want you to know the *why*, as well as the *how*.

We have seen rapid and recent changes in the technology and business of radio. It's amazing to see how students seem to immediately understand the computers used in modern radio production. Perhaps it's the result of a generation of playing video games and doing homework assignments on word processors, but whenever a computer replaces a manual way of performing a radio production task, students embrace, understand, and always prefer the computer method. It's happening faster than anyone ever realized. The economic structure and the audiences of the American system of broadcasting have also changed. New program formats and new delivery systems will ultimately influence the content of what is produced for the new listener with new expectations from radio.

Finally, we want to give you a sense of feeling for what it is like to be a part of the creative side of radio. Whenever possible, we have placed you inside the radio station, in programming meetings, meetings with sponsors, on the air as a disc jockey, even at city hall for a news interview. We'll show you how to survey the jobs in radio and how to put together an audition tape and resumé. We want to help you know the people who work at the radio station, what they do and why. And because we want you to look realistically at the possibility of a future career in radio, we have tried to present it as honestly as possible.

We have also looked at college and university programs in radio and television and found that while most students are in television they will take at least one course in radio. We want mass communications and journalism students to see the similarities between radio and television technology, programming, and production. We want television production students to understand audio production for radio. We want radio students to get a good background before going on to a radio internship or entry-level job. Call it the big picture. If electronic communications using the various delivery systems—radio, television, cable, and satellite—has such a profound influence on our lives, then shouldn't we put its production processes in as real a context as possible? We have tried to add content to the abstract technology of radio. We want to give radio production a sense of purpose, a home, a face, a name, a history, and a hope for the future. It is because of our belief in the importance of presenting the activities of radio production in the context of how the radio station works that we have written this book. We hope that we can help you to understand all of radio better.

Acknowledgments

Thank you, thank you, thank you. Many radio stations and their professionals and manufacturers of broadcast and production technology have contributed to what we believe is a realistic and up-to-date book. For the historical photos, thanks to Gene D'Angelo of WBNS in Columbus, Ohio, and the Perham Foundation Electronics Museum in the Bay Area. We were able to photograph the activities of San Francisco broadcasters KCBS, KRQR, KGO, KSFO, and KYA, and for that we thank lifelong broadcasters and old friends, Jerry and Phyllis Gordon, for introducing us to the folk at those stations. In San Jose, Kelly and Kline at KHQT let us sit in on their morning show, and Michael Zwerling and Larry Johnson welcomed us at KSCO in Santa Cruz. Manufacturers' photos were provided by Della Northcutt of Computer Concepts, Mary Stevens of AKG, Michael R. Dosch of Pacific Recorders, Robert Easton of 360 Concepts, Davida Rochman of Shure, N. Tokutake of Denon, and Orville Green of Eventide.

At San Jose State University, we thank the many students, faculty, and staff who contributed to the production of this book. Our award-winning college radio station, KSJS-FM, provided the background for many of the production and on-air photos used to illustrate this text. Thanks to station manager, Pol VanRhee, and program director, Jeannine Parshall, and the hundreds of students who contribute to the 24-hour-a-day operation of what has become one of the most respected student-operated radio stations in America. Working as faculty advisors to KSJS-FM has provided us with knowledge, insight, and experience in radio at the university level. Each day we see programming ideas become production reality. Thanks also to radio-television facilities coordinator, Jim LeFever, for always being there with the right piece of equipment and for demonstrating it for our students and our cameras. We would also like our computer guru, Don Perrin, to know how much we appreciate his generosity of hardware, software, and advice. And thanks to lifelong radio enthusiast, Terry Hackney, for taking all the photographs used in this book. Terry remembers that first day many years ago when he sat behind the microphone of college radio station WOUB at Ohio University. He'll never forget it; it has influenced his life as well as ours.

At Brown & Benchmark Publishers in Dubuque, Iowa, and Madison, Wisconsin, we thank editors Stan Stoga and Mary Rossa for their enduring patience. We thank Marilyn Frey, copyeditor, Jayne Klein, production editor, and our reviewers: James Cathey, Arkansas State University; Cynthia Lont, George Mason University; Linda Rhodes, California State University, Sacramento; David Sedman, University of Arkansas, Little Rock; Andrew Skitko, Jr., Kutztown University; and James Sneegas, Southwest Missouri State University.

Most of all, we thank those who know us best, who live with us, who support and help us, who love us. We dedicate our work to our families.

Michael H. Adams
Kimberly K. Massey

The Excitement of Radio

Picture this: You are in your car driving east on Interstate 70, a few miles from the Ohio border. You've been at it for ten to twelve hours a day for the past four days. Drive, stop, eat, drive, stop, sleep, drive again. And worse, it has been raining for the past three days. Both your sanity and your windshield wipers are beginning to fail. Still, you remain alert, almost at attention. A dozen different ideas have been churning around in your mind during this lonely drive to nowhere: How much longer will this old car really last? Will I ever find West Virginia? Will I like it there, will they like me? Mostly, though, you've been thinking about radio. Real radio. Not the college station where everyone played the music they liked and said what they wanted to say, but a real radio station where you get paid to be on the air. Unlike the college station where your audience was in the hundreds, you could be listened to by thousands in West Virginia. Unlike the college station where you were on the air for only four hours a week, you are heading for an eight-hours-a-day, six-days-a-week, full-time paying job in broadcasting. A career in radio production.

Back to reality. Comfortably inside Ohio, you reach for the map to reinforce the directions given you on the phone by the person who hired you. About two hundred more miles to West Virginia, then south on US 250 from Wheeling, and follow the signs to Moundsville. You laugh out loud, and in your best announcer voice you say, "WMVA in Moundsville, the gateway to West Virginia." Soon you'll make the complete transformation from full-time college student to full-time working stiff. You are looking forward to the experience, but your emotions are mixed. The nervousness you feel is not unlike that first day you sat behind a microphone. As a person growing up and going to college in California, you somehow believed that you would get a job at a big station and be a star. Maybe not Los Angeles or San Francisco, but at least

Fresno. You were going to the best school, and you were a shining star in local college radio.

So why, you ask yourself, are you less than two hours from Moundsville, West Virginia? The answer, of course, is opportunity, and you know it. Faced with graduation, you carefully assembled the best pieces of your radio tapes and, along with a letter of introduction, sent copies to fifty stations. Music programming experience? Some. News? You did minor in journalism. Sports? This is how you got the job and why you are only a few hours from West Virginia. And even though your forte in college broadcasting was football and basketball play-by-play, and even though you were probably hired because of your sports experience, those high school games will only be a part of your first job in radio. You already know that at WMVA, you will be a combination DJ/news/production/writer/sportscaster. You don't know it yet, but you'll probably answer the phones and sweep out the studio. You'll do it all. You'll love it!

That first job in radio production. Truly there is no excitement like that found at a small, local radio station. It is the small station in the proverbial southern or midwestern small town that will hire the fresh-out-of-college broadcaster, so this is where a broadcasting career often begins. Of the many thousands of radio stations found in all fifty states, most are in small towns and many will welcome a talented, motivated graduate right out of school. The best reason for pursuing a job at a small station is that it allows you to see the big picture. By performing all the production and on-air jobs, you will begin to know what you like and don't like, what you are good at and what you are not. You'll learn fast in an atmosphere without ratings and the pressures of competition. Most importantly, many of your co-workers there will be just like you, so you'll find out quickly about new challenges at larger stations.

▲

Introducing Radio Programming and Production

There are more than 12,000 licensed radio stations in the United States today, most operated as profit-making businesses. The rest are nonprofit public and community stations or teaching labs. At each station are a few, to several dozen, to several hundred, people engaged in a variety of administrative, technical, and creative tasks. All of these people have one goal in common: to present to an audience a product using the processes and equipment of audio production, a product usually defined as either a continuous offering of music, news, and talk, or a collection of longer programs. Whether the manager or a disc jockey, one who writes commercials or news, one who sells time to advertisers, or one who repairs and installs equipment, every person in the radio station is there to support the programming of the station in some way. Support of a station's product, its programming, is the specific purpose of production. As a student of radio, your first job in a small local station probably will be mostly in production.

PRODUCTION TASKS AND CHALLENGES

As a radio production professional, you'll probably spend much of your work day engaged in real-time, continuous production as an on-air disc jockey or air personality. An air shift of from four to six hours daily, six days a week, is not uncommon. It is here that you'll soon find out whether you are cut out for the highly repetitive world of radio. More importantly, you'll meet other radio production people in various stages of their radio careers. From them you'll learn about on-air styles, production techniques, and other jobs at other stations. If you remain interested, you'll make tapes and begin to listen carefully for an emerging style. As an on-air disc jockey, you'll be in a public position, communicating to an unseen audience. Many in that audience will perceive you as a friend, a trusted member of the community.

Communication using radio.

The job of the live DJ is the most publicly visible in radio production, but there is another part of the production process that is potentially more important and usually more creative. In a room called the production studio, you'll be expected to create, write, read, record, and prepare for air many of the commercials and other short announcements used during the broadcast day. This other part of the production process is often a daily responsibility, one performed before or after the air shift is complete. This production will be assigned and supervised by programming and promotions people, salespeople, and advertisers. For this part of the production process, you'll get to shift gears and slow down a bit. Instead of the constant attention required in the service of an on-air format, there will be time to try out new techniques, write scripts, and experiment with music and announcer delivery styles. It is here that most of the creativity in radio production can be realized.

RADIO PROGRAMMING INFLUENCES RADIO PRODUCTION

The programming done by a radio station—its type of music, the style of the announcing—is the factor that most influences, even dictates, the type of production done at the station. The kind of music that will be used as background for a commercial announcement, the speed at which the copy is read, and the kinds of sound effects that may or may not be used will mostly be tied directly to the overall station sound, based on a programming philosophy called a format, and all planned in advance and supervised by the program director and general manager of the radio station. That is why this book is going to place the technical and creative tasks of audio production for radio into a programming context whenever possible. There is a reason behind the sound of every radio production.

THE GREATER PICTURE

This book is designed for the student who will elect a single radio production class, the student who may now be interested primarily in television production but wants or needs to know about radio production. There are more similarities than differences between radio and television. The audio portion of television is like radio, and it uses much of the same equipment. Both aim at serving a mass audience for profit. Both require the production person to follow a similar process of preplanning, producing, and editing. Both often use a similar cast of talent and technical people: actors, directors, writers, producers, engineers, and editors. Both require a sense of timing and a desire to creatively entertain or inform the listener and viewer. And while most of the equipment is certainly different, any production experience, audio ·or video, will add to the general communications experience. Plus, any skills you learn in audio are guaranteed to make your next television project *sound* better.

During your professional lifetime, you may work in a dozen different production venues, both radio and television. You may also use your production experience for a totally nonmedia career, law or business for example. There are dozens of successful attorneys who owe part of their skill at speaking before judge and jury to their on-air experience in radio. So whether you see radio production as a career in itself, as an adjunct to a career in television, or as just an interesting piece of the liberal arts puzzle, you will see radio in a new perspective after reading this book. You will be a better consumer of radio, and you will begin to see it from an industry standpoint.

Another real advantage of most of what is defined as audio production for radio is its low cost. You could go into any one of thousands of radio production studios and produce a very competent-sounding commercial for no real expense on personnel, music, or special equipment. Using audio only, you can experiment with script writing, different voice styles, drama, comedy, informational, all without paying for a camera crew and equipment, lighting people, and the typically larger number of people needed for a similar effort for video. An idea that you, as a student, have for a creative project that is not possible using video or film, because of the high cost of equipment and people, may be adapted and done very inexpensively for radio. And since it is more likely that a college or university will have a radio station than a television outlet, your audio production could be heard by thousands, while your video project may never be viewed outside of the classroom. You can learn a lot from radio production, and your production can be heard by an actual audience.

HOW TO USE THIS BOOK

This book is organized into sections designed to lead you from equipment to production techniques, and from production techniques to programming applications. The order of chapters within these sections is planned so that once the basic terminology and equipment for radio have been learned, several different levels of productions can be attempted. Once there is a familiarity with where and how production is done, the practical application of programming will make sense. You won't do production in a vacuum; you'll be encouraged to learn a bit of the history of a particular radio programming idea or production technique. You'll be given much of the background needed to generate ideas and turn them into radio production, all in the service of programming. You'll be placed inside the thought process used in the radio station to turn radio programming into radio production. *Introduction to Radio: Production and Programming* is about audio production as performed at the radio station.

The chapters in Section Two introduce the basics of sound. Learn how you hear and why, then how to define what you hear, and finally how that knowledge applies to audio production. Both the physical characteristics and the terminology of sound are presented as an important part of the necessary background of audio; it is here that the basics of sound are related to audio production. Next in this section, the audio chain as it is used in the radio station is introduced. Soon you'll understand which devices pick up and produce audio, like microphones and compact disc players; which devices route and change the shape of that audio, like mixing consoles; and what types of equipment are used to edit and store it for later broadcast. Individual pieces of audio equipment will always be shown in the context of the complete audio signal path; for example, what happens between the time a person speaks into a microphone in a radio station and it finally is heard by a radio listener. Each piece of equipment is organized into logical categories, along with an explanation of how it works. First sound, then audio equipment.

Finally in this section, those individual tools that are the technology of radio production will be put together and presented as complete production systems. It is here that you will see the studio and control room as those working in radio see them every day, as functioning facilities dedicated to the production that supports the programming of the station. You will learn the differences between a control room designed for live, continuous on-air broadcasting and the studio used for the preparation of announcements and programs to be broadcast later. These studios and control rooms will be shown as actual facilities in real radio stations. Finally, you will learn how to select equipment that is most appropriately used for on-air playback or that is better suited for recording and editing.

Section Three is about actual, usable production techniques. In the beginning you will learn how to approach and organize a production project. A process will guide you step by step as you consider script, treatment, selection of music and sound effects, what people to involve, and how to select each. Next you will enter a simple studio in preparation for actual production and will be presented with a simple assignment designed primarily to familiarize you with the location and operation of basic equipment as a production system. This requires you to undertake the introductory tasks of production: selecting and preparing music, identifying playback and recording equipment and supplies, setting correct volume levels for each device, and then, one step at a time, assembling a simple project.

Next you'll be ready for the more advanced production activities, those techniques used to complete more complex projects. You will learn how to plan for and produce a project with a production group, one that may require more than one

You may learn how to edit using a computer.

voice, special music, and special facilities and equipment. Presented here are techniques used by professionals, like multitrack recording and the planning and recording of original music and sound effects. Unlike the basic project described in the previous chapter, the advanced project will need to be done by a small group where each person has specific tasks as part of a final product. To complete this section, you'll see how to edit projects both by physically cutting and splicing tape and with the use of a computer-controlled digital audio workstation.

Section Four, turning radio programming into production, is about the practical application of production in the direct service of radio programming. This section is going to make the tools and techniques of radio production seem more real. The chapters in this section tie together what you've learned about production technology and processes with how to use it to support the kinds of programming decisions that a station must make. First, the radio station itself. Learn about the programming role of radio today: how and why a station selects a particular type of programming or format and how it decides whether that programming choice is effective. Find out which people at the station level are engaged in production. Once you understand the role the radio station plays as a programmer, you'll be introduced to the creative process that results in production there. You'll learn how to create commercials and public service announcements, how to produce news and documentaries, how to use drama and comedy, and how the on-air disc jockey uses continuous production in the service of the format.

Finally, there is a look ahead at what to expect in the future of radio business, programming, and technology. Will production equipment become more computerized, and will the conventional tape recorders and CD players used in radio slowly become obsolete, replaced by the next big thing? What about the way a station selects its music, determines its programming? How will delivery systems change? Someday, the term broadcasting may mean much more than just a person in a studio with a transmitter and antenna on a hill or tall building. But no matter what equipment is used, no matter what the delivery system, some things will never change. Audiences will still want information and entertainment, and someone will have to produce and present them. That person may be you. Read on. You have an exciting challenge ahead.

The Technology and Tools of Production

The initial step in solving problems, performing tasks, or beginning new projects is to first become familiar with the tasks and tools needed to create a product—in our case, the production. This section will take that first step toward learning creative radio production by describing the physics of sound and the process of hearing, as well as the basic principles of sound design.

In audio production, the route that sounds take from their source to their destination and any manipulation (processing) along the way, is known as the **sound chain.** Of course, the sound chain always depends on the medium, the equipment being used and the audio being produced.

In a sound studio, audio signals also follow a prescribed path called the **signal flow.** In order to efficiently organize an audio project, you must be aware of the sound chain and become familiar with the signal flow within the studio and individual components. This section provides an introduction to the lexicon—equipment and facilities that are used in audio production.

▲

2 ▼

Understanding Sound and Audio

Whether you realize it or not, you already have a working knowledge of sound. For example, you know that the sound of a person shouting seems much louder and tends to echo much more in a gymnasium than it does outside after a freshly fallen snow. You have probably noticed how the flash of lightning and its accompanying thunderclap don't seem to happen at the same time. Even as you read this page, you can cup your hand behind your ear and target specific directions to change your perception of the sounds in the environment. What you probably don't know are the words to describe these various characteristics of sound.

UNDERSTANDING SOUND

Sound consists of waves that travel out from a source, similar to the waves created when you drop a pebble into a smooth pool of water. But instead of water being the medium, the sound waves that are perceived by your ears travel through the medium of air.

How and Why Do You Hear?

Sound waves are created when a moving source vibrates the air next to it. When you speak, your vocal cords vibrate the air in your throat, creating a wave that, in turn, vibrates the air next to it, and so on until it reaches the air in the listener's ear. The sound waves consist of changes in air pressure. The ear detects these variations in pressure and translates them into pitch and volume. The eardrum vibrates the tiny bones inside the middle ear called the hammer, anvil, and stirrup. These bones transfer the vibrations to the inner ear, where a group of tiny nerve sensors reacts to the vibrations and sends electrochemical signals along the auditory nerve to the brain for identification. Characteristics of the waves allow the brain to identify the sound and determine the direction of its source. Assuming a static head position, one ear cannot determine direction but two ears can. This is called the **binaural effect.**

If you have been around extremely loud sounds, you have probably become aware of air pressure movement. If you listen to a car stereo with the volume up high or if you stand next to a car playing loud music, you can actually feel the *boom* vibration of the bass as it moves the air around you. This is an example of changing air pressure.

Audio begins with a basic understanding of the characteristics of waves because it is waves that are electronically created, recorded, reproduced, transmitted, and amplified during the production process. Before you can manipulate waves, you must understand how they work. The first step is identifying types of waves such as sound waves and electromagnetic waves, which includes light waves.

Sound waves travel at a constant speed of approximately 344 meters, or 1,130 feet, per second in air at 70 degrees Fahrenheit. Temperature is a factor in sound speed because the barometric pressure of air changes with temperature. You will recall that sound is caused by a vibration and that sound waves travel through the medium of air (sound cannot travel in a vacuum); therefore, air pressure affects the speed of sound, although only slightly.

Unlike sound waves, light waves and electromagnetic waves travel through the atmosphere and, therefore, do not need air as a medium. The speed of electromagnetic waves is referred to as the speed of light or 186,000 *miles* per second—much faster than sound, which explains why you *see* lightning before you *hear* thunder.

Defining What You Hear. What's in a Wave?

Whether sound or radio, all waves function basically the same way. A wave begins at a zero point, moves up to a positive peak, then back down through the zero point to a negative peak, returning upward to zero to begin the process again. One complete wave is called a **cycle.** A cycle can actually begin at any point on the wave but must pass through the zero line and end at the beginning point while moving in the same direction.

One complete vibration cycle/wave. The number of cycles that a vibration completes in one second (ab) is called its frequency. *The height or breadth of a sound wave (cd) is called its* amplitude.

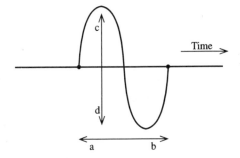

The size of the wave is called its amplitude. *Since wave A has a higher amplitude, it will seem louder than wave B, which has a lower amplitude.*

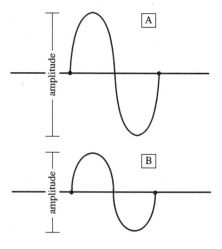

Every sound wave has specific characteristics that make it unique or different from other sound waves. Become familiar with the characteristics of waves in order to better understand how sound works.

Amplitude and Loudness

One important concept describes a wave's peak above or below the zero line. This peak is called the wave's **amplitude** and determines the sound's strength. We physically interpret amplitude as the loudness or softness of a sound. The greater the amplitude of a sound wave, the louder the sound.

If you've ever stood too close to a speaker or had someone shout very close to your ear, you know from that somewhat painful experience that there is only so much sound your ears can take before distortion or even hearing loss, known as sensory neural damage, occurs. At the same time, if a sound is too weak, your ear will not be able to hear the sound accurately. The ear has an incredible ability to hear wide variations in loudness, yet everyone's ears hear differently. Loudness or signal strength is measured in **decibels (dB).** The decibel scale corresponds to a logarithmic law that relates sound intensity (sound pressure levels, or SPLs) to the sensation of loudness.

The **threshold of hearing** for most people is placed at 0 dB. The area in which the SPL will cause discomfort is called the **threshold of feeling,** about 118 dB. Finally, the **threshold of pain** is near 140 dB. When dB increases by 10, humans perceive sound as being approximately twice as loud.

▼

BOX 2.1   *Amplitude, Loudness, and Volume*

Though they are related, do not confuse the three terms: amplitude, loudness, and volume. Each describes a different aspect of sound.

1. **Amplitude** describes sound pressure.
2. **Loudness** describes hearing.
3. **Volume** describes signal intensity when using audio electronics.

Frequency or Pitch

The number of waves that occur during a certain amount of time is called the wave's **frequency,** and it is measured in cycles per second, which are expressed as **Hertz (Hz).** If a wave is vibrating at 80 cycles per second, its frequency is 80 Hz.

▼

BOX 2.2   *Talking in Hertz (Hz)*

Hertz were named after Heinrich Hertz, who proved James Maxwell's theories predicting the existence of electromagnetic waves known as radio waves. Hertz are the same thing as cycles per second or waves per second. When expressing frequencies into the thousands and millions of Hertz, further shorthand is used. For example:

1 wave per second	is expressed as 1 Hz
One thousand Hertz	is expressed as 1 kiloHertz (kHz)
One million Hertz	is expressed as 1 megaHertz (MHz)
One billion Hertz	is expressed as 1 gigaHertz (GHz)

Just as there are limited volume levels that humans can hear, there are also frequency limits. The psychological interpretation of frequency is **pitch,** which determines the highness, the high frequency, or lowness, the low frequency, of a sound that you hear. In theory, young, normal humans are capable of hearing between 15 Hz and 20 kHz. In practice, the continuous exposure to an increasingly noisy environment has created a generation of people who do not hear high frequency sounds as well as they would have in the quieter world of the past. Aging also causes similar hearing loss.

The difference between light waves, radio waves, and x-rays are their frequencies. It is interesting to note that oscillation releases energy. The higher the frequency, the greater release or radiation of energy. X-rays are at a much higher frequency than radio waves, so an x-ray's oscillation emits higher levels of radiation—such a high level, in fact, that overexposure to such frequencies and their radiation can be damaging to your health.

Note that frequency and velocity are not the same thing. **Frequency** is the *number* of waves (cycles) traveling in a second. **Velocity** is the actual *speed* at which the waves are traveling. The frequency can change, but the velocity is usually considered to be constant.

Wavelength

The **wavelength** is the actual distance between the beginning and end of a cycle. The wavelength is somewhat connected to the frequency because as the frequency increases the wavelength decreases or becomes shorter.

Sound and electromagnetic waves travel at a constant speed. So it is logical that if more waves—that is, a higher frequency—need to travel in a given amount of time, and they travel at a constant speed, those waves must be closer together in order to fit within the specified time measurement. If the waves are closer together, they have a shorter wavelength.

Phasing

Since a wave can begin at any point, it is possible for waves to affect each other. When two waves begin their journeys at the same time and their peaks coincide, they are considered to be **in phase.** Waves that are in phase reinforce each other. This **phase augmentation** increases amplitude, just as two people pulling on a rope in the same direction would be twice as strong as one person. But what if you have

Shown are two waves with different frequencies. Note that as the frequency increases, the wavelength decreases.

Wave with a frequency of 1 cycle per second (1 Hz)

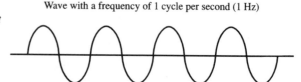

Wave with a frequency of 2 cycles per second (2 Hz)

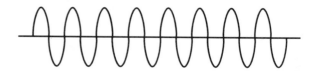

one person pulling in one direction and another pulling in the opposite direction? The forces would cancel each other out and the rope would not move. Similarly, when waves are **out of phase** they can partially or totally cancel each other out. This is called **phase cancellation.** In the production studio, it will be important to understand how waves can affect each other through phasing, since some of the more popular special-effects technology is designed to manipulate this information.

When waves are in phase, they can augment or reinforce each other.

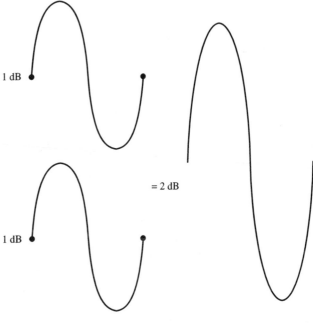

When waves are out of phase, they can cancel each other out.

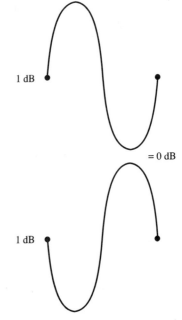

These two instruments playing the same frequency (like the musical note A) sound different because of timbre.

Overtones or Harmonic Structure

You now know that loudness is determined by a wave's amplitude. And pitch is determined by frequency and wavelength. But what if you play the same frequency, the musical note *A* for example, at the same volume on two separate musical instruments? Why don't these notes sound *exactly* the same? The difference between a particular note played on a saxophone or a piano or a guitar depends on the shape of the waveforms the sound sources produce. The way in which we perceive these waveforms determines our perception of the sound's quality, or **timbre.**

This is how it works. If you created a sound wave that vibrates, or **oscillates,** at 500 cycles per second, you would describe it as having a frequency of 500 Hz. Since this is the lowest frequency the sound produced, it is considered the sound's **fundamental pitch.** Simultaneously, however, other weaker sounds are also generated at higher frequencies above the fundamental pitch. These other frequencies are called **overtones.** When these overtones are integer multiples of the fundamental frequency, for example 1,000 Hz or 1,500 Hz, they are called **harmonics.** It is the harmonics or overtones of waveforms that give sound a certain quality. Thus, stringed instruments have different waveform characteristics than do reed, brass, or percussion instruments. And male voices differ from female voices.

It is possible to produce a single frequency devoid of harmonics and overtones. This wave is known as a *sine wave* or a *pure tone.* However, most sound consists of several different frequencies that produce a complex **waveform.** A waveform is a graphic representation of a sound's characteristic shape that is usually displayed on test equipment.

Envelopes

Another characteristic of sound is the *envelope* of a waveform, which describes its intensity based upon amplitude and time duration. An envelope is composed of three parts:

1. **Attack** is the way in which a sound begins.
2. **Internal dynamics** describe changes in volume as it increases, decreases, or stays the same (sustains).
3. **Decay** is the way in which a sound stops.

A snare drum has a short attack followed by a quick decay, a very snappy percussive sound. A flute, on the other hand has a much slower attack and decay, which makes the sound seem much smoother and softer.

Noise

The final concept that you must be aware of is **noise,** which is defined as random sounds that cannot be interpreted or are not useful. For example, you might be unable to hear a specific sound clearly because some other very loud sound is overpowering your hearing. This would be considered environmental noise.

In audio production, noise is typically defined as **interference.** When working with electronic communication systems or audio equipment such as those in a sound studio, noise describes any unwanted electronic signal that exists during production.

Psychoacoustics—How Sound Affects You

Hearing sounds does much more for you than provide information about the immediate environment. For example, hearing allows you to participate in oral communication with others, whether in person or over the telephone. Or sounds can be used to create moods or recall emotional responses. **Psychoacoustics,** as the name implies, are concerned with the psychological aspects of sound. Music is a prime mood-setting example. Nearly everyone can think of a song that evokes a particular mood or works as a referent for a particular event from the past. The importance of the impact of sound cannot be overemphasized. Sound provides physical information about time and space, and it also works as a tool for mental and emotional construction.

UNDERSTANDING AUDIO AND ITS LEXICON

Sound travels through the medium of air and decreases in intensity as it proceeds. Were it not for the audio equipment in your homes, your cars, or at radio stations, you would have to be in the presence of every sound source in order to hear it. This means the only way you would be able to hear music by your favorite band would be to hear it *live* in concert. The only way to hear a political candidate speak would be to see him or her face to face. Audio equipment provides the means to create, detect, amplify, duplicate, combine, and record sounds from anywhere. In addition, audio equipment allows you to combine sounds or create new sounds that may not already exist in our natural world.

BOX 2.3

Sound or Audio?

ATTENTION: Just a reminder! Sound is not the same thing as audio! **Sound** is a vibration through air or another medium; **audio** is the electrical signal used in reproduction or transmission of the original sound.

Understanding the basics of how sound works is important in order to be able to use radio production technology to manipulate that sound. However, this is only half of the story because before you can become versed in using the available technology you must first understand basic audio concepts and vocabulary. These terms are closely related to and are the electronic equivalent of the physiological interpretation of sound, such as loudness, pitch, and noise.

Transducers

Just as your ears detect and translate sound, the primary task of some audio equipment is to take sound out of its medium of air, change it to electronic energy, transfer it or amplify it, and turn it back into sound waves so your ears can receive it. The tools that are used to convert one form of energy into another are called **transducers.**

Microphones are transducers that detect and convert all of the frequency and amplitude ranges of normal sound into an electronic signal. There are several different types of microphones that accomplish this conversion in various ways; these will be discussed in the next chapter. Loudspeakers are also transducers that do just the opposite of what microphones do. Speakers take electronic signals and convert them back into sounds that then travel through the air to your ears. The limitations of speakers lie in their inability to reproduce all frequencies equally. These problems have been solved by creating different sized speakers to transform specific frequencies. For example, **woofers** are normally larger and handle lower frequency sounds,

A microphone is a transducer that converts mechanical energy into electrical energy.

Most modern speakers have a woofer for low frequencies and a smaller tweeter for high frequencies.

while **tweeters** are smaller and reproduce higher frequencies. In addition, frequency reproduction also can be affected by positioning the speakers carefully in relation to the environment.

Frequency Response

If you have ever watched television closely you have probably noticed that several types of microphones are used. News commentators or talk show hosts typically have tiny microphones called lavaliere mics pinned to their clothing in the chest area. Talk show guests are typically *picked up* by large, moving, overhead microphones called boom mics. Even during regular comedy or drama programming, the boom mic might accidentally drop low enough to be seen or to create a shadow that the television director does not catch. Microphones are certainly chosen for their maneuverability and *hide ability*. After all, it would be very distracting to watch a movie where the actors and actresses kept microphones in their hands the entire time.

However, in addition to the way a microphone is or is not integrated into a television program, microphones are also chosen for their ability to reproduce or enhance certain sounds.

All microphones are especially designed to respond to a specific range of frequencies. This **frequency response** manifests itself in terms of one of the performance characteristics of microphones, which are typically described as bright, rich, crisp, flat, or muddy. The lavaliere microphone meant to be worn against the body has been designed so that the low frequencies of a vibrating chest will sound normal rather than boomy. To accomplish this, the lower frequency response of the microphone is minimized. Conversely, the high frequency response of the same microphone is increased because the person wearing the microphone is not speaking directly into it.

This woman is wearing a lavalier microphone.

On late night talk shows from decades past, you might have noticed the host using a microphone on his or her desk while the guests were "picked up" by a large microphone hovering over their heads. In some cases, the hosts utilized a microphone that tended to enhance the deeper tones or lower frequencies, making their voices seem much richer and fuller than those of their guests. The audience might have perceived psychoacoustically this *richer* voice as more appealing or more powerful, which could have provided the host with a sense of authority. Contemporary talk show hosts still might have big microphones visible on their desks, but these may be nothing more than props to give a degree of depth to the set and may not always be used for picking up any audio.

Volume Levels

Volume levels are a bit more complex when dealing with audio equipment. When you listen to a particular sound, your ears are mostly concerned with the strength and clarity of that one particular sound. However, in audio, sufficient volume levels must be maintained throughout the production process as signals are sent to and from various pieces of equipment. Do not concern yourself with knowing all about the audio equipment quite yet. These specifics will be provided in the next chapter. It is simply important to introduce the following volume level concepts now in order for you to be better able to relate them to an overall understanding of the relationship between sound and audio.

Dynamic Range

Just as there are limited frequencies humans can hear, there are also volume limitations. Microphones, amplifiers, and audio storage devices are also limited in the
range of signals they can handle without distortion. Every sound source generates
a specific volume range. This difference between the softest and loudest sounds that
an instrument is capable of producing or recording is called its **dynamic range.** Although no machine can replicate every sound perfectly, your task as an audio producer is to understand the limitations of the technology while still creating the desired
effects.

Mic Level

Once the desired mechanical sound has been detected and changed by a transducer
into a different form (electrical), you must then be concerned with whether the electronic components are communicating with one another effectively. Microphones
are limited to the amount of **output**—the voltage of the signals going out to their
destination—they can generate. The amplitude of signals a microphone is capable
of generating is called its **mic level.** This is a very tiny volume.

Line Level

Because the electrical signal that the microphone generates is relatively weak, it
must be amplified in order to be processed by **audio consoles.** The function of the
audio console is to mix and route the output of production equipment. The console,
like your ears, must have a certain level of amplitude, called the **line level,** in order
for the input, or those signals coming in and their source, to be received correctly
or *understood.* This is why all stereo systems have an amplifier—to boost output
levels of audio sources such as phonographs, CD players, and tape players. Devices
called preamplifiers bring mic level signals up to line levels, while amplifiers boost
a line level signal to speaker level. Understanding the difference between mic level
and line level is important in radio production. If you connect a mic level device like
a microphone to a line level input of a mixer, it will be too soft to hear. If you connect
a line level device to a mic level input, distortion will result.

Once the microphone has transformed sound into an electrical audio signal and
the signal is amplified to line levels, it is then sent to an audio console. From this
electronic board the signals can be amplified, or **boosted;** decreased, or **attenuated;**
mixed with other inputs, altered, or processed; or sent to destinations like tape recorders, monitors, or computers. Since you will probably be working with several
different inputs coming into the console at different power levels, it is important for
you to be able to keep track of how strong the various signals are in relation to each
other. Remember: You cannot depend on your own interpretation of loudness to
determine volume, or the power of an audio signal, because sound and electronic
audio signals *are not* the same thing. The **Volume Unit meter, VU meter,** provides
a visual objective reading of an audio signal's average strength in discrete volume

units. This device allows you to depend on the audio console to tell you when signals are too strong or too weak in order for you to avoid distortion, overlap, or loss of sound levels. More on this equipment and its use will be provided in the next chapter.

Signal-to-Noise Ratio

Turn on your stereo system at home. Don't play any music. Just turn up the volume and see what happens. Even though you are not sending any information through the system, you can still hear sound, a distinctive electronic hum or hiss coming out of your speakers. This is because electronic components introduce both distortion and noise into the audio process. Noise is always present in these components, and when the signal volume is too low, the noise becomes more apparent. The ratio between the strength of the wanted audio signal and the background noise in the equipment is called the **signal-to-noise ratio.** The higher the signal-to-noise ratio, the better the sound.

BOX 2.4   ### The Formula for Signal-to-Noise Ratio

$$\text{signal to noise ratio} = \frac{\text{signal in a channel}}{\text{noise in a channel}}$$

SUMMARY

Even though you may be quite familiar with specific aspects of sound, you now have a working knowledge and vocabulary to express what you know about sound and audio. Sound is a vibration through air or another medium; audio is the electrical signal used in reproduction or transmission of the original sound. By learning the basic characteristics of sound, you will better be able to manage and manipulate audio in creative production.

Sound is made up of waves. The amplitude of the wave determines its loudness. The wave's frequency determines pitch, and the characteristics of waveforms determine sound quality, or timbre. Audio utilizes transducers to electronically create and interpret sounds. Audio equipment and processes are characterized in terms of their volume level capacities and frequency responses. Finally, neither sound nor audio exists without encountering some outside interference or noise, which must be controlled.

By understanding the basic ingredients with which you will be working, the next step in creative radio production is to become familiar with the audio technology and equipment that you will be using to replicate, manipulate, and store sound and audio.

ACTIVITIES

1. Sit alone in a room and listen to all of the *natural* sounds that exist in your environment. Visualize whether they have high or low frequencies and how loud you perceive them to be.

2. Turn on your television but close your eyes and try to concentrate on the audio portion. Pay special attention to commercials, because they must communicate an idea to you in a very short time, usually from ten seconds to a minute. Concentrate on the psychoacoustics of sound. What kind of voices do your hear? Why do you think those voices were chosen over others? What kind of music do you hear and under what circumstances? How are moods established with these sounds?

3. Look at the volume level indicator on your home cassette player. Play a favorite song and notice when the signal is strongest and weakest.

Audio Production Tools

Before you can see audio production as a system, and before you take on an actual audio project, you must first become familiar with the tools you will be using in the process. Learning to select and identify audio production tools and knowing how they work is very important because you will not be able to apply the production skills presented later in this text if you cannot identify, or do not understand the purpose or application of, a specific piece of equipment. The better acquainted with the equipment you become, the more creative you can be with your productions. And, frankly, you will also have much more fun if you are not bogged down by confusion with the technology. The equipment is categorized into sections:

1. Microphones
2. Playback and recording devices
3. Audio control devices

MICROPHONES

The microphone was the first tool of radio broadcasting. Decades before stations began playing prerecorded music, microphones were the only audio pickup device used for announcers, actors, live music, and sound effects. The very first microphone used in radio was a converted telephone connected to a wireless telegraph transmitter. Today, with hundreds of microphone types to choose from, the basic principle remains the same: A microphone is a **transducer,** a device that converts one form of energy into another. As a transducer, a microphone converts the mechanical energy of moving air into electrical energy. When sound occurs, the resulting moving air vibrates a diaphragm in the microphone, which generates a tiny voltage resembling, or analogous to, the original air vibration. Unfortunately, microphones do not have brains so they detect all sounds equally within their range. Therefore, all sound, whether important or not, is converted by microphones.

The first radio microphone was a telephone.

Even though all microphones perform the same basic function of converting acoustic energy into electric energy, different types of microphones accomplish this in very distinct ways. Therefore, you must become familiar with each microphone's *specialty* in order to make the best of every audio production situation. There are three basic characteristics that distinguish one microphone from another. They are:

1. Physical design characteristics. Microphones are categorized by their physical designs, called **operating principles.**
2. Directional characteristics. Microphones are designed to focus on specific sound locations, referred to as the **pickup pattern.**
3. Sound characteristics. What the microphone *sounds like* based upon its **frequency response.**

Operating Principles

Once the acoustic energy is changed into electric energy, the signal flows through a circuit as voltage, where, depending on the microphone, it encounters various levels of resistance called **impedance.** Low-impedance microphones, or those that create less resistance, have two important advantages over high-impedance microphones, or those that have more resistance: They are less likely to be affected by electric noise and hum, and they can be connected to longer cables without risking increased noise levels. All of the microphones presented in this chapter are low-impedance microphones. Microphones used in radio production are almost always low-impedance microphones.

There are three common operating principles that are based upon the type of *element* mounted in the microphone head, the part of the microphone that picks up the sound.

Moving Coil Microphones (Dynamic Mics)

The most widely used type of microphone is the **moving coil,** often referred to as a **dynamic** microphone. This microphone contains a mylar diaphragm attached to a small coil of wire that surrounds a tiny fixed magnet. When sound waves strike it, the diaphragm vibrates in relation to the fixed magnet. A tiny voltage is generated because of the interaction between the stationary magnet and the moving coil. The same principle is employed in the tone arm and cartridge used in a phonograph; the *stylus* or needle may be attached to a moving coil of wire that interacts with a fixed magnet.

A dynamic moving coil microphone.

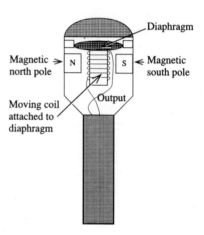

Popular moving coil dynamic microphones are used in audio and radio production.
(Courtesy of Shure Brothers, Inc.)

Ribbon Microphones

A second operating principle describes the **ribbon** microphone. Instead of a moving coil element, an extremely thin corrugated metal ribbon is suspended between two fixed magnets. When sound waves strike the ribbon and cause it to vibrate, a tiny variable voltage, which resembles the pressure of the sound wave, is generated. Since both sides of the ribbon are activated by air pressure and velocity, these microphones are sometimes called **velocity,** or **pressure gradient,** microphones. Ribbon microphones were widely used in the radio studios of the 1930s and 1940s, but their fragility has kept them out of modern on-air studios. The delicate ribbon can be easily damaged by a loud, fast-talking disc jockey. In the past these microphones were considered the best at providing the highest-quality sound, but that is no longer true. Currently, microphones of equally high quality can be found in both moving coil and capacitor varieties.

Capacitor Microphones (Condenser Mics)

Whereas moving coil and ribbon microphones transduce energy using electromagnetic variations, **capacitor mics** transduce energy using voltage or electrostatic variations. This microphone's element consists of two electrically charged plates separated by a *dielectric,* either air or other nonconductive material. One plate moves while the other stays fixed. When sound waves strike one of the plates, its distance away from the opposite plate changes accordingly, thus altering the voltage output

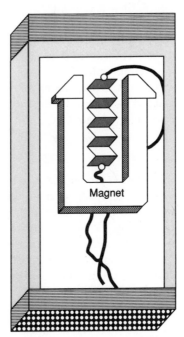

A ribbon microphone is also called a velocity, or pressure gradient, microphone.

A ribbon microphone.

A condenser/capacitor microphone.

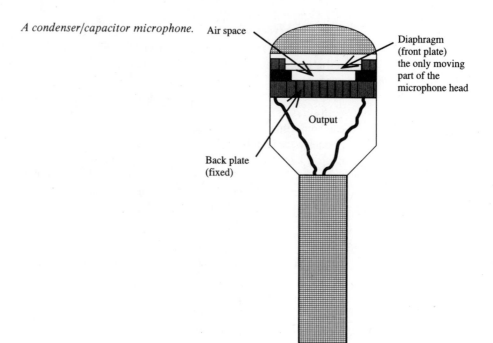

of the microphone. The signal output has a very high impedance, which requires a preamplifier as part of the microphone to make it usable. This preamplifier requires its own power supply, which may be provided by one of three sources: an external power supply, a phantom power supply initiated at the console or input circuits, or a small battery contained inside the microphone.

The original term used to describe the capacitor microphone was condenser. Consequently, many still (technically) inaccurately use the name **condenser** microphone when referring to capacitor microphones.

Microphone Pickup Patterns

The major task of a microphone in audio production is to be able to detect or pick up the sound you want to use. Since microphones do not discriminate between desired and undesired sounds, they have been created with **pickup patterns,** which allow a user to focus on specific sounds. Pickup patterns describe from which direction most sounds are "picked up" or heard by the microphone. The pickup pattern of the microphone directly determines the placement of the microphone in relation to the sound source. There are several commonly used pickup patterns that describe all microphones.

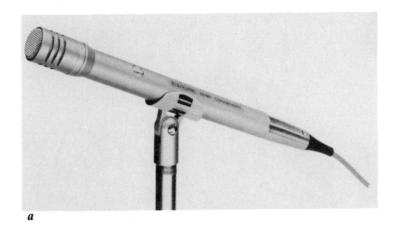

a

b

A condenser microphone (a) and a lavalier (b). (a: Courtesy of Shure Brothers, Inc.)

Omnidirectional Pattern

If the microphone allows sound to enter equally from all sides, it is described as **omnidirectional.** In a quiet production facility, a microphone that is omnidirectional is often an advantage if two announcers must share the same microphone by standing or sitting next to each other. When it is each person's turn to speak, he or she simply moves close to the microphone. Cost is another possible advantage of a microphone using this pickup pattern. Adding special baffles and other devices to a microphone to make it more directional certainly adds to its price.

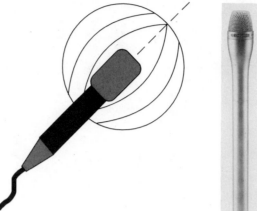

Omnidirectional pattern.

An omnidirectional microphone. (Courtesy of Shure Brothers, Inc.)

Unidirectional Pattern

A **unidirectional** microphone allows sound to mostly enter from the front of the mic by canceling out some of the sound from the sides and back. The more common of this type is called a **cardioid** microphone because its pickup pattern is heart-shaped. Even narrower unidirectional pickup patterns result in designs known as **supercardioid** and **hypercardioid** microphones. In noisy studios or control rooms, a cardioid pickup pattern allows the announcer to be heard while minimizing the unwanted sound of nearby people and equipment. A simple method for determining if a dynamic microphone has unidirectional characteristics is to look for holes on the side. If the body of the microphone is smooth, it's not directional; if it has slots or ports on its side, it's directional. Looking for holes is a good way to determine if dynamic or ribbon microphones are directional, but this does not apply to capacitor microphones. Capacitor microphones are made directional by alterations in the plate configurations and charges.

Bidirectional Pattern

The pattern is **bidirectional** if the sound enters mostly from the front and back of the microphone and less from the sides. Sound affects this type of microphone mainly from *two* directions. In early radio, it was common for two announcers or actors to

Cardioid (unidirectional) pickup pattern.

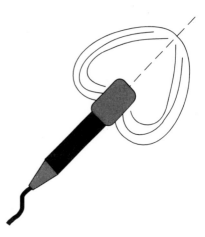

A unidirectional microphone showing the slots.

face each other with a bidirectional microphone suspended between them. Volume could be altered by moving the microphone closer or farther from the announcers, depending on their voice levels.

Multidirectional Pattern

Microphones that have changeable pickup patterns are considered **multidirectional.** These microphones typically have either a switchable diaphragm or two diaphragms that can be turned on and off.

Bidirectional pickup pattern.

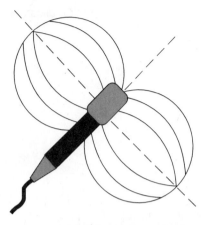

A bidirectional microphone.

All microphones fit into one of the above categories. Later, when production systems and the process of production is presented, much information on the selection and use of microphones will be detailed.

Accessories and Mounting Devices

In the on-air facility, more than in the production studio, the way the live announcer/disc jockey works with the microphone suggests certain accessories and specialized mounting devices. The most common accessory is a **wind screen,** sometimes called a pop or blast filter. A popping sound is created when the explosive nature of the breath pushes the microphone's diaphragm beyond its mechanical limit. Because a live announcer tends to work close to the microphone, a foam wind screen

a

b

c

d

(a) *A selector switch on the back of this multidirectional microphone allows its pickup pattern to be changed;* (b, c) *These are two popular microphones used for on air and production;* (d) *A combination microphone and headset is used by sportscasters for play-by-play.* (d: Courtesy of AKG Acoustics, Inc.)

is attached to the microphone. Also, microphones in on-air facilities must be mounted in a secure way to avoid movement that could translate into unwanted noise picked up by the microphone. Usually, a device called a *shock mount* is included to isolate the microphone from the rest of the room. In an on-air facility, the most popular mount is flexible and adjustable to meet the needs of many operators in many positions.

a   *b*

(a) This air personality at KSFO/KYA San Francisco is using a boom-mounted microphone; (b) Microphone stands in the studio.

AUDIO SOURCES—PLAYBACK AND RECORDING DEVICES

Listen carefully to your favorite music station. Notice that as soon as a commercial ends, the music begins with no pause in the sound. Notice, too, that when the announcer stops talking, music begins immediately. The act of transition from one audio source to the next without pause is called **tight production** and eliminates what radio people call **dead air.** Tight production is possible only because the source of music can be either manually or electronically **cued up** to right before the music begins and then started immediately. Consumer music playback sources, like the LP and CD, have been adapted for broadcast production. Others, like the compact cassette, cannot be easily used on the air because they cannot be cued with precision. Music playback devices like the cart and those that are digital-based were developed specifically for broadcasters.

Turntable

The phonograph record is dead. The two consumer black vinyl recorded music formats, 33 1/3 rpm long-playing LP and the smaller 45 rpm, were introduced in 1949 by Columbia and RCA. By the mid-1950s, these two formats had replaced the 78 rpm disc, in use since the 1920s. Of course, the 78 had replaced the earlier Edison cylinder in the unavoidable march of technology. The first music playback device used by radio stations was the 78, and the phonograph record was the main source of radio programming by the 1950s.

Most radio stations still have a turntable or two in the on-air facility. Maybe they're just there because the room was built years ago and there is no reason to change. Perhaps management worries that someday the CD players will break and, in an emergency, records will have to be played. Or, the format is so eclectic that

Broadcast turntables have been replaced by CDs as a music playback storage medium.

music is played from all sources, like at a public radio or community station where volunteer programmers still bring in their own music on black vinyl. Nevertheless, as more and more of the best music from the past is remastered onto CD, there won't be many good reasons to replace turntables when they break or even buy them at all for the new on-air facility. It's the end of an era.

CD

The compact disc, or CD, began life as a home format and was immediately successful. And why not? Didn't music lovers hate broken needles, scratchy records, and dubbing desired selections to another format (cassette) for the car?

It is no wonder that in just a few years, the popularity of the CD as a replacement for the LP caused the record companies to cease production of vinyl. The revolution consumers caused by embracing the CD forced broadcasters to convert their own facilities to play back the new format. In fact, radio stations used consumer models until broadcast equipment suppliers caught up with the technology.

a

b

A broadcast CD player (a) and a type of player that holds two CDs (b). (a: Courtesy of Denon America, Inc.)

The CD is a digital format. Most sounds begin as analog so they must be converted to the digital domain. The sound created by a person speaking or hitting a drum, for example, causes vibrations of air that resemble or are analogous to the sound created. The way we speak and hear sound is called analog. To convert analog sound to digital, the loudness, the duration, and the frequency of music or sound is sampled many thousands of times per second and converted into a binary code, bits and bytes, the 1's and 0's of computer language. The computer-sampled sounds on the CD are stored as "pits" on aluminum protected by clear plastic. These pits are read by a laser beam, which converts the digital information back to its analog form for listening. The advantage for consumers is a longer-lasting, rugged, music playback source free of the scratches and pops characteristic of vinyl. For radio stations, it is a music playback source that can be electronically cued to the desired selection and instantly aired.

Cart

The continuous loop tape cartridge, called the **cart,** is one of the devices found in a radio station that was developed exclusively for broadcasters. Its development began in the late 1950s as an alternative to the cuing up and airing of commercials, jingles, and other brief announcements on individual reels of tape. Evolving out of the basic reel-to-reel design, quarter inch tape is loaded into a plastic housing as a continuous, never ending loop of tape. It travels at the same speed as reel-to-reel, but it differs in a few important ways. First, it lacks an erase head, so it has to be **degaussed,** or bulk erased, using a large electromagnet. Second, it contains a system for automatically cuing the cart right to the start of the music or spot. Early models used a piece of aluminum tape as a sensor; a few years later, a series of electronic tones were placed on an unused track of the tape, tones that cued the tape, fast-forwarded it to the audio, even indicated when the recorded material was about to end and then start the next machine. An electronically cueable, broadcast device was born, and it was instantly embraced by radio stations.

Most radio stations still use the analog cart.

It was envisioned that the major role of the cart would be the playback of commercials and other production aids. But in the early 1960s, some *top-40* stations, those that played the same thirty or forty songs over and over, saw the cart as an ideal playback device for music. Even then, the cart was high fidelity enough for the limited frequency response of AM radio, and the cart allowed programming to be tighter, even lending itself to early automation: no scratchy records to cue up, less production error. And believe it or not, some large-market radio stations had a protected group of union employees called **record spinners.** In the highly unionized environment of the 1950s, a typical control room and studio-based disc jockey program required one person to cue up and start the records, another person to operate the console, and a third to announce. The use of carts for music made it possible to phase out the record spinner, and the facilities of music-formatted radio were well on the way to being operated by a single person.

While the analog tape cartridge is used by some stations for playback of prerecorded music, its major use is the playback of short announcements and other promotional and production aids. In the typical control room, the disc jockey has at least three cart playback devices, all of which must be loaded with the production elements necessary to support the format. Even if the station airs music on CD, it is between music selections that the cart is used the most: for jingles, spots, public service announcements, promos, and liners. Those five-, ten-, and thirty-second production aids that give radio its *sound* make the cart still the most popular piece of on-air equipment. Add to that the advantage of being able to record any locally produced audio onto it, and you can see why it has been an industry standard since 1960. Even digital replacements for the cart have been made to look and feel like the familiar cart.

Since most radio programming is the playback of prerecorded popular music, it makes sense that a radio station would follow consumer trends and use CDs, whether aired directly or transferred to cart for broadcast. With exception of the

Six cart players at KGO San Francisco.

cart, most of the currently used music playback formats are playback only. What about the playback of locally produced commercials and public service announcements? What about network news and other programs from satellite? What about half hour and hour public affairs programs and documentaries? What would a disc jockey use to tape the phone response of a contest winner and instantly play it back on the air? For nonmusic playback on-air there are several formats long familiar to all radio stations, and others more recently introduced.

Reel-to-Reel Tape Recorder

Reel-to-reel tape machines, sometimes called **open-reel,** are available in every possible size, shape, and track or channel configuration. This format really has an exciting and long history; in fact, its introduction in 1948 literally *saved* broadcasters. As early as the 1930s, inventors had been trying to develop a high-quality magnetic storage medium, but none had been very successful. Recording artists recorded directly to 78 rpm discs. Radio programs were either done live or *transcribed* onto large 16-inch discs at 33 1/3 rpm and played back later. This format was not popular with producers because the fidelity of so-called *transcriptions* was less than AM quality, plus the medium could not be edited.

Meanwhile, World War II was under way and the allies were wondering how Hitler was reported to be in one country while his voice heard on the air, sounding as clear as a live broadcast, was originating from hundreds of miles away. The answer was that German engineers had invented the first practical open-reel tape recorder. After the war, a young soldier/engineer named Jack Mullen found the perfected German machine, called the Magnetophon, and brought it to the United States. By the mid-1940s, Ampex Corporation had developed an American version of the device. The future of the new device was guaranteed in 1948 when singer Bing Crosby first used the device in order to be able to produce and edit his weekly half-hour radio program. No more bad-sounding transcriptions. This was another example of how the demands of programming influenced the technology. The modern open-reel analog tape recorder is still compatible with that first Ampex Model One.

There are two good reasons why the analog open-reel deck is still the preferred device for playing back programs longer than a single musical selection or commercial. First, compatibility: Open-reel equipment is found everywhere, and while the format has been around, even improved for over forty-five years, a tape recorded in 1948 can still be played on a modern machine. Second, while the cart cues by itself and doesn't have to be threaded, cart tape lengths longer than five to seven minutes are impractical because of the size of the tape housing and the mechanical limitations of the tape loop configuration. In the on-air facility, open-reel tape still remains a universal and high-quality device both for airing longer programs and for *instant production,* like a listener phone response to a contest question or request, while on the air.

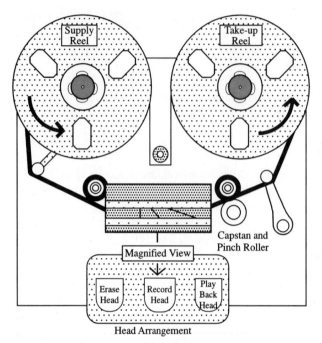

A reel-to-reel (or open-reel) tape transport system.

An operator prepares tape for on-air playback using a typical open-reel machine.

UNDERSTANDING MAGNETIC RECORDING

Whether reel-to-reel or cart, tape recording works like this: Sound waves from a microphone or other sound source are converted to an electrical signal that varies to resemble or be analogous to the original sound wave. This signal is sent to a tape head, which selectively magnetizes a moving strip of plastic on which has been coated an oxide of iron, the magnetic medium. The sound, now a magnetic pattern, is stored on tape until played back or erased. The open reel tape deck typically has a mechanical transport for moving the tape past the heads and the necessary electronics for erasing, recording, and playing back the tape. Look closely at how magnetic tape devices work. There is the storage medium—magnetic tape—and there are the tape heads—those devices that put a magnetic signal on the tape during recording and then convert it back into audio during playback.

Audiotape

The basic magnetic storage unit used with the reel-to-reel tape machine is called audiotape. In order to understand the basics of recording and editing, you must first comprehend this object you will be handling and manipulating. Magnetic tape is made up of millions of tiny iron oxide magnets bonded to a ribbon of plastic. If you look closely at most audiotapes, you will notice that one side is shiny, or at least smooth, while the other side has a duller, rougher surface. This latter side contains the oxide treatment. Note that dullness is not a foolproof indicator of the oxide side; there are some tapes where the duller surface is the back of the tape, not the oxide-treated side. As the microscopic magnets move past the record heads, the magnetic patterns on the tape are changed. The tape's magnetic pattern duplicates the changes in electrical current that is fed from the audio sources like microphones and CDs. Tape used for recording and playback for broadcast is usually 1.5 mils thick, 1/4-inch wide, and is usually stored on plastic or metal reels that are generally seven inches or ten inches in diameter.

Since magnetic tape is resistant to change, it requires energy to place a magnetic pattern on tape. If recording signals at low volume levels, there may not be enough energy to create a magnetic pattern and, therefore, the recording process could sound distorted. In order to solve this problem, a high-frequency signal called tape **bias** is added to any information being recorded to boost the signal. Bias is too high to be heard; its only function is to overcome the tape's resistance to change its magnetic pattern.

Tape Heads

How does the audio signal get onto the tape? It is accomplished by sending the electronic signals that are audio to tiny magnetic devices called heads. Electronic signals are recorded onto or played back from audiotape in the form of magnetic patterns on the tape. Tape heads are simply small horseshoe-shaped magnets. The two ends of the horseshoe are called the *poles*. The space between the two poles is called the *gap*. The other end of the horseshoe is wrapped many times with a small wire. This coil of wire is connected to an audio amplifier. Tape heads should be kept clean to prevent build-up of oxide particles or dust, which can affect sound quality.

Professional reel-to-reel tape recorders have three heads: erase, record, and playback.

The three tape heads in an open-reel machine are erase, record, and play, always in that order.

A small reel of tape on a degausser.

The Erase Head

When the tape recorder is in the record mode, and before the tape passes over the record head, the erase head prepares the tape by removing previously recorded information on the tape. The erase head does this by saturating the tape with a high-frequency tone that cannot be reproduced by the play head. However, some of the old audio signal may still remain, so it is always a good idea to demagnetize or degauss the tape with a bulk eraser before using it.

Audiotape with random magnetic pattern

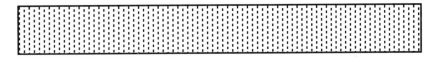

The magnetic pattern becomes organized after being exposed to the record head

A magnified look at audiotape magnetic flux (particles).

BOX 3.1   ### The Degausser at Work

Tape can be degaussed over and over again. To operate, simply turn on the degausser machine, lower the tape into the magnetic field and rotate it several times. Remove the tape from the field *before* the degausser is turned off to avoid any magnetic glitches on your tape. Both sides of the tape reel must be degaussed. Make sure you are not wearing a watch or other jewelry that might be affected by the strong magnetic field. The signals on the magnetic strips of credit cards can also be erased, so watch your wallet!

The Record Head

How is sound recorded? First an audio signal is sent to the record amplifier and then it travels onto the wire coil of the **record head.** When electricity flows through a coil of wire, a magnetic field is created in that coil. The horseshoe-shaped record head focuses the magnetic field into a small space in the gap. As audiotape passes the record head at a constant speed, it touches the head at the gap. The magnetic field in the head gap changes the magnetic pattern on the audiotape and a replica of the electrical audio signal is reproduced in the oxide coating of the magnetic tape. The record head then acts as a transducer, changing an electrical signal to the gap's magnetic field, which magnetizes the tape.

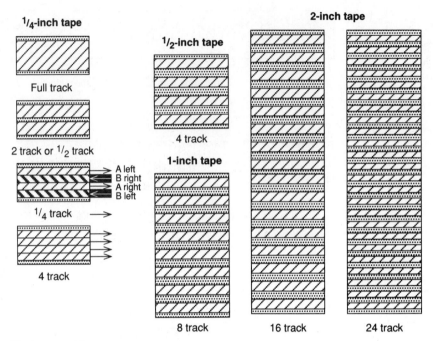

Various tape formats.

Recording heads differ in size and in the number of tracks they record onto the tape. Tracks involved use only a small portion of the tape width as it passes by the record head. This explains why your cassette machine plays one set of songs traveling in one direction and then, when you turn it over, it plays different songs traveling in the opposite direction, yet it still reads the same dull oxide side of the audiotape going both ways. The trick is, it only records or plays back half of the tape width at a time.

The Playback Head

Playing back audio information that has been recorded works in reverse order from recording. As audiotape passes the playback head, the magnetic pattern on the tape creates a magnetic field across the gap that travels through the horseshoe to the coil of wire, causing an electrical current to flow to the playback amplifier. Thus the playback head works as a transducer, changing the magnetic pattern on the tape into electronic signals. It's very important to become familiar with the location of the playback head, as it is the location where you will perform manual editing.

The Mechanical Transport

Reel-to-reel machines move the tape past the heads at either 7 1/2 or 15 **inches per second,** or **ips.** The faster speed allows the information to be stored in a larger space, increasing the frequency response and the fidelity of the recording and allowing for easier editing. Cart machines use the 7 1/2 speed only. If the magnetic tape is the

The transport controls on a popular open-reel machine include record, play, stop, rewind, and fast forward.

A close-up of the capstan and pressure roller.

software used to store audio, and the tape heads convert the electrical signal of audio into a magnetic pattern on that tape, how does the tape move past those heads? The system of motors and wheels is called the **tape transport.** Just as important, just as necessary to the tape recording process as the tape and the electronics, the transport is responsible for the tape passing by the head at a steady and standard speed. Most modern reel-to-reel tape recorders have three motors, which are controlled by the push-button functions called forward, fast-forward, rewind, and stop. These motors allow the tape to get from the reel on the left, called the **supply reel,** to the empty one on the right, called the **take-up reel.** In the cart, of course, there is only one reel, as the tape is a continuous loop contained in a single housing. Carts cannot be rewound; they can only go forward, which means they also can be fast-forwarded.

The most important motor is the one that determines the speed at which the tape travels past the heads. This motor is electronically controlled and is usually capable of travelling at the two standard speeds used in radio production, 7 1/2 and 15 ips. This motor is either mechanically coupled to a shaft called the **capstan** or, on some machines, the motor shaft is the capstan. When the forward button on the open-reel tape transport is depressed, the tape is held firmly to the capstan by a rubber roller called the **pinch or pressure roller.** It is this action that allows a tape recorder to travel at a constant speed throughout the recording and playback process. A similar action occurs in the cart.

It is important to remember that analog tape recording is not an exact process. The magnetized audiotape is not a perfect reproduction; it has lost a minute amount of the sound information in the transduction process. And if you record this copy again, you will lose even more information. This is called **generation loss,** or **degeneration.** The original would be the first generation. A copy of the original would be second generation. A copy of the second would be the third generation, and so on. It works much the same way paper-copying machines work. Every time you make a copy of a copy, you lose some level of detail. Eventually, if you keep up the process, the results will become more distorted from the original. The loss in quality suffered during the analog magnetic recording process is one reason for the popularity of digital recording devices.

DIGITAL OPTIONS

Both the reel-to-reel and the cart are analog tape formats. Sure, both have improved greatly during the transition from the frequency-response restricted days of AM radio to the high quality of today's FM. They have taken advantage of the benefits of better tape, better engineering, and more features.

But what about the new digital recording and playback formats finding their way into radio stations? Will they replace the open-reel for the recording and playback of longer shows? Eventually. Will the cart, with its inherent problems of tape hiss and speed variations, survive as a music playback format? Not likely. Those stations that play complete albums, like classical music and jazz, will probably continue to use CDs. It will be those stations that formerly **dubbed,** or copied, music from CDs and records onto carts that may convert to one of the many digital devices now being marketed. Large-capacity optical and magnetic hard disks store an entire radio station's music and commercials, and they are listed on the menu of a computer screen. Click the mouse and the song is ready to be started from the console.

Why didn't the consumer *compact cassette* catch on as a playback device for broadcasters? There are at least two reasons: low fidelity and lack of cueability. Enter **DAT.** Now broadcasters have a viable cassette replacement for the reel-to-reel tape format. It is called R-DAT for **rotary digital audiotape.** Known simply as DAT, it is a high-quality audio recording, storage, and playback format And because it has cuing features, it has become popular with broadcasters. Its small size means easier placement in on-air facilities and easier storage of the tiny tapes. Now stations can set a timer that records, from a satellite feed, an hour show on a DAT right in the on-air room in a space no larger than that used by a CD player.

If the DAT may replace the open-reel, how long will stations continue to embrace the analog tape cartridge as the most-used playback format for spots and other short production aids? In the short term, it may depend on the economics of broadcasting or the type of format, but sooner or later some universal digital storage medium as convenient as the cart will emerge. Because there are several contenders

The Digital Commercial System (DCS) allows on-air playback of digitally stored commercials using a computer. (Courtesy of Computer Concepts Corporation)

Tape is inserted into a DAT machine.

and no clear standard, most broadcasters are not rushing to dump their familiar and trusty cart machines yet. What are the options likely to be? Perhaps some form of recordable CD would be popular, since most stations now have easily cueable CD playback devices in their on-air facilities. Some are even designed using the logic of the cart player. Another possible option is a hard-disk storage system with a computer screen for easy retrieval. Like the CD or the cart, the right format will capture the market and become the new standard.

OTHER ON-AIR AUDIO SOURCES

An important audio source is the telephone. For the news and talk station, or the public radio or community station, sometimes there is little or no music played. For these types of stations, many switching, frequency-enhancing, and delay devices are used to allow the on-air operator to bring up live phone calls just as quickly as playing a cart. Many news stations have equipped their on-the-scene reporters with cellular telephones for live actualities that add immediacy to a broadcast. Even music formatted stations use the phone for remote call-in broadcasts and often put a listener-caller directly on the air.

Other nonmusic, nonmicrophone audio sources include so-called receivers for **RPU,** or remote pickup, transmitters used for high-quality origination of remote broadcasts; satellite feeds for news on the hour; **EBS,** or emergency broadcast receivers and required test-tone generators; and the outputs of other consoles in the facility.

A small telephone control console at KGO San Francisco is used to put a caller on the air.

AUDIO CONTROL DEVICES—THE AUDIO CONSOLE

The audio playback sources used in an on-air radio facility—the microphones, turntables, CD, cart, DAT, telephone, satellite, remote receivers, and more—all must be sent to the transmitter at the exact moment required by the operator. Some sources must be aired one at a time; others must be **mixed,** or combined together, as when a disc jockey talks over the instrumental opening of a song. All audio sources must be aired at a proper volume level, and the person controlling all this must be able to do it with the least energy and motion possible. Between the audio playback sources and the transmitter is the console.

a

b

Two on-air consoles are shown here: (a) a modern, high quality console, and (b) its 1940s predecessor. (a: *Radiomixer,* courtesy of Pacific Recorders Engineering Corporation)

Control of all outgoing audio sources is accomplished by means of the **console,** sometimes called a *mixing console,* a **mixer,** an **audio control board,** or just a **board.** Whatever it is called, it is the heart of all radio production facilities, the device that ties all the discrete pieces of production equipment together.

Consoles have these elements in common:

1. A way to select which audio playback source or microphone will be controlled by which volume level control.
2. A way to vary the volume level of each audio source, and a method to visually determine that exact level.
3. A way to manipulate or change a signal using some special effects technology and techniques (production consoles only).
4. A way to start the transport of each audio source (on-air consoles only).
5. A way to preview sound before it is aired, **audition;** a way to find the beginning of a sound before playing, **cue;** and a way to listen to it while it is being aired or recorded, **monitor.**

Patching

All but the most basic boards offer the operator some choice as to which microphone or which audio source goes into a particular volume-level control, or fader. As discussed earlier, the audio signals generated from these sources must be brought into the audio console so you can work with them. Some consoles are connected to **patch panels** or **patch bays** as a way of connecting the playback of any turntable, CD player, cart machine, telephone, network, or remote source into any fader/level control on the console. Some have at least an A/B switch above each input channel that gives the operator a choice of at least two sources for every fader. If these two choices are permanently connected, they are said to be *normalled* to the consoles. Usually the *A* position has a frequently used audio source, like a CD or cart, and the *B* position has a seldom used source, like a turntable or a remote line.

If an audio console is not already connected to meet the needs of a production, patching may be necessary. Patching allows you to route a signal in a different way than is already provided by the audio board. Patch bays are usually wired together in a very logical and straightforward way. For example, inputs and outputs of a specific component are usually lined up vertically, which makes them convenient to use and understand. Patching allows you to add or bring in additional equipment and patch it into the board or reroute a source because of equipment damage. When no patch cords are used and you are relying solely on the original configuration of the board that was wired together by your engineer, it is called a *normal connection.* If you patch around a connection, you are *breaking normal.*

A patch panel.

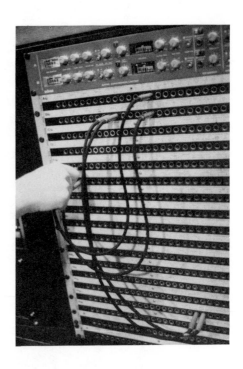

Cables and Connectors

Signals from microphones and other sound sources travel through the audio console by way of *balanced lines*. These travel in cables that use two conductors plus a shield, so noise signals induced by surrounding electrical signals are canceled out. These cables are attached to the microphone with a three-pronged connector called an **XLR.**

There are other types of plugs that are used in audio production. Luckily, if a cable doesn't fit with a compatible connector, an adapter can be used to make it work.

VU Meter

The console also allows you to amplify signals to a usable level. Microphones, phonographs, and so on, send out a very weak signal that must be boosted up to line levels before they can be utilized by the audio console. All consoles have a **fader** or **potentiometer,** which is also called a **pot,** to control the volume level of each audio source. Older consoles had so-called **rotary pots,** round knobs like those found on old radios, but most modern consoles have straight-line volume controls called **faders**

a

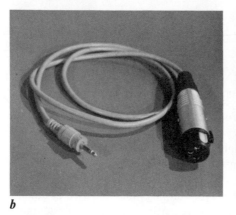

b

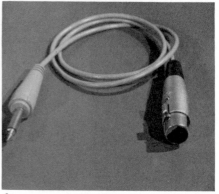

c

The standard microphone cable with XLR connectors (a); adapting the XLR to a mini plug (b); and adapting the XLR to the ¼-inch phone plug (c).

or **sliders.** Both operate in identical ways to increase or decrease, that is, fade up or fade down the level of one sound source relative to another. The less expensive consoles use a simple volume control-like carbon resistor and a slider to vary the volume. The more expensive ones use a voltage-controlled fader that is electronic and isolated from the actual audio source and offers smoother control of the level.

The console also provides a way to visually "see" the level of each audio source, usually a **VU,** or **volume unit, meter** that uses a needle to indicate when the level is too low, too high, or just right. Some level meters use **light emitting diodes (LEDs)** that indicate levels with corresponding lights instead of a meter pointer. You might be more familiar with these level indicators since they are more commonly used on consumer stereo equipment.

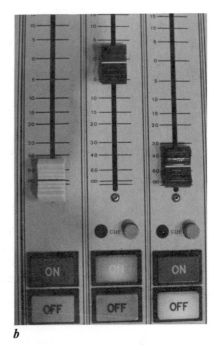

a   *b*

A rotary pot shows an A/B selector and audition/program switch (a), and three faders show a remote start switch (b).

Left and right channel VU meters.

Zero VU is considered the standard operating level or the reference for proper volume. The difference between the maximum volume level that can be handled without causing a faulty reproduction (distortion) and 0-VU is called **headroom.** If volume levels of signals are too high, you run the risk of distortion. And if volume levels are too low, they might not be clearly reproduced.

Signal Processing

In addition to working with the volume of an audio signal, you can use the console to manipulate or change a signal with some special-effects technology and techniques. **Equalizers** alter the frequency response of an audio signal and, therefore, can be used to cut or boost specific frequency ranges making an audio signal lighter or more bassy, for example. A **graphic equalizer** actually allows you to set a graphic representation or picture of the response curve you want to effect.

Filters knock out entire frequencies all together. A **low-pass** filter allows lower frequencies through but cuts off most higher frequencies, eliminating hiss. A **high-pass** filter eliminates lower frequencies to get rid of rumble, or low vibration.

A **harmonizer** allows you to vary pitch, harmonics, and tempo. These alterations can change a normal voice into a computer-sounding voice, for example.

A **flanger** creates a mirror image of a sound and then shifts it a bit, changing the phasing and time and creating a water-rushing-through-a-voice effect.

An **echo** can be achieved by manipulating a signal from the record and playback heads of an audiotape recorder.

Reverberation is both a technique and a specific component. The device creates a delay and then adds it back to the signal. And since it is electronic, not like the echo technique, it can be fine-tuned to a very small amount.

The specific use of these devices will be learned in the sections on production. As described earlier, effects can add depth and emphasis to the message you are trying to communicate. However, be careful not to overdo it. Too many special effects can be distracting. Meaning might be lost, or, even worse, you could lose your audience's attention completely.

Remote Start Switch

A true on-air console has provisions for remote-starting a CD, turntable, cart, or other tape source. Often located right under the fader control, the **remote start switch** both turns on the audio source and the motor of the turntable or cart, or puts the

A production person adjusts one of the many signal processing devices available.

CD player into play. On older boards with rotary volume faders, the switch is called a "key" and is often located right above or below the level control. For fast production while on-air, remote control of all sources is important. Often the remote start controls are connected to a timer so that the operator knows when a tape is about to end.

Mixing and Routing

Once the audio signal has been received, it is the function of the console to allow you to manipulate the signal. The console can put out two or more signals at once, and **mixing** allows you to work with the volume of these sources separately. For example, if you are working with an announcer and music, you would want to be able to adjust the volume to make sure the music doesn't drown out your announcer. In addition, every mixing console provides several ways to "monitor," or hear, the audio of all playback sources. You can also choose the path of the audio signal by **routing** it to a specific channel. There are several monitoring options. One system is called the *cue system,* which is usually activated by moving the fader to its down or counterclockwise position until it clicks. Using cue, an operator is able to find the start of a record, to hear how an unfamiliar cut on a CD fades out, or monitor the remote line from a sports venue before broadcast. Many consoles have a tiny loudspeaker built into them dedicated to the cuing function. **Audition** is similar to cue in that it allows an operator to listen to and preview any sound source before airing, either on the main speakers or through a headset. The other system is the **air,** or **line monitor,** and this is the program either as it comes out of the console or the way it sounds directly from a radio receiver. On-air operators should always monitor the air. Besides loudspeakers, headphones are used so that the operator can hear the level of the music relative to his or her voice while the microphone is on. When the microphone is switched on, the monitor speakers are silenced, or **muted,** to avoid a loud squealing known as **feedback.**

A production person at KSFO/KYA San Francisco wears a headset.

Will the familiar broadcast console endure? The answer probably depends more on operator acceptance than available technology. Even though it is possible to buy an on-air facility with only a computer screen, it has not been met with joy by disc jockeys used to working with their hands, manipulating volume, and shaping the sound of the station. One computer-only facility has only a single monitor, and every on-air function from turning on the microphone to looking at the log to playing music and commercials and controlling the level is done with a user-friendly touch screen. If current announcers and operators are used to the old ways, the disc jockey of tomorrow may have already trained for the tasks of modern radio on a Nintendo or word processor.

SUMMARY

Before you can learn the tricks of the trade, you must be familiar with the tools of the trade. The individual pieces of equipment needed for audio production were presented in this chapter, along with details on how they work. Using a microphone is the first step in converting acoustic sound to electric energy. There are several types of microphones to choose from, which are characterized by two basic criteria: their operating principle and their directional pickup pattern. In addition to the microphone, there are also many different audio sources you can use in your productions, such as turntables, CDs, carts, reel-to-reel tape recorders, and digital systems. Once you have determined what sound and audio components will comprise your project, the audio console will help you put it all together. You will be able to process the sounds, adjust the volume, combine the audio sources, and preview the results.

Now that you understand the individual components of what is called the sound or audio chain, it will be easier to see how they work as a system in the production of radio programming. Because each audio production is unique, the type and selection of equipment utilized will change with every project. Understanding the performance characteristics of available equipment will help you choose the best tools for the job as you proceed to do creative radio production.

ACTIVITIES

1. Try to find a vinyl phonograph record and look closely at the grooves that represent sound information. Do the same thing by looking very closely at the multicolored back of a CD and the dull emulsion on some audiotape or videotape. Don't destroy new tapes for this purpose!
2. Plan a mock audio production project. Consider what equipment you would need to successfully produce the project. What kind of microphone would you use? How many sound sources would you need? Will you record the final project for replay in the future?

4 *Studios and Control Rooms*

▼

The audio chain consists of individual components such as tape, CD, microphone, and console. When you put them together as a system, you get radio. Think about how you might *see* that system when you listen to the radio. A person in a large room talking into a microphone, surrounded by records and CDs? Is it possible to tell when one audio source ends and another one begins? Have you noticed how the announcer always talks immediately after the music or commercial ends, with no periods of silence between sounds? Even if you have not gone behind the scenes at a radio station, you probably really do *see* some of it in your mind's eye as you listen. Now consider this: It is all perceived differently by a majority of the audience. To listeners, radio is an illusion, a seamless wall of entertainment, music, voices, and commercials. Unlike you, the student of radio, they may not *see* it.

The carefully crafted illusion of sound that is radio is created using selected tools of production, but combined at the on-air and production facilities found in a modern radio station. On-air. Production. Two different facilities with different purposes. On-air is where the announcer, operator, or disc jockey presents the discrete elements of information and entertainment programming in an order that conforms to a plan or format that is decided upon by the station. It is usually done live, in *real-time,* thus contributing to the immediacy of the medium. Production, on the other hand, is typically used to combine voices, sound effects, and music into a pre-packaged product that will be scheduled and played back later on the air. Two different facilities: one for continuous live radio, the other to prerecord some of the programming elements that will be played back on-air. Now look at the tools of production as a system, the on-air and production facilities found in the radio station.

DEFINING THE CONTROL ROOM AND STUDIO

While the words **studio** and **control room** evolved from radio, these terms now have a clearer meaning in television than they do in radio. In television, a studio is where the talent performs and is picked up by cameras and microphones, and a control room is where you find the technology of production and the people who operate it, all coordinated by a director. In television production, there is a complexity of equipment and technique that requires more than one person to accomplish. In the studio and control room, television production is a team process.

Most radio is done by a single individual operating in a single room that is a convenient combination of studio and control room. When productions require several people and multiple microphones, these people may be in the same room with the equipment and operator. In radio, the term **control room,** or **master control,** often means the on-air room, while the production facility may be called a **production studio.** Whatever it's called, it is almost always a single room where the equipment is designed to be operated by a single individual. Modern radio facilities, on-air or production, are combinations of studio and control room. When one person operates the equipment and announces, the combination of production tasks performed are said to be **combo.**

But it wasn't always this way.

In the Beginning

Long ago, when radio programming and production resembled, or even suggested what television has now become, very little production was performed by a combination announcer-operator. Throughout most of the 1930s and 1940s, radio invented much of the long-form broadcast entertainment, the half-hour and one-hour program formats that eventually made their way to television by the 1950s. Early radio was the half-hour sitcom and drama, the variety show complete with live studio audience, the full-length documentary, and news broadcast. Sound familiar? It's television without the pictures. In early radio, a small live studio audience was able to view a staged live theatrical or musical event as it was being broadcast live to a home audience of millions. The pictures had to be created in the minds of the listeners.

It was the programming that defined what the studios and control rooms looked like, and why they were different from those used today. Because early radio programming was so different, so too were the number of creative people needed and the skills required of its technical people. Unlike today, early radio required a team of writers, actors, announcers, control board operators and engineers, sound effects people, live musicians, directors, and assistants. Yesterday and today, programming determines the design of the production facilities of the radio station.

If the nature of early radio programming and the people required to put it together are so different from those of today, what about the production facilities? For starters, they used to be much larger. Many studios used in early radio were either converted theaters or rooms designed to resemble them, complete with stage, lighting, seating, and a lobby. The entire studio was soundproofed to reject unwanted sound from the outside that might be picked up by sensitive microphones and inadvertently made a part of the live broadcast. The interior walls were covered with sound-deadening material so unwanted echo would not interfere with the intimacy of the program. If the studio was not designed to accommodate an audience, it had to be large enough for a group of actors, sound effects equipment, and a piano or organ.

The early control room was adjacent to the studio, sometimes placed where the balcony would normally be and visible to the on-stage or in-studio talent through a giant soundproof glass window. There, a director followed the script while looking through the window at the studio talent. Also behind the window were the audio control console and an engineer or board operator. The show's director, with the help of assistants, told the audio person which microphones to turn on and when, and cued or pointed to the appropriate talent when it was time to speak, sing, or play. Often, an early radio facility designed for network origination would consist of a master or main control room surrounded by a group of studios, some large enough for audiences and some designed only to accommodate a single announcer. If television inherited many of its characteristics from these early broadcasts, radio, with its variety shows and dramatic presentations, certainly began as a copy of the dominant medium of the time, theater and vaudeville.

Now consider the differences between that facility called the on-air control room, or master control, and that facility called the production studio. Both have very specific purposes. Both the use of the room and the equipment used may also be very different. Different facilities. Different outcomes. Both are used in the total radio production process.

ON-AIR FACILITIES TODAY

Changes in programming have redefined the concept and design of studio and control room. Now it's one person in one room, a basic combination of studio and control room containing compact disc players, tape players, a microphone, and a mixing console. Music-dominated radio programming requires only a disc jockey to weave and mix music, commercials, and promotional announcements into a **format,** or station sound that never varies. Because of this, a modern radio station's on-air facility is designed so that a single operator can carry out the repetitive nature of the format in the easiest possible manner. The facility and its equipment must be rugged enough for continuous use, it must be appropriate to the format, and it must be convenient enough for sustained operator comfort.

Often the station format determines the design of the facility. Classical music or jazz? Classic rock? A basic on-air facility for these formats may have two CD players, several cart players for commercials and other short announcements, a microphone, and a simple console. Oldies, contemporary hit radio, or country? Because these are formats characterized by short play lists consisting of single records, perhaps carts or an all-digital hard disk system will be used for the majority of music playback. Even though some of the hits of the 1950s and 1960s are available on CD, many stations already have extensive libraries of music on cart. Public radio? News/ talk or information radio? Facilities for these stations may include extensive telephone systems, reel-to-reel tape, analog or digital, and DAT for playback of half-hour and hour prerecorded shows, and a receiver used to air a live satellite network broadcast. College and community radio? Because of the often eclectic nature of their music programming, these stations will have a large library of 12-inch vinyl LP records and at least two turntables in their on-air facilities.

An air personality at KHQT San Jose.

All on-air equipment is in a single rack, within easy reach of the operator. In this rack are the transmitter controls, the telephone interface, a CD player, and three cart machines.

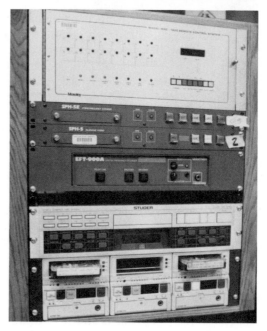

On-air facilities are getting the benefit of the science of ergonomics, the design of a work space for maximum operator comfort. Experts study the movement of a person while working and note how that person relates to the equipment needed to perform each task, all in an attempt to make the activity more "user-friendly." Does the operator have to get out of the seat to get a tape or CD? Does the disc jockey have to reach too far to push a button that starts a turntable? The modern on-air facility has all equipment, the "hardware," tapes and CDs, and the "software," within reach of the operating position. Some wrap-around furniture for on-air now resembles the cockpit of a Boeing 747 jumbo jet. Instead of starting each piece of equipment by pushing its play button, most on-air consoles now incorporate remote starts with their level control faders.

Selecting Equipment for an On-Air Facility

Look at the many variations of on-air facilities. Sure, it may depend on the format, the type of music or talk done by the station, but for now, look at what's available. What would a typical system include? In the previous chapter, you were introduced to individual pieces of equipment and learned how they worked. Now see them differently, as part of a system, an on-air facility. Notice that there are microphones for live voices, playback devices for music and recorded announcements and programs, consoles that control and mix each source, and monitoring systems that allow the operator to hear sources one at a time and in combination.

While most of the digital innovations in radio already have found their way into the production studio, there is also the possibility that much of the familiar equipment currently used on-air will disappear altogether. As more radio stations move into computer-controlled digital systems for on-air playback of music and recorded announcements, equipment will become *invisible,* and less maintenance will be required. Finally, the mixing console may be replaced by a computer screen and mouse. All audio will be stored in computer memory.

Getting the Audio to the Transmitter

Usually, the transmitter is on the highest building or mountain in the area, not where the studio is located. For this reason, part of the equipment in the on-air facility that the operator must use and be familiar with is the remote control of the transmitter. The Federal Communications Commission, **FCC,** allows a broadcaster to use a small UHF radio transmitter and receiver to send audio from the console to the transmitter and to turn on and off and monitor the technical parameters of the transmitter. Devices called **STL,** studio-to-transmitter link, and **TSL,** transmitter-to-studio link, are used for this purpose. Their controls must be in the on-air facility where the duly-licensed operator/disc jockey records pertinent transmitter information on an **operating log.** Rules require that the operator must actually be able to see those meters showing the performance of the broadcast transmitter.

a   *b*

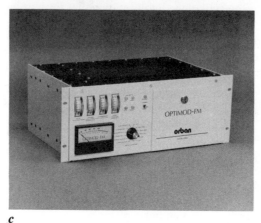

c

An operator monitors the broadcast (a); the modulation monitors (b); and the audio processor (c) used by most modern stations. (c: Courtesy of AKG Acoustics, Inc.)

PRODUCTION FACILITIES TODAY

Production may be defined as those creative activities that support and enhance the on-air sound of the station. Most production is simply the **mixing,** or combining, of music, voice, and other sounds into a thirty- or sixty-second package. It may be a **spot,** commercial spot announcement; a **promo,** a station promotional announcement; a **PSA,** public service announcement; or even a short dramatic or comedic segment for the morning show. When completed, the final package is usually transferred to tape cart, given a label with a number, scheduled on the program log, and finally played by the on-air person. At most small- and medium-market stations, an announcer may spend four hours on the air as a disc jockey and two or three hours in the production facility.

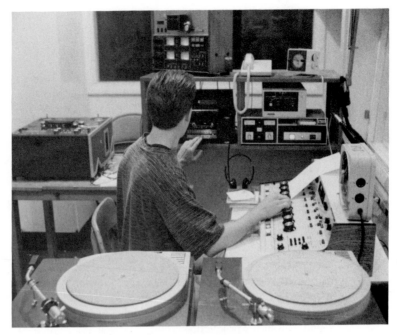

A student completes a production assignment.

There are several levels of production studios. Production of so-called national or regional spots, those commercials that air on many stations, may be done at large, dedicated recording studios rather than at a radio station. As this type of major production facility is also used for recording live music, it will have samplers, sequencers, synthesizers, and keyboards, as well as dozens of sound shaping tools. Most local stations will not have this type of facility; when it is needed, it can usually be rented on an hourly basis.

Facilities designed for production at the local station are smaller versions of the traditional recording studio, and, like the on-air facility, are designed to be operated by a single individual. Production facilities differ from those used for on-air in important ways. While on-air is playback only, production facilities include the ability to record onto tape cart, reel-to-reel, and a DAT or other digital storage device. Usually, production includes some editing, either physically cutting and splicing magnetic tape or using the mouse of a digital audio workstation to move, add, and delete sounds. Mixing consoles are also different. Remote start of equipment may not be possible and each channel may have equalizers or other provisions for accepting signal processing devices like reverberation. Finally, a station's production facility may be used to record talk and interview shows. For this purpose, perhaps a separate studio with a table and several microphones is adjacent to the production control room.

This is the large production studio and control room at KSFO/KYA San Francisco.

Selecting Equipment for a Production Facility

The production facility is often the best-equipped room in the radio station. It is here that you will do much of the creative production that satisfies both advertisers and the public service community, and, in general, defines and supports the on-air sound. It is in the production facility that you as a radio person might single-handedly produce a commercial. It is also possible that a group of writers, musicians, voices, and technical people might spend an entire day here in the production of a truly creative and unique thirty second promotional announcement for your air. And while the on-air facility is designed to play back only, it is in the production facility that much of what is played back is recorded.

There are similarities and differences between the equipment used for on-air and that used for production. Microphones? Both facilities have them, but in production there is a greater variety of them and often more of them. Console? It is more elaborate and has more features with many extras not found in the on-air facility like inputs for sound processing and shaping devices. In on-air, because everything must flow and fit together, most playback sources must exist in twos and threes. In a production facility, there may be only one record player, CD player, or cart machine, because in production sounds are often added one at a time. For a visual comparison, look at some of the devices that are added in a typical production facility, those not found in an on-air facility.

Microphones and Accessories

On-air is simple. It has one person, one microphone. Production is a bit more complex. Here, you may use several voices, and they will need separate microphones, all with their own separate mounting device, perhaps a floor stand or a small boom. They may even be in a separate studio. What about on-location recording of events? You may need a highly directional microphone, a **shotgun.** You may also want to use a wireless microphone when high mobility is important and cables could get in the way. Will a production require original music? There will be times when a production project is so important, so special, that prerecorded library music will not

Two XLR connectors, one mounted in the end of the microphone and the other on a cable.

suffice. Special microphone setups in a large studio will be required to record a live band. In a larger studio, often a round piece of screen is mounted in front of the microphone to eliminate breath popping from a speaker or singer.

Using microphones in the production studio is different from on-air because it is here you can finally get creative, it is here that you are able to take an idea and turn it into a piece of audio for radio. Now, instead of one microphone to announce records, read station ID, weather, news, and commercials, you begin to think about actors, musicians, and interesting sound effects, all in a single thirty-second promotional announcement for your station. Now you have the luxury of time because you are not live on the air, feeding carts and CDs into their machines in service of the format. You begin to explore the various types of microphones available for your production. You have plenty of choices.

Microphone cables and connectors will suddenly become important. While the on-air facility is characterized by simple, permanently installed equipment, it is in the production facility where you may work with microphone cables and connectors. Since all microphones have built-in XLR male and all professional consoles used for production have XLR female connectors, production facilities will have various lengths of connecting cables with an XLR connector on each end, one that connects to the microphone and one that plugs into the console.

Consoles for Production

The mixing console found in the production facility is quite a bit more elaborate than that needed for on-air. First, the number of possible audio sources is greater in production. In addition to more microphones for more than one voice, any recorded music and sound effects or the samplers, sequencers, the drum machines and synthesizers of a live music group may need their own volume level control. Control and manipulation of each sound is important, and the production console usually has built-in equalization for control of the high, mid, and low frequencies of each audio source. And instead of a single stereo output like the on-air console, the production console may have several **submasters,** or outputs, for sending selected audio sources to the input channels of a multitrack recorder.

A production console. (*Productionmixer,* courtesy of Pacific Recorders & Engineering Corporation)

It is in the production facility where you are likely to find an elaborate patching and routing system, one that allows the flexibility to connect any mic level or line level source to any volume fader. Other apparent differences on the production studio console are functions like **echo return** and **solo.** These will not be found in an on-air facility. What is echo return? Normally, audio sources are recorded *dry,* that is, without any form of equalizing or signal processing. When the sound is played back to be mixed into a production, the echo return can be used to add common effects like echo or reverberation. When more than one channel is being mixed, solo is used to listen to as a single track of a tape or a single audio source without hearing the other channels or interfering with the mix.

Another characteristic of a production console that sets it apart from that designed for on-air is the variety of outputs needed to send audio sources to selected recording devices. The on-air console is simple. Stereo playback of CDs and carts goes to the transmitter. In the production studio, buttons located above each volume fader marked *send,* or *assign,* allow you to send or route the output of a volume level fader to a selected track of a multitrack recording device. This feature is neither useful nor desirable for an on-air console. Finally, the production console may not include remote starts for the audio sources since the repetitive tasks of format radio are not carried on in this facility.

a   *b*

*The on-air console (a) is simple. It has a volume control fader and a remote start switch for each playback source.
The production console (b) adds equalization, pan of left and right channels, solo switches, and more.*

Production Storage Devices

The output of the production console must be stored on a recordable format. When
you are on the air, you are only playing back sources of audio, already-produced
commercials, PSAs, and promotional announcements. But somebody has to record
it all ahead of time and copy it onto the proper playback format for airing. This is
another way that production activities and the technology that serves them are different from on-air. In production, everything has to be recorded, edited, and stored
for mixing into a final spot or show, all before it can be dubbed onto a cart for the
on-air facility. There are a number of analog and digital devices used in the production facility for that purpose. Some are also used as playback devices in the on-
air facility. They are, in order of audio quality, the reel-to-reel, the cart, and, occasionally, the consumer compact cassette. If the reel-to-reel is used to record, edit,
and master a commercial or other short announcement, the final product is then
recorded onto a cart for airing and to a cassette for the sponsor.

a   b

Two open-reel models; a basic two-track for on-air playback (a), and a 24-track digital used in high level production (b).

In Chapter 3 you learned how these devices work. Now look at them as an integral part of a system.

Reel-to-Reel

The most popular production format found in the studio is still the reel-to-reel tape recorder, or open-reel. Those used in production can be either identical to those used on-air, or they can be quite different from the basic two-track playback device used to air a station's half-hour public affairs program. Radio stations have standardized on the quarter-inch, two-track open-reel format for playback on-air, while in the production facility there are a number of configurations still employed. Four tracks on quarter-inch tape is probably the most common. There are even specialized models with mechanisms that are easier to use that are designed for rapid **tape editing,** the act of physically cutting and splicing the tape.

Tape Cart

Tape cartridges played back on-air must first be recorded in the production facility. The technology of the popular analog cart has probably evolved to the highest level of technical quality possible. While the earliest models only recorded and played a

A cart recorder.

tape and cued it up to the beginning of the audio, today's carts *read* the tape and adjust the electronics for an optimal recording every time a cart is inserted. Tape is better too, with better lubrication for less friction and better magnetic coating for lower noise. As an analog format, it is still good enough for the majority of broadcasters. While the on-air use of the cart is limited to the playback of prerecorded material, it is in the production facility that you have to select the proper tape length for the recording, properly erase it, set the levels, and finally record it and label it for air.

Compact Cassette

In 1963, Phillips introduced the compact cassette. Standardized the world over, it has become an inexpensive way for the radio production person to play his or her work anywhere, without the expense of setting up an open-reel or bringing a sponsor into the studio. Just as the VHS videotape has become a universal distribution format for television and film, the compact cassette is the radio producer's format of choice for sharing and archiving creative work originating on a larger format. Still, even with Dolby noise reduction and better tape quality, the compact cassette has never made it as a professional production format. Compact cassettes are found in the production facility to play back audio recorded on location and to make copies of productions for sponsors and others.

Of these three analog formats, only the reel-to-reel can be considered a true production format. It is in this format that you will likely record all the various bits and pieces of audio—the voices, the music, and the sound effects of a production. Once on open reel, audio on separate tracks can be equalized, replaced, edited, and, finally, mixed to a final product on a cart.

a

b

A broadcast-quality cassette deck (a) and the popular consumer compact cassette (b).

Digital Options

All of the recent activity in radio production, storage, and editing formats is in the digital domain. While large recording studios long ago converted to 24-track digital reel-to-reel formats, radio stations are largely embracing the smaller DAT and the new tapeless formats. But like the long-used analog storage devices, some digital devices are better designed for production while others are primarily for storage for later playback on air. Digital storage devices can be divided into two categories: those that record and play back in the digital domain and those that allow the production person to actually manipulate or edit the audio in the digital domain. Once edited, the results are copied onto a second digital format for the on-air control room.

A DAT is used for on-air playback.

Digital formats designed for basic recording and playback of already-produced audio, from short announcements like commercials and PSAs to full length programs, have been designed to replace the old tape formats like reel-to-reel and cart. Like the reel-to-reel, the DAT is capable of recording and playing complete programs of an hour or more. Because of its search functions, it is also possible to put a group of short produced announcements on a DAT tape. And while the DAT is a high-quality digital storage device featuring rapid access and cueing of recorded material, it has only recently been adapted for multitrack editing.

While the DAT is a high-quality format used by both recording studios and broadcasters, radio production people can now choose from several storage devices that have been designed to replace, even physically resemble, the cart machine. Several newly introduced models are exactly the same size as a cart machine so that they will fit into the same space. But instead of a cart, the audio is stored digitally on the 3 1/2-inch disk used in a computer. Each disk can hold from several to a dozen or more thirty- and sixty-second announcements. When the disk is inserted, an electronic label appears on the front of the machine, its menu. By designing these devices to resemble the cart, it is hoped that operators making the transition from analog cart to digital will not *feel* like they are dealing with a foreign object.

Now that broadcast folks have gotten used to the CD format for the playback of consumer music, production music, and sound effects libraries, there is much action toward making the CD a recordable format. It sounds like the perfect format. Production and on-air facilities already have them, and some CD players for broadcasters even allow stations to put the CD into a cart-like holder with a place for a label. As an optical device, the technology for recording audio onto CD is quite a bit more complex than putting it on a magnetic medium like a computer disk.

All of these digital devices designed to store both long programs and individual short announcements like commercials and PSAs require the production person to place each announcement or group of announcements on an individual tape or disk, label it, and put it within reach of the on-air operator. There may be something better. Entire systems that are invisible to the operator have been introduced. After putting together productions in the studio, they are loaded into a high-capacity hard-disk memory of a personal computer and the produced announcements are listed as a menu on a computer screen. With most of these systems, all the on-air operator

The digital cart will eventually replace the familiar analog tape cart. (Courtesy of 360 Systems)

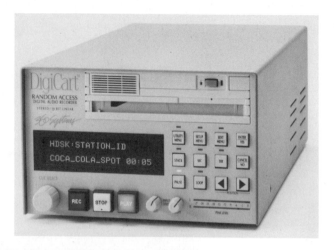

A recordable CD is used by broadcasters. (Courtesy of Denon America, Inc.)

has to do to play back the scheduled announcement is to point and click a mouse to cue, to make ready for airing. The audio stored in the computer is converted to analog and assigned to a volume level fader just like any audio source.

While there are many formats vying for acceptance as the digital standard to replace the cart, there is another category of digital production format designed to replace the multitrack reel-to-reel tape recorder in production—**digital audio workstations** or **DAWS.** This format also uses the hard-disk technology of the computer to record and store for playback all audio information. The difference between a digital playback format and a workstation is function. As opposed to the format that allows recording and playback only, the workstation features an on-screen menu that allows the production person to record and manipulate each piece of audio,

*Digital production at
KCBS San Francisco.*

assign it to its own location as a track, and finally mix it into the desired final production. It can then be dubbed onto a record-play system for airing. In the future, it is likely that workstations will be used for production, and a hard-disk-based or recordable CD format will be used to play back that production over the air.

NEWS PRODUCTION FACILITIES

A station's facility for news will depend largely on the format. If the station has one newsperson, a reader who is part of the morning show team, a small room with only a microphone may be enough. Some stations incorporate an extra microphone into their main on-air facility, and others place the news reader in an unused production studio. Music-formatted stations with major commitments to gathering, writing, and reporting news will have complete facilities for news production, including recording and editing equipment, right in the newsroom. All news-formatted stations will have a number of workstations for reporters and reader/anchors so that **packages,** prerecorded news stories, can be assembled using both live copy and **actualities,** the voices of the people in the news as gathered by reporters in the field and over the telephone.

THE INTEGRATED RADIO STATION

A radio professional could go into any of the radio stations in the United States and quickly be in familiar surroundings. The modern radio station likely will have a room for on-air origination or playback of talk, music, and short announcements, longer prerecorded programs, or a satellite feed. It also will have a second room for the production of these elements, and possibly a third room where news can be prepared and read. The space, equipment, and the complexity of the facility will primarily depend on the format requirements of the station, and, to a lesser degree, the size of the station and market. As a student of radio, you'll begin to see how programming will have a direct effect on production and the design of the facility.

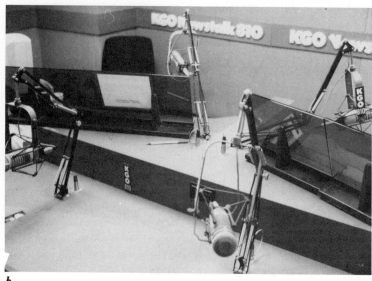

a   *b*

At KGO San Francisco, the engineer controls the volume of guest microphones, phone calls, and commercials (a), while the talent sits in a separate studio (b).

SUMMARY

On-air and production facilities: two different systems with two different purposes. From the 1930s era with its separate control rooms and studios for half-hour variety and comedy shows to the all-digital combo facility of today, the technology of radio has evolved greatly. And while the equipment used is still in transition, its evolution cannot be viewed as strictly technical. The equipment needs of the radio production person have always been directly influenced by programming needs. Is it easier to *see* yourself in radio, on the air, in production? Can you see the studio of the 1930s, the actors and sound effects technicians around large microphones? Could you see yourself in a modern on-air facility with CDs, carts, and console? Now picture yourself seated in an on-air facility with only a computer. Touch the screen. You're on the air.

ACTIVITIES

1. Visit several radio stations, and observe the activities and tasks necessary to be on the air and produce a spot in the production facilities. Ask questions about the equipment. Have someone demonstrate how it works as a system.
2. Get on the air at your school radio station. Many of these stations are very good and offer many professional experiences.
3. Listen to several radio stations, and try to imagine what the on-air operator is doing as one audio source ends and another begins.

The Techniques of Production

Now that you understand basic sound and audio terminology, and now that you are beginning to master how the technology works and how it is selected and put together as a production system, it's time to do something practical—to actually create a product. First, look at radio production as a type of communicative process and ask these questions:

What is the message you are trying to convey?

What kind of audience will be receiving the message?

How can you ensure that the audience understands your message?

What technical, economic, and creative limitations might be imposed upon you?

Are you prepared to produce the project?

In some situations, the message that you are trying to present will be predetermined by a sponsor, either before the production process or as part of script development. For a class production, perhaps you will be assigned to write a script for a product or service. In other radio and classroom production situations, you may be asked to come up with the idea, write the script, and produce the production; it all may be up to you. The audience that receives your message will be the easiest to understand because the style of programming done by the station, its format, will already have an audience well known to your station. When you know something about that audience, you'll have a better idea of whether it will understand the message. And while the technical and economic limitations will depend on the scope of the project and the size of the station's market, there may be no creative limitations placed on you as a producer. You may be left alone, even encouraged, to give it your best and most original effort.

Within the last question, "Are you ready to produce the project?" lies one of the most important aspects of the production process. In fact, compared to producing for other communication media such as television, magazine, and newspaper, audio production for radio can be affordable and creative. But that does not mean it's always easy. Audio production ranges from one person in a simple studio or with a portable recorder interviewing out of the studio to two dozen people working at a live musical event with thousands of dollars worth of equipment. And it's not only the radio station where audio production takes place; you can find audio production in television stations, film studios, and concert halls, as well as less obvious places such as private businesses, hotels, restaurants, night clubs, schools, all levels of government, and religious organizations. Whether for radio, television, or film, there is an obvious and definable process: preproduction, production, postproduction.

Look at the organization of a production for radio in the same general framework as television, film, and even print. No matter what level of production you are associated with, all production requires some advance planning and preparation, called **preproduction,** in order to be successful. The next step is the actual **production** of your project. Once production begins, problems will arise and changes will be made to the original plan. However, the better prepared you are, the easier it will be to solve problems if they occur. The first time you try to produce audio without doing the necessary preproduction, you'll realize how a little time planning saves a lot of waste later. Finally, once production is completed, editing or other changes will be made before the project is ready to be distributed. This last step is called **postproduction,** but is most often referred to as simply editing. Again, even postproduction will go much more smoothly if your production is organized and planned well.

A word about the creative process: Throughout all three steps of production you will be required, even encouraged, to add your own ideas to the project or at least creatively implement the ideas of others. It isn't enough to simply be the technician that turns the machines on and off. You must be able to make the technology work for you in a creative and satisfying way. Based on your knowledge of audio production, you should be able to accomplish your project, satisfy the sponsor or your boss at the station, and feel good about what you are doing. And if you lack enough content or technical knowledge, you'll want to know how to find out what you need to know. It is difficult to be creative if you are not in a state of constant learning and if you are unable to implement an idea you are not familiar with or that you do not understand.

Briefly consider some of the tasks you will have to perform in order to do your best audio production for radio.

Preproduction

1. Idea: either the sponsor's, yours, the station's, or that of an instructor.
2. Script: you are given already-written copy or a fact sheet from which to write a script. If there are facts absent, must you do any research to gain them?
3. Treatment: comedy, drama, straight voice, music and voice.
4. Facility selection: for most productions, there will be little choice but to use the station or school studios.
5. Talent selection: you, fellow announcers, class members.
6. Materials selection: CDs for music and sound effects, blank tape.

Production

1. Rehearse and record all original audio, voice, and music.

Postproduction

1. Edit voice and music if needed.
2. Organize and copy each audio source onto separate tracks.
3. Mix to final product and dub to on-air playback format used.

With this background in mind, you are now ready to plan, prepare, and complete an audio production for radio.

▲

5 ▼ *Organizing the Production*

Preproduction is a series of planning and organizational steps toward a successful audio production. Preproduction begins with the formulation of an idea and ultimately leads to the final script of a project. Of course, there are many steps in between, such as focusing on the intent of the production, identifying the intended audience, planning what form the production will take, acquiring talent, reserving equipment and studio facilities, and identifying distribution outlets. Once these aspects are assembled, you must prepare a treatment that includes all of these components for approval before you proceed to finalize the script. It is important to remember that many ideas are already predetermined by the client or sponsor; that is, the audience has already been determined, the production techniques have been chosen, and the script has been written. Decisions are made about the potential audience, production techniques, and even the final script before the project even makes it to production. Consequently, production personnel must be able to follow the parameters set by the creators and the technology in order to effectively initiate the desired message.

THE PREPRODUCTION PROCESS

The importance of the preproduction stage cannot be emphasized enough. The better prepared you are, the better the final work will be.

Goals and Outcomes

If the idea is not already provided, first and foremost you'll want to decide what it is you want to accomplish with your production. Your communication message should have a *purpose*. It is this purpose that will guide you in deciding how the project will proceed and what type of response you want to get from the audience.

Typically audio messages have one of three purposes: to entertain; to persuade; or to inform.

To Entertain

Music programs, comedies, and dramas are examples of entertainment programming. The audience response that is most desired with entertainment programming is to keep the audience interested, listening, and enjoying itself. Entertainment puts people in a good mood and makes them more receptive to new ideas.

To Persuade

Public service announcements urge people to believe or act in a particular way, like wear your seat belt, don't litter, or learn CPR. Promotions urge people to tune in to upcoming programs. In the case of a station promo, the goal is to gain public attention and to separate your station from the competition. And commercials, of course, are designed to persuade consumers to buy a particular brand or product, or service.

To Inform

News and public service programs fall into this category. News reports are designed to present information in a clear and objective manner so that people can understand the circumstances surrounding an event. Public service programs also seek audience comprehension of particular issues or problems.

Understanding the purpose of your message will greatly affect the form it takes and will determine what type of response you expect from your audience.

Audience Analysis

Once you have determined the purpose of your production, you must then think about who will receive your message. You must take into consideration the potential market for your station or you can tailor your message to *speak* to a particular segment of the audience, called your **target audience.** You have to consider the demographics and psychographics of your audience. **Demographics** are characteristics such as age, race, gender, economic status, and so on. **Psychographics** refer to the values and beliefs held by people. You will have to decide how to interest your listeners and ultimately what effect your message might have on their lives.

An announcer reads the morning news on KSJS San Jose.

Content or Idea

As mentioned before, audio communication is extremely important, and a production, no matter how sophisticated and precise, will only be as successful as the idea that drives it. Research is the key to focusing an idea. To be sure, you should rely on your own knowledge and experience, but no one can know everything about every subject. You must develop research skills to find the information you cannot provide yourself. The library is always a good place to start. Interest groups associated with your subject matter are also good resources. Make phone calls, write letters, ask questions, use referrals. Details can make the difference between an average and a great production. As you begin to get organized, you will find that your idea will be changed by outside influences you'll come across. Keep in mind, once again, that many times the content will be provided by sponsors or the programming department.

Treatment

Once you come up with an idea, you must commit it to paper. A **treatment** is a type of proposal that outlines an idea. Information that should be included in the proposal are: the purpose of the project, a script synopsis, a production time-line, budget requirements for casting and equipment, and the projected target audience. The treatment gives the reader a clear understanding of the project, including music, sound effects, voices, pacing, and mood, and whether it will be comedy or straight. Treatments are necessary to identify potential problems before the project goes into production. In addition, treatments are prepared to acquire approval or funding for productions.

Script

Once you come up with an idea, you have to transfer it to a form useful to others. It would be too difficult and time-consuming for you to verbally explain to your production crew, one by one, what you have in mind and how you would like your idea to work. The **script,** often called **copy** in radio production, is a written record of how an idea or communication message should sound. Many times you may be working with someone else's script. Under these circumstances, your responsibility would be to recreate sounds as closely as possible to the script's requirements.

Scripts provide directions about sound effects and music, including their implementation, such as fade-in music, segue to other music, or EFX loud. Directions are also relayed to characters on the script, such as slowly, angrily, coyly, or pause. Scripts use specific language to represent the process of production. Scripts are normally made up of three components:

1. Dialogue (**ANN**), which is provided by the announcer or talent.
2. Music (**MUS**), which is played in the background or as an exclusive part of the program.
3. Sound effects (**SFX**), which are any sounds other than music or speech that are used to reinforce the message by creating an image, setting a mood, or compressing time.

The way in which these three sound sources are combined are indicated in the script language. For example, fade corresponds to the increase (**FADE-IN**) or decrease (**FADE-OUT**) of volume of a sound source. A **segue** is often used as a generic term for any transition. However, transitions may take the form of a **crossfade,** which moves gracefully from one sound to another, like television or film's visual dissolve, or a **hard segue,** which abruptly stops a sound source and immediately follows it without interruption with another sound. This latter type change is analogous to a visual cut in television, but is typically called a segue while the dissolve is called the cross-fade.

▼

BOX 5.1   *A Script Example Utilizing Various Cues*

Script formats vary. Some are more detailed than others. There are three basic levels of scripting. A full script notes every detail of the production, including exact dialogue, music sound effects, intros, exits, and so on. Commercials, promos, PSAs, or newscasts typically require a full script. Partial scripts provide an outline of the production only. Interview programs couldn't possibly script the responses to every question because they are not specifically planned in advance; consequently, a partial script would be used to highlight such things as entrances, prerecorded segments, and exits. The last type of script is a run-down script, which is typically used for programs with established formats. The various segments are listed with projected length times, but the rest of the program is ad-lib or live performances by talent.

When writing your script, remember to write for the ear and not the eye. By reading your dialogue out loud you will be able to tell if the words work well when spoken.

Selecting Talent

Once you have decided on your message, you must acquire **talent** that is capable of communicating your message effectively. You might think this is quite simple. However, audio communication is not just sitting any person down in front of a microphone. It takes good communication skills, timing, emotion, characterization, confidence, and certainly experience, to work comfortably and successfully in audio. Keep in mind, if you are producing for a radio station, your talent must fit within the boundaries of the station's overall sound.

Straight Announcers

Straight announcers are basically program hosts or narrators as opposed to actors. Why are DJs called announcers anyway? Because when radio first began, on-air people were literally announcers; they announced events, programs, music, and so on. Now, announcers are considered more as entertainers or radio friends than they are as straight announcers. Announcers must be able to speak clearly without any voice defect in order to be understood by the audience. Announcers should speak

A prodution person at KGO San Francisco gets ready to read a commercial.

as though they are addressing one person so that the individual audience member believes the announcer is speaking to him or her personally. This does not mean that a low-energy or unenthusiastic speaking style should be used. On the contrary, announcers must sound confident and natural. Those artificial *radio voices* are a thing of the past unless they are a parody. Overdramatic, or unnatural voices distract the listener and thus detract from the all-important message. So do mispronunciations and grammatical mistakes. Announcers need to be literate, have a working knowledge of the language, have some general education, and be up to date on current events. Announcers are expected to read scripts, station logs, announcements, news reports, and memos from other departments. At times, they might have to engage in a conversation about contemporary topics or interview others about specific issues.

Actors

On the other hand, if you are producing a radio comedy or drama program, the requirements of your cast members are quite different from those of a straight announcer. Voice affectation, for example, is exactly what you will need from your characters. Surprisingly, the best person for the job may not always be the best actor. It is voice *quality* that is the important factor in audio production. A voice is capable of conveying so much more information than just written text. Avoid casting similar voices for the same production, especially if they are to play in a conversation with each other at some time during your script. Cast for voice contrast. Try to audition as many people as possible for your production in order to take full advantage of the talent that is available to you.

Recruiting for talent can be done just about anywhere. Place an ad in the school newspaper, post flier announcements, or even produce an audition announcement to be played on your college radio station. You should keep written records for those who do apply. Make notations about an applicant's name, address, phone number, voice quality, experience, audition performance, availability to work, and so on. These records will allow you to recall people for future productions as well.

Selecting Music

Music will provide various functions for you during your production. It will create a mood, provide a background, or a **bed,** provide an effect, and set the tempo. Beware not to use music out of habit. Sometimes messages without music in the background can create quite an effect. Consider what contribution the music will make to the overall message theme before you include it in your project. There are several music sources available to you. One is the cleared music library. It is somewhat generic in nature and is designed to be used as background music for productions. If you are not associated with a radio station or if you cannot find appropriate music for your project, music can be produced specifically for a production. If you are not musically inclined, you can hire musicians who specialize in writing original compositions.

Selecting Sound Effects

A sound effect (SFX) is considered to be any sound element other than music or speech. These effects can be used to enhance your message or take the place of words. Sound effects can be background sounds that create a specific environment or particular sound, such as a door slamming, the clinking of glasses, or a phone ringing. Virtually any sound you can think of—and some sounds you've probably never heard before—are available for you to use. Again, consider how the sound effect will allow you to communicate your message more effectively. Too many sound effects can confuse the listener and detract from you message. Along with music, stations also pay for the right to use sound effects. These sound effects are cataloged and kept in a library. Selection and use of both music and sound effects is detailed in Chapter 8.

Budgeting—What Will Your Idea Cost?

Even the most basic production will cost something. Equipment, talent, studio space, editing time, script materials, music, and so on all must be considered when assessing your budget. Time is also money. The more complicated the project, the more time it takes to complete. When you are renting studio time by the hour or your interview subject has a tight schedule, time can become your worst enemy. Once again, organization is the key to making the most of the time and money you do have.

The kinds of decisions you must make in order to run an efficient production are what the budget process is all about. A budget should reflect every element of the production with a prediction of how much each will cost, including equipment, studio time, salaries for talent, equipment, supplies, distribution costs, secretarial services, even photocopying the script. By laying out the project in this way, you can see the "big picture" and make decisions about how much emphasis in the form of money is being distributed to the various areas.

Once your budget is finalized, it still has to be flexible enough to accommodate some level of change, especially if unforeseen problems occur. Keep in mind, however, that many budgets have an overall bottom line. That is, there may be a maximum amount of money you are allowed to spend. In this case, if some aspect of the production goes over budget, you will have to adjust another element to absorb the loss.

SUMMARY

Now that you have been introduced to audio production, it is time to begin the first step of the process. Preproduction is a series of planning and organizational steps toward a successful audio production. The better organized you are, the smoother your production will proceed and the more easily you will be able to handle problems. The various components of preproduction include: formulating an idea, focusing the intent of the production, identifying the intended audience, planning what form the production will take, acquiring talent, choosing music and special effects, reserving equipment and studio facilities, identifying distribution outlets, preparing a treatment, and finalizing the script. Since production does cost money, all preproduction planning and decisions must be made according to budget limitations. However, budgets must be flexible enough to accommodate change if problems occur.

ACTIVITIES

1. Listen to some radio commercials and transcribe their scripts onto paper. Pay special attention to what kind of voices, music, and sound effects are used to communicate ideas in such a short amount of time. What are the goals of the commercial? To persuade? To inform? Who was the target audience for this message?
2. Create a script of your own. It does not have to be complex. Simply toy with some ideas and put together a spot that complies with a specified time constraint. Most radio spots are usually thirty seconds in length.

6
▼

Beginning Production Techniques

You've listened to radio your entire life, and now you're a student of radio. Maybe you have spent some time observing at a college or commercial station. Perhaps you're training to be on the air at the local community or public radio station. You understand a bit about programming, and you know the equipment in your facility. As a result, you begin to see that there are two types of radio production activities taking place in two separate facilities: on-air and production. Each has different tasks, different purposes, and different outcomes, but for the same radio station.

The activities of an on-air disc jockey are best described as live, real-time production. Everything is organized on a *program log* that provides a minute-by-minute schedule of programs, commercials, promos, and PSAs. The log guides the airing of every element in the broadcast. One format tells which songs are to be played and how often, and another tells when the announcer must talk and what he or she can and must say. As an on-air real-time announcer/disc jockey, every minute of every hour is always planned in advance.

On the air at KSFO/KYA San Francisco.

The production of those short announcements that are played over the air takes place in an environment different from that of the live, real-time production of an on-air program. First, when doing production to be broadcast later, everything is recorded, and that means that you are able to keep trying until all the elements of a produced piece are perfect. If you are on the air live and you stumble over a word while reading live copy or fail to fade the music down enough to talk over it and still be heard, you can't go back and do it again. Second, unlike being on the air where the clock never stops, when you are preparing production for air, the clock is only running when you want it to run. There is time to work with ideas, write a script, and find the right music, voices, and effects. And finally, there are technical differences. In production for air, you are recording something that may be repeated dozens, even hundreds, of times, so it must start the instant that the on-air operator presses the button and it must sound technically perfect.

Now production begins. You'll learn how to create, and prepare on cart for air, a thirty-second produced announcement using basic production techniques and simple equipment. For this you will need a thirty-second script, your voice, a single piece of music, some open-reel tape, and a cart. It will be a combo exercise, so you'll operate the equipment while announcing. Because this is a first production, there won't be any extra effects or editing. The goals of this exercise are to see the steps involved in production, to be able to identify and operate equipment, to select simple production materials, and to mix your voice with music. The process will be more important than the final product.

BASIC ORIENTATION TO THE PRODUCTION FACILITY

Before the production can begin, you'll want to spend some time identifying the location and understanding the operation of the equipment found in the typical production facility. Once you understand how it can work together as a system to support a production, you can start to select some of the materials needed for the basic production. Sure, every facility is different; yours may even have more equipment than you'll ever use for this exercise. It won't matter. For this production, the equipment and materials required are basic to every facility.

Identifying the Equipment

You'll need a small combo production facility consisting of at least a single microphone, a turntable or CD player, a console, an open-reel recorder, and a cart recorder. Spend some time learning the location of each piece of equipment, and note which volume level fader on the console is used to control its audio. Try each piece of equipment. Play a record or CD, speak into the microphone.

TABLE 6.1   *Basic Equipment Needed and Purpose*

1. Microphone	Pick up announcer voice
2. Turntable or CD player	Playback music selected for background of production
3. Console	Control and mix all audio sources; includes monitor speakers and headphones
4. Open-reel recorder	Record the mixed output of the console and then play back the completed production when dubbed to cart
5. Cart recorder	The final destination of the completed production. The cart goes into the on-air control room for broadcast

This is basic equipment found in the typical production facility. It is designed to be used as a system. Other production equipment includes a bulk-tape eraser or **degausser,** a cart splice finder, a typewriter for making cart labels, clocks and timers, and cassette recorders for making copies of your work.

TABLE 6.2   *List of Materials Needed and Where to Find Them*

1. Live copy	See the examples in Appendix A or ask the college radio station for outdated PSAs
2. Record or CD	Your school's production music library or the library of the radio station. For background in your production, it should be an instrumental, not vocal
3. Reel of tape	Local broadcast or electronics supply house. For production, the preferred tape is a 7-inch reel containing 1 1/2-mil tape
4. Cart	Local broadcast supply vendor or campus radio or TV station. For PSAs and spots; most are 40 or 70 seconds in length

---

Identifying Needed Materials

The materials, the **software** of production, consist of a script that sells a product or service, or promotes the activities of the radio station or a nonprofit public service organization, a piece of prerecorded music from a vinyl record or a CD, a reel of blank tape for your particular reel-to-reel recorder, and a tape cartridge of a length sufficient to hold the complete production.

A final element of any production is the talent, usually actors or announcers. For this simple production, you are the talent. Later, a more advanced production will be attempted, one where you may write an original script, use more than one voice, or actually produce an original music track or create sound effects. In the future, you will always edit your production, perhaps even using a digital workstation. But no matter how complex, a short produced announcement or a half-hour or hour program for radio will always consist of some combination of voices, music, or sound effects, combined according to a script and designed to entertain or inform a listener.

BASIC PRODUCTION TECHNIQUES

Now that you've identified each piece of production equipment and all the materials needed, it's time to use it as a system. Before you begin, consider your operating position. It's somewhat like driving a car. You are in the "driver's seat" and, from that position, it should be possible to control all the equipment. Like the driver, everything should be at your fingertips. Whether you sit or stand depends on how the facility is set up. At one time, most consoles were mounted on a desk-height table, thirty inches from the floor. Turntables and tape decks were less than an arms-length away if you were seated in the facility's swivel chair. Of course, most consoles then were shaped differently, and all had round knobs to control the volume level.

Today, there are more facilities designed for the stand-up operator, usually with a desk height of thirty-two to thirty-four inches from the floor. In the stand-up facility, the CD and tape players are often at eye level. Why the recent popularity of the stand-up facility? It might be the lower, gradually sloping design of the console to accommodate slider-type volume faders, or the more compact nature of playback devices like CD players, or even the fast paced, aggressive sound of modern radio. Compare the act of loading a CD into a player with the physical movement necessary to cue up and ready a 12-inch vinyl record for broadcast. For the operator, the person in the driver's seat, radio production equipment is easier to use. Look closely at each part of the production system and determine the best way to relate to it as an operator.

Using a Microphone

Every announcer and disc jockey *works,* or uses, the microphone differently. Some believe that they sound best when their mouth is six to ten inches from the microphone, while others believe they have to talk into the side of the instrument to avoid the popping caused by breath. Still others see the microphone as their favorite listener, one to be whispered to or shouted at, their mouth touching the microphone. Experienced announcers even have very definite preferences for microphone type and may actually bring their own microphones when they go into a new facility.

Is there a right way and a wrong way to relate to a microphone? Probably not, since all voices are different, and it only has to sound right when it comes out of the monitor speaker. Good technique is usually accomplished by trial and error. Each time a new situation is encountered, record your voice and play it back. Listen for extraneous noises. The aim of the combo announcer-operator is to reach the perfect balance between being so close to the microphone that the mechanical sounds that accompany speech are noticeable and being so far away that the background noise of the motors and fans in the facility are picked up easily. Also, if you are too far from the microphone, sound reflected off the studio walls and windows may cause a hollow, over-reverberant sound as if you were speaking from inside a trash can.

Using the microphone correctly.

The usual dynamic and condenser microphones found in a production facility are designed to be talked into from as close as several inches. Most have a built-in windscreen to eliminate all but the most explosive breath sounds, and most are designed to take a lot of abuse. Not all are created equal, however. Look at the microphone housing closely for any switches or controls. If it is a condenser microphone, there may actually be an on-off switch to control power to the microphone. It could be battery-powered or it could use so-called **phantom power** from a power supply built into the console.

Another microphone-mounted switch is used to give the operator some control over the **proximity effect,** or the tendency of some microphones to overexaggerate the bass or low frequencies of a voice when the person speaking is extremely close to the instrument. Some microphones have a simple two-position bass filter, indicated by a straight line for *flat,* or no effect, on the sound, and a line curved downward to indicate less bass. Other microphones have switches marked voice and music. Select the switch position on the microphone that sounds most natural with your voice.

Identify the microphone volume level control on the console. **Open the mic,** or turn it on. Learn to *set* or *get a level,* or to adjust the microphone volume of your voice. As you read the script into the microphone, try not to vary the mouth-to-microphone distance more than an inch or two. Also try not to vary the volume of your actual voice so that some words or phrases are noticeably louder or softer than normal. If you suddenly raise your voice, distortion will result, and if you just as

Dust must be removed from the record to eliminate noise.

suddenly lower it to a whisper, it will be too low to properly record without unacceptable background noise. The appearance of loud and soft on the radio is mostly a practiced illusion, since the volume-controlling devices between console and transmitter, called **limiters** and **compressors,** really keep all sounds at about the same real loudness. The voice actor who can "do" loud and soft has learned microphone techniques that create these audio illusions.

Using Turntable and CD

For this simple production, prerecorded music from a single CD or record will be used. Eventually, a more creative and complex production may require playback of several carts and cassettes, digital samplers and workstations, DATs, telephones, and other sources of audio. Now, learn how to cue and use two of the more common sources for music playback, the turntable and the CD player. Depending on your facility, at least one of these sources will be available.

As found in radio station production facilities, common turntables usually have the two playing speeds, 33 1/3 rpm for the twelve-inch LP and 45 rpm for the seven-inch single with the large center hole. Because the spindle of the record playing turntable is small, an adapter is needed for the 45 record. Read the label because some twelve-inch records are recorded at 45 rpm and some seven-inch records are at 33 1/3; some even have an LP-size center hole. If you are using a commercially recorded production music library, it will be recorded at the twelve-inch, 33 1/3 format.

In order to use the turntable for production music, you must be able to **cue,** or find, the desired selection of music to the beginning sound, and you have to be able to start it at the exact second needed. Find the turntable volume-level control on the console, and, while a record is playing, turn up the volume so that the music can be heard. This also may be accomplished using the cue position on the volume fader. Next, locate the desired **cut,** or band or track, of music on the record. Locate

The 7-inch 45 rpm record has a large center hole.

For a slip-cue start, the operator holds the record on a spinning turntable.

the motor on-off switch and start the record spinning. Place the needle on the disk at the start of the desired cut, and, as soon as the audio begins, stop the motor using the on-off switch. With two or three fingers, very carefully move the turntable backward until the needle is positioned several inches to a half-inch before the start of the music, depending on how the record will be started. The better turntables start quicker so they don't have to be backed up so far.

Now you have two choices, mostly depending on the design of the facility and the type of turntables used. One option is to **slip cue** the record. To accomplish this, gently rest several fingers on the disk, holding it still while the turntable spins under it; for this, you need a specially designed **cue mat,** a slippery piece of paper or felt between the record and the turntable platter. Now, the music can be started the instant you remove your fingers from the record. This is how cuing was accomplished from the early days of radio until the popularity of remote starting in the 1960s. Try this method a number of times until it is comfortable enough to do.

Option two is to start the turntable using its built-in on-off switch, or the remote-start option if available. Newer turntables are designed to start instantly, and get up to correct playing speed in less than a quarter rotation of the turntable platter. To cue a record on a newer turntable, or one without a cuing mat, find the first note of the music and stop the turntable as above. Now manually reverse the platter to a position from one-quarter to one-third revolution away from the exact place where the music begins. The turntable will start the moment you press the on-off switch, whether remotely at the console or at the turntable itself. With this method, you must anticipate the length of time between when you press the button and when the music will actually start, often a second or two. In order to accomplish tight production using this cuing method, you'll have to press the button before you actually want the music to start.

A broadcast CD player is being loaded.

Both cuing methods for vinyl records require plenty of practice.

Compact disc players designed for broadcast production cue electronically. Most consumer models do not. Try this at home: Press the start button on a home CD after you have selected a track. Note how much time elapses before the sound is actually heard. It might be less than a second or it might be as long as three or four seconds. Every CD is recorded differently. Conversely, the chances are good that the CD player in your production facility has a feature called *auto-cue* or *cue-to-music*. Load the CD you are going to use into the player and select the desired track. Press the auto-cue or cue-to-music button. The timer should indicate that several seconds or less have elapsed on the track and the player should go into pause. Now it is ready to be started instantly.

Both the record and its replacement, the compact disc, are well-suited to tight production because they can be easily cued and instantly recalled for playback the second that they are needed. Select one of these two audio playback sources for this production.

Using the Console

Chances are you know where the microphone and other audio sources are on the console. You may have actually used them to audition music or to set a microphone level. Now, take a closer look at the heart, or the brains, of the audio facility, the console. The mixing console is necessary, since the discrete pieces of audio technology must work together as a system in the service of a production. The console is a logical device for controlling all these sources of sound. Use the console in this production to select audio sources, audition those sources, set proper levels and monitor them, combine or mix them together, and finally assign the console's output to a cart recorder.

This production facility is at KSFO/KYA San Francisco.

There are two ways that audio playback sources find their way into a production audio console. One is with the use of a patch panel. Patch panels provide the most versatile use of a facility's technology; they allow you to hookup practically any audio source to any available volume level fader. If you don't like the order of sources that appear at the faders, change them. If faders two and three are turntables and you want them to be CDs, just use a patch cord to connect the two CD players to faders two and three. It's really that simple. The same is possible with microphones. Want five microphones for a live recording session? No problem. Just connect a patch cord from the appropriate microphone connector in the studio to the desired volume level fader on the console. Remember to match line level audio devices to line level volume faders, and mic level to those faders designed to be used with microphones. Some faders are single purpose while others have mic/line selector switches.

Patching is not necessary when all the possible audio sources in the facility are normalled into the console. Look closely at a complete input module and its volume level fader. Somewhere near the top of each module may be found a *mic/line* selector. This switch is important for two reasons: it is the first place where an audio signal goes once inside the console, and its position determines whether the signal will go directly to the fader as a line level source or to a preamplifier as a mic level source and then to the fader. In the typical facility, each input module has two normal sources, one line level and one mic level. For this exercise, you'll need to identify the correct faders for microphone, turntable or CD, open reel, and cart. Remember, these faders are used to play back an already recorded audio source.

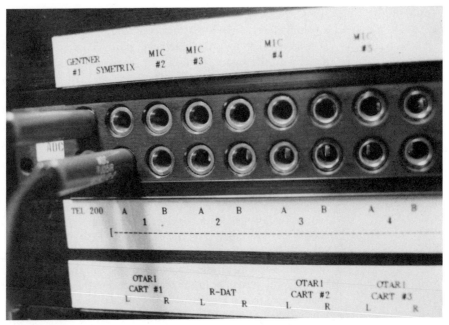

Using a patch panel.

On-air consoles have a cue position. In this example, the pot is rotated counterclockwise until it clicks into cue.

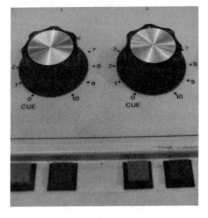

Next, you may use the console to cue audio playback sources before putting them *on-line* to be recorded. The major purpose of the cue channel is to allow an operator to preview an audio source using an isolated speaker or headset while another audio source is being recorded. A cue feature on a console is mandatory in an on-air facility, because the console is always on-line.

In the exercise on page 98, where only one music source must be cued, the fader used to set the level can be in its normal playback position for cuing before the production begins. If you decide to use the cue channel of the console, determine whether it is selected right on the volume level slider or pot, and if its signal goes to a headphone, the studio monitor, or a separate speaker.

Once an audio source has been selected and previewed, the next step is to set a volume level, reflected by a meter reading of 100 percent or "0" VU, **volume unit.** If a level is too low, the electronic noise inherent in every console may be heard along with the signal. Also, if you record a less-than-normal signal onto an analog tape recorder, the "hiss" or noise that is an artifact of all analog tape will be more noticeable when that recorder is played back and the already low level is raised to normal. The opposite of a level too low is one that is too high. If the VU meter continuously indicates a reading of +3 or more, or stays *in the red* area of the meter, the level of the audio source may distort because it has overloaded the recording device. Most cart and open-reel recorders will not have automatic volume limiting devices like those found in the on-air audio chain.

For setting accurate levels, production consoles will have some combination of trim pot, level fader pot/slider, and VU meter. On consoles with sliders as level faders, there is usually a **trim pot,** a small volume control between the input selector switch and the fader. The trim pot is used if a particular source is too loud or soft to easily match the system, or when an operator wants all input source faders to be at about the same physical reference place on the console. Trim pots need to be used in conjunction with both the level fader and the VU meter when setting a level. The easiest way to set a level is to turn the microphone on and move the fader to the normal, "0," or gray area near the top of the fader's path. Speak into the microphone or play the record or CD and adjust the trim control until the meter indicates close to its optimum 100 percent. On those consoles with rotary faders, simply advance the pot until the desired level is reached.

All audio facilities have a pair of monitor speakers. As a production person, you are also going to need a good-quality headset. Actually, you may already have one with you at all times if you carry a portable cassette or CD player. Since consoles use the larger *1/4-inch phone* connector, and portable stereo headsets are equipped with *mini-plugs,* an inexpensive adapter will be needed. If you buy a high-quality headset specifically designed for audio production or at-home stereo listening, it may have a combination 1/4-inch and mini-plug so it can be used with all devices. Headphones are important when you have to mix your live voice with music. When the microphone is turned on, either the monitor speaker will have to be turned down manually or it will be muted automatically to prevent acoustical feedback.

Headphones are often equipped with a combination plug, which can be used with both consumer and broadcast equipment.

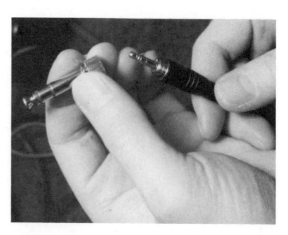

TABLE 6.3	**Correct Order for Getting Audio In and Out of Console**

Task	Location
Select input source	Mic/line switch, patch panel
Cue or audition source	Cue position on console, headphones, extra submaster
Set proper level	Main slider or rotary pot, trim pot, VU meter indication, test tone to recorder
Monitor source	Speaker or headphone, VU meter
Mix sources	Two or more faders up to desired level
Assign	Submaster or master output to inputs of selected recording device, pan to selected channel, test tone to equalize levels

There are two remaining production tasks that can only be accomplished using the console. They are mixing and assigning. **Mixing** is what happens when you fade the volume of music down so that a voice can be clearly heard. It is called mixing because both audio sources are on at the same time, even though their levels are not equal. Even though you may start the music at a 100 percent VU indication, it will have to be faded down before talking so that the music level is "under" that of the voice. Sometimes the music is faded up using the slider, while other times it is *keyed,* or switched, on. It depends on the type of console you are using.

Once you have decided how the various audio sources will be mixed together, the resulting mix must be *assigned* to a tape source to be recorded. Every board has either a simple stereo master output, four or more submasters and a master, or separate recording and monitoring master outputs. The output of the submaster and master is the *mixed line output* of the console. This audio goes to the monitor section of the board, where it feeds various headphones and monitor speaker combinations. It also goes to a **DA,** or distribution amplifier, a device that sends sound from the console to all recording devices in the facility. These include open-reel, cart, DAT, cassette, DAWS, and other consoles in the station.

How will you know if the level coming out of the console matches that going into the tape recorder? If your facility does not have preset levels, perhaps there is a test tone built into the console. Find the test tone, usually appearing at a line level input, and set it to read 100 percent or "0" VU indication. Later, it will be used to make certain that the open-reel and cart recorders "see" or receive the same level as that indicated by the console VU meter.

Finally, there are some features on the production console that will be used later, when a more ambitious project is attempted. EQ, or equalization controls, pan pots, and effects returns should all be in the off, detente, or normal position for this first exercise. In fact, it is a good idea when you approach the console at the beginning of production to make certain that all switches on all input level modules are *normalled.*

Table 6.3 gives a review of the order of tasks necessary to get audio from each playback source to its final destination, a recording device.

These EQ switches are set to normal.

Using Reel-to-Reel

For this first basic production, a simple two-track, two-channel, open-reel deck will be used. Tracks versus channels: What does it mean? Very simply, a track refers to how the tape head lays down information onto the magnetic medium itself, and channel is the electronic path from the console to the tape recorder. A professional open-reel tape recorder capable of recording two, four, or eight tracks simultaneously will have as many channels. Whatever the track/channel configuration of open-reel decks, all will have a speed selector, some will have a reel tension adjustment, and all will have monitor selectors, in addition to the record, play, rewind, and fast forward functions of the transport.

Learn to correctly thread the reel-to-reel deck in your facility. In fact, learn as much as possible about the deck you'll be using. Your facility probably has standardized tape type, tape speed, and other operating parameters. For this first exercise, you may be using a seven-inch reel of 1 1/2 mil tape, and you may record at either 7 1/2 or 15 **IPS,** or inches per second. At the faster speed, the audio quality is better, there is less chance of distorting the tape, and, when editing, the faster speed makes it easier to find where words begin and end. A seven-inch reel of tape will give you fifteen minutes of two-track recording time at the 15 ips speed. For seven-inch reels, set the tape tension selector to *small.* The *large* position is for ten-inch reels.

Probably the most confusing feature on a reel-to-reel deck is the monitor selector. Labeled *source/tape* or *input/output,* it monitors the heads before and after recording. Remember that in a three-head deck, the erase head is first, followed by the record head, and then the playback head. When the monitor position is in source or input, the VU meters and the audio output of the deck—the sound you hear—is what is going into the recording head. If the position of the switch is in tape or output, the meter and sound from the deck is what is heard by the playback head, after the recording has taken place. Use the monitor selector in the source or input position only to set a "0" VU tone level from the console but in tape or output the remainder of the time. When recording, the monitor can be in either position.

Using the reel-to-reel in your facility, practice setting levels and recording and playing back an audio source from the console. Identify its *record safety* switch. It must be in record before a recording can be made. If applicable, learn to use the auto-locate features and memory rewind and return to the 000 feature found on many deluxe models. Learn to use the tape transport in a way that puts the least stress on the tape. Instead of going directly from rewind to stop, for example, go from rewind to fast forward and then finally to stop when the tape has nearly slowed down to a stop. This gentle braking action has been used by the pros for decades to keep tape from stretching and breaking.

The cart uses a continuous loop of ¼-inch tape in a plastic housing.

Using the Cart

If you have spent any time on-air at a radio station or in some television production facilities, you may be quite familiar with the tape cartridge, the **cart.** Perhaps you have only played back those carts that are prerecorded. Now, you are going to record onto them. Unlike the on-air carts that are ready to be played back, recording onto them requires that you select the proper length for the production, manually erase it, and put the deck into record, all before you play it back to check its quality. Some facilities actually have a combination tape eraser and **splice finder,** a device that first erases the entire tape and then stops the erased cart at a point just beyond where the two ends of the continuous tape loop are spliced or joined together. By not having to record over the splice that every cart has, you can really be assured of a recording without a noticeable **dropout,** or loss of audio, at the point of the splice.

If your first production is going to be thirty seconds or less, select a standard-length cart, say forty seconds. Because most spot announcements for radio are either ten, twenty, thirty, or sixty seconds in length, carts are sold in lengths of at least twenty, forty, and seventy seconds. This allows a comfortable few seconds before the tape recues for its next airing. It also means that each time an announcement is over, it will cue quickly so that the player will be free for the next cart. Carts are also available in multiples of seventy seconds, like two minutes and twenty seconds, three-thirty, and four-forty, in case a sponsor wants to air in equal rotation two or more sixty-second spots.

a

b

Two carts lengths are 5½-minute (a) and 70-second (b).

A cart is erased before use.

Once a cart is selected, it has to be erased, and if possible, the splice located and bypassed. Because the cart system uses a continuous loop of tape, an erase head cannot be used, since there will always be a half-second or so of unerased material due to the continuous loop nature of the medium. Here's how to erase a cart. Remove your wristwatch since it can be damaged by the strong magnet in the degausser. Now, while holding the cart several feet from the top of the eraser, turn on the power. Lower the cart slowly to the device while continuously moving it in a circular motion. Without stopping its motion, move it to the sides and then the back of the cart. Still without stopping, gradually raise the tape from the device, and when it is several feet away, turn off the degausser. If you play back an erased cart and you hear a "blip" or a rushing sound at regular intervals, erase it again.

After the cart is correctly erased and cued past the splice, place it in the player/recorder and advance the tape in play for several seconds. This takes up the slack in the tape loop. Now press stop, followed by the "record set" button and you are ready to record. Set a level by generating a 100 percent or "0" VU tone on the console and adjusting the meters on the cart machine to match. Now, when the start button on the player is depressed, recording will begin. The combination of record set and play also places a cue tone on a separate track of the cart; that way, the cart will always stop at a point immediately before the audio begins. Some machines even have tones that fast-forward the cart to the next record cue tone; others have a third tone used to indicate when the audio is ending. This tone is sometimes used to start a second player in automated radio stations. Practice with the cart machine in your facility. When using a cart, the goal is always to record the audio tightly so that the sound begins a fraction of a second after the start button is pushed.

A BEGINNING ASSIGNMENT

Now that you understand the production facility a bit better, it's time to do a practical exercise. Here are the steps in the process required to record a PSA, using your voice and music, onto open-reel and then to cart. Because the exercise is going to be produced on open-reel and then **dubbed,** or re-recorded, to cart, a countdown will be used so that the cart can be recorded tightly. The skills learned while doing this exercise provide the basics needed for every project.

Here is a summary of the assignment: First, find a comfortable operating position. Start the open-reel tape recorder. Turn the microphone on. After a 5..4..3..2..1.. countdown, pause a second and start the music. After several seconds to establish the music, fade it under and read the live copy. When you have read the copy, fade the music out, turn off the microphone, and stop the open-reel tape. Play it back, and if it's OK, dub to a cart.

TABLE 6.4	*The 10 Illustrated Steps for a Simple Production*

Check each step off when completed:

_____ **STEP 1:** Gather all the materials needed: You'll use live copy, a selected music cut from record or CD, a blank open-reel tape, and a blank cart.

_____ **STEP 2:** Select volume faders and set levels: Check to see if all input selectors, equalization, pans, and effects returns on the input module are in the normal position. Using a combination of trim control and slider, find a "0" VU level on both music and voice.

_____ **STEP 3:** Cue music: Place the music playback slider into cue. When using a record, find the start of the music, stop the turntable, and back the platter up to a third of a turn before the music begins. If a CD, select the cut and cue it to music.

_____ **STEP 4:** Rehearse: Read the live copy aloud several times until you feel comfortable in its reading. Once the reel-to-reel is rolling, plan to use one hand to start the music and then turn on the microphone and the other to control the level of the music. Once the music has been started, use that same hand to turn on the microphone while the other hand fades down the music. Practice starting the music one second after the 5..4..3..2..1.. countdown. Using the headset, try several practice runs to get the feel of operating the console while reading copy. Try to fade the music under your voice so that it will not be too loud as to overpower the voice or too soft so as to not be heard at all. Try this several times.

Setting the microphone level.

A CD is loaded into the player.

TABLE 6.4	*continued*

_____ **STEP 5:** Prepare reel-to-reel for recording: Set up the deck by selecting the correct speed and tape tension. Thread the tape. Turn on the record function and select input or source on the monitor. Send a "0" VU test tone to the open-reel. Set the level so that the VU meters on the open-reel match those of the console. Return the monitor selector to tape or play. Make sure that the playback level control for the open-reel is all the way down or off; otherwise the recorded signal will be played back through the console a fraction of a second after it has been recorded and an echo will result.

_____ **STEP 6:** Record: Put on the headset. Start the open-reel tape and make sure its record lights are lit. Prepare to start the music with one hand while the other is in position to control the level of the music. Turn the microphone on. Do the countdown, pause a second, and start the music. Fade the music under, then read the live copy. Fade the music out, turn off the microphone, and stop the open-reel tape.

An announcer reads the copy.

_____ **STEP 7:** Playback: Rewind the tape. Select the proper monitor position on the open-reel deck for playback and turn on the playback volume level fader for the open-reel playback. Listen to the entire production to determine if the levels are good and the music is correctly mixed with the voice. If not, repeat the entire process again. If the exercise is OK, play it back and set a "0" VU on the console meter.

a

_____ **STEP 8:** Prepare cart: Erase the cart you have selected for this exercise. If your facility has the proper technology to find the splice in the continuous loop cart, cue past it for a dropout-free recording. Place the cart in the machine and press start, let it run several seconds in play, press stop, press record set. Again, send a "0" VU test tone from the console and make sure the cart recorder's VU meter reads the same. In the absence of a test tone, play back the reel-to-reel and set a level that is as close as practical to the "0" VU or 100 percent. Make certain that the playback volume level fader for the cart is off or down, otherwise an echo may dominate the recording, as with the open-reel.

b

Starting the reel-to-reel tape (a), with a closeup (b).

_____ **STEP 9:** Record cart: Place one finger on the start button of the cart recorder and one on the play button of the open-reel. Here is where a tight recording is important, for if you start the cart recorder on the "1" of the countdown or too soon after the countdown ends, there may occur a one-second pause between when the on-air operator pushes the start button to play back this cart and when the sound actually begins. This is the dreaded loose production. If the cart is started too late after the countdown ends, like on the first note of the music, the recorder will cut off that first piece of the music and when cued up after airing, a brief *blip* will be heard.
The best way to correctly record a cart is to start the open reel, and at a point halfway between the audible "1" of the countdown and when the music begins, push the start button on the cart.

The record set is pressed.

_____ **STEP 10:** Playback cart: Is it tight? Does it cue quietly? If not, erase the cart and try it again.

By going through the steps necessary to complete this simple production, you have learned many basics about production equipment, materials, setting levels, using the console to mix two audio sources, recording it onto open-reel, and dubbing it to a cart.

SUMMARY

Now you are beginning to get an idea of the process of production. You have combined live announcer copy with music, and you have worked with common recording mediums—reel-to-reel tape and carts. You also have a good understanding of how the equipment contained in a production facility is used to support a production. You have learned to select audio sources using the console, and you have completed a basic production exercise.

Now it's time to get a bit more creative. While the just-completed thirty-second produced announcement shows the process, it has used an already-existing script and commercially recorded music. There's much more. To be truly satisfied in audio production for radio, try an original idea, write a script, perhaps use more than one voice, even produce original music and sound effects, all in the service of a simple announcement. You may want to try a comedic or dramatic treatment using actors, and you'll want to try a variety of special audio effects at a more complete facility. And you'll record and edit all these pieces into a final product using the latest digital workstation. Someday, you'll be tuning the car radio while driving and suddenly there it'll be, your masterpiece, on the air. Stay tuned.

ACTIVITIES

1. Practice reading copy for a variety of spots and PSAs. Record them onto open-reel tape and play them back for other class members to hear.
2. Record your voice reading copy with several microphone types. Do you notice that some make you sound better than others?
3. Observe experienced announcers at work on-air and in the production studio. Note their microphone technique.
4. Play back a variety of music and tape audio sources and experiment with levels. Use the "0" VU level test tone on your console to set a level for recording.
5. Become familiar with your facility. Learn to operate all the equipment and know where its audio output appears on the console.

Advanced Production Techniques

For most radio production, the basic combo facility is all that is needed. But what about more complex forms of production, like a full-length radio documentary or drama? What about those promos, PSAs, and commercials that require several voices and more than one microphone in a large studio? Or productions that require more creative attention to directing talent and technical people? Or those that require extensive use of multiple audio sources that must be put on as many tracks of a tape format or a digital workstation? And what about those productions where you need to have at your command every possible digital and signal processing option invented? For maximum creative choice, you'll want to know about the more advanced techniques of production and how to operate the equipment found in a major production facility. And whether a class group project or a major professional effort, you'll need to know how to select the talent and technical people needed to complete a more advanced audio production for radio. There will be times when an audio project for radio needs a larger production team than just a single person recording a spot. Professionally, both the equipment and the techniques used in the big recording studios are finding their way into the radio station.

DEFINING THE ADVANCED PRODUCTION

Think back to that first radio production assignment in a combination control room and studio, the one called a combo facility. Here, you were able to stand or sit in one spot and operate a few pieces of basic equipment while reading a script. You did it all yourself. It seemed easy enough, and for most projects in radio production, a combo facility is all that is needed. There will be a day, however, when an idea for a production will require skills and equipment beyond that found in the combo facility. There will be a time when the coordination of multiple voices, audio sources, and technical effects will be more than the familiar combo facility can handle. The more advanced production may have to be done in a facility with a separate control room and studio.

How will you know when to seek out this type of facility? More than any other factor, it is the type of show or project that you are planning that will point the way to the equipment, facilities, talent, and technical resources needed.

First, people. Look at the number of actors, announcers, or interview subjects needed for the production. Will you have two or more voices that must be on separate microphones? Will they have to work in a large space, one beyond the capacity of the typical combo production facility? Does your proposed project call for a group of actors who must read a dramatic script? Or will a half-dozen community leaders and politicians need to be grouped around a large table in order that a lively discussion can be recorded for broadcast? Will the program be a comedy and variety show, complete with live audience? In any production where a group of voices must interact with each other as performers, actors, or interview subjects, they should be in a room separate from that of the production equipment.

Second, consider the technical complexity of the production. Even if you must work with a large group of people in an interview show, you may not need more than a few microphones, a console, and a basic recorder. The opposite of that simple talk show might be the complete comedy/variety/musical show for radio like those found on National Public Radio. These shows require plenty of microphones, a director and assistants, several engineers, and maybe even multitrack recording and signal processing. Even a thirty-second commercial using several actors, sound effects, and music may require some postproduction, or editing, and signal processing before it can be mixed to the final spot. Look at the script to determine whether a production can be completed in a basic combo facility.

Separate engineer and talent. Separate rooms. Perhaps now you are able to visualize the type of facility needed for some of the larger, more advanced radio productions, a facility designed to handle a production more demanding than that possible in a combo facility. And unlike the studio-control room combination, the more advanced facility is often known as a *dual operation* because a separate control room and studio are used. In a dual operation, like a recording studio, the mixing and recording technology of production is in a control room and the microphones are in a connecting studio, visible to the control room through a soundproof window. Like live television production today, talent is in the studio, and the producer, director, and engineer are in the control room. If you have visited a television station or recording studio, you've already seen some of what goes on in a facility designed for dual operation.

DIRECTING A PRODUCTION

Directing a radio production requires learning new skills and plenty of preplanning. Of course, in the early days of radio, a program always got on the air this way; a director would select and work with engineers and talent as they learned the script. The microphones in the studio would be set up, and rehearsal would take place several days prior to the live broadcast of the program. Finally, the director would coordinate it all using a familiar language and prearranged *hand signals,* a way for the talent to know when to speak their lines while looking at the director through the control room window. You can imagine one evolutionary result. In the middle 1940s, owners of radio stations received their television licenses and proceeded to design their control rooms and studios for *radio with pictures.* Radio inspired the process of directing for television.

To direct, you'll have to change roles from that of combo producer to that of leader. A one-person effort, if that's what you've mostly done in the service of radio production, won't be possible for some advanced productions. Now, you'll have to learn the studio and control room and its more complex equipment setup, and you may have to select a few people to help. Now, you'll be the producer and director instead of the combination talent and engineer that you were in the combo production. Now, you'll need to learn the process and language of production; a studio will have to be set up with microphones for your chosen talent, and you'll need to communicate the results of what you're doing to an engineer so it can be recorded. Whether you are playing a role as part of a classroom group assignment or involved in a production for air, there is a process to follow, one that can take you from idea to finished production, from studio to control room to air.

In the Studio

In television, the studio is where the cameras and microphones pick up the talent's performance so that it can be selected in the control room and put onto tape. In some radio productions, the talent, the microphones, and an occasional sound effects person are found in the studio. Whether radio or television, each person needed as talent must be selected, rehearsed, and directed, and an engineer must set up the equipment so that the talent's performance can be correctly picked up as it is being directed from the control room. There are at least three categories of people who

TABLE 7.1   *Who's Who in the Studio*

Person	Task	Type of Production
Announcer	Reads copy	Simple voiceover or narration for all productions
Actor	Reads dramatic script	Full-length drama or spot using drama
Host/interviewer	Introduces, interview guests or talent	Talk/interview show, variety show
Guest	Answers questions, performs, sings	Talk/interview or variety shows
Sound effects technicians	Creates live effects	Drama
Audio technicians or engineers	Sets up microphones before production	All productions
Studio audience	Sits, participates	Variety shows

are found in the studio part of a radio production. Talent can be described as announcers for a commercial, narrators for a documentary, hosts or interviewers for news and information programs, and actors, musicians, and other performers. Guests are those people who have been invited to the studio to be asked questions for an interview program. Technical people include the engineers who set up the microphones and the occasional sound effects person needed to re-create an old-time radio drama. You will have to select and prepare these people for the production.

Finding Talent

Announcers will be the easiest talent to find, select, rehearse, and finally record for your production. Your class production group, the campus radio station, and even the local volunteer public or community radio station will be home to dozens of people with satisfactory voices who may not be trained but are at least interested. If a studio production requires two or three voices reading fairly straight copy, your experience in combo production will have prepared you well for working with these announcers. The selection of announcers will partly be determined by the voice qualities that you are searching for, like *authoritative; light and friendly; male, female, child;* and *old person* or *young man.* For a class assignment, selection will be primarily determined by who is available.

Hosts and interviewers are another matter. Are you producing and directing a news and informational type of program where the subject matter is of primary importance? Does the person you select as the host have to be knowledgeable about community or local government issues? To select talent for this type of program, you might try recruiting at the journalism department of your school. Sometimes, those individuals who report and write for another medium are the best qualified to interview local newsmakers. This includes people who write for the campus and community newspaper or reporters for the local television station. The selected individual will be a journalist first, a radio announcer second. Selection of hosts and interviewers will always be decided by an individual's content expertise and interviewing abilities, not by the quality of the voice.

Of all the people you will have to select, prepare, and direct for a production, actors will provide the greatest challenge. While there are plenty of announcer types willing to read straight copy and enough broadcast journalist types who can handle interviews with newsmakers, finding an actor experienced in radio drama is not going to be as easy. Where do you begin?

There are two possibilities. One is that you simply use your friends, the people you know from your broadcast classes, and attempt to direct them in a performance of your script. For a beginning project, this often provides good experience for you and the talent, and, because they are your friends, they'll give you plenty of time. They'll be patient with you. Another possibility is to go to the theater department and explain your script to instructors and their students. You may even find that there is actually a class in dramatic techniques for radio. There also are community drama groups with dozens of trained actors who will be glad to volunteer for the chance to get into a studio.

Technical People

The studio technical people are the same people who will end up in the control room during the actual production. Before that, they'll have to set up the microphones so that each voice can be accurately recorded. How many microphones will your technical people have to set up? The best advice is to use the minimum number required to pick up all the voices, since every time another microphone is added, there will be an increase in the amount of sound picked up. The rustling of script pages and the movement of chairs and bodies, no matter how silent, will always have a greater chance of being heard as more microphones are added. If, for example, six people are acting in a play, how many will need to speak together at one time? Two, three? For this, three microphones can pick up all six performers.

The only other technical person found in a studio during a production will be the rare sound effects technician. Of course, for your production, most of the sound effects will be prerecorded, probably from a CD-based sound effects library. But, when producing a re-creation of an old-time radio drama, some producers call for sound effects created in the studio to accompany the dramatic dialogue. What about footsteps or the opening and closing of doors? In the studio of the past, a piece of wood floor and a door mounted in a frame were used during the show to add a realism not possible with recorded effects. Because the actors could not *stay on mic* and walk or close doors at the same time, a sound effects technician performed these difficult-to-synchronize effects live, in front of a microphone. You may need this individual if yours is a real-time production. Otherwise, these effects can be added later during postproduction.

In the Control Room

Once you have selected the studio talent and technical people needed for an advanced radio production, it's time to consider those support people you are likely to find in the control room. As director, you'll need technical people to operate the equipment, and you'll need some assistance with the script and the continuity of the production. Depending on the complexity of the show and whether it is a real-time

TABLE 7.2   *Who's Who in the Control Room*

Person	Task	Type of Production
Producer	In charge of the project; may be the director, sponsor, even the radio station's programming or promotion director	Most large and sponsored productions
Director	Directs talent and technical people	All
Assistant director	Assists director with effects, other details	Most larger productions
Continuity person	Helps the director interpret and follow script	Longer dramas
Board engineer	Operates console, but the director may do this in simple productions	All productions
Assistant engineer	All technical production tasks, from running sound effects and music to operating tape recorders and other equipment	Larger productions
Editor	Postproduction and editing	Large, multitrack productions
Mastering engineer	Mixes all shows to final version for duplication and distribution	Large shows with multitrack, edited audio
Sponsor and advertising agency people	Observe, approve	Any

production or one recorded in segments for later editing, there will be from two to a dozen people needed in the control room. If it's a class project involving a group, everyone will have to perform one or more of the tasks shown in table 7.2.

The control room could be a busy place. While the purpose of having the talent in a separate, soundproof studio is to isolate it from the technology of production, the control room serves the recording, directing, sponsoring, and every other support need of the production. And while most advanced productions could be accomplished with a single engineer and director, many sponsors request and pay for plenty of creative, supervisory, and technical support. It is the usual procedure for an advertiser to contact an agency during the initial creative stages of a production. Once the concept is approved, a production team—administrative, technical, and creative—may be called in and the project further refined. The necessary talent is auditioned and picked, a studio is selected and scheduled, and the production is completed.

The **producer** is the person responsible for the entire radio production. Sometimes the producer and director are the same individual. A separate producer is likely to be found when the production is sponsored, when the project involves a great number of spots or a series of longer programs, and when many people must be coordinated in preproduction. The producer is responsible for selecting and supervising writers, approving scripts, hiring talent, finding facilities, and working with the director and technical people to make certain that the final product will satisfy the people who have provided the financial support. The producer is the chief liaison between the money people and the creative people. For your first advanced production, you'll probably be the producer, director, even the engineer and editor.

In the real world, a *director* of a radio production will usually be someone who is at a radio station or has in the past worked in radio production at all levels. In an advanced production, the director is the creative person in the studio and control room who puts the best possible performances from the talent into a final product for air. The director, aided by an assistant in large productions, will select actors and rehearse them in the studio before going into the control room for the recording. A director is often helped by a person who follows the script so that the director can concentrate on the actors and the audio. Often called a continuity person, this individual knows when to tell the director to get ready to start a sound effect or open a new microphone. The director has a language for communicating with the engineer in the control room and a series of hand signals to direct the actors in the studio.

There may be several technical people in the control room. You will need at least one technical person to operate the console. Known as the *engineer* or *board operator,* it will probably be the same person who set up the microphones in the studio. There may be a second technical person to run the sound effects, start the tape, set the levels, and do other routine technical tasks. In the recording studio, this person is known as the *second engineer.* In major projects, the technical people who set up the studio microphones and operate the equipment during recording will be joined by other technical support personnel. If a multitrack recording, there may be an individual to operate the recorder or digital workstation, there may be an editor, and there may be a mastering engineer to combine all audio into a two-track master for release. For productions that must be sent to a multitude of stations, someone will have to duplicate, type labels, and prepare for mailing.

The Directing Process

Now that you have some idea about who does what in the studio and control room, how will you direct them all into a finished production? Where do you begin? How do you know when to stop rehearsing and begin recording? How will you know when all the technical and other support people are ready to follow your creative lead? There is a process that every director will want to follow before he or she has the necessary confidence to put all the production elements together for that final product. Table 7.3 shows what a radio production person-as-director might consider for the production of a series of thirty-second announcements—using several voices, both straight announcers and actors, and music and sound effects—which will be distributed on tape to several dozen local stations.

TABLE 7.3   *Order of Directing Process*

1. **Idea.** As director, you may be asked to originate the idea, or it may come from a sponsor, a program director, or a promotions director at a station.

2. **Script.** A producer may hand you a complete script or assign a writer to work with you. You may write the script yourself or in concert with talent, sponsor, or the producer. If in-house, you may work with the promotions director or an account executive at the station.

3. **Select talent.** The producer may do this, or it may be as simple as asking a couple of announcers on your staff to be talent. For more complex productions and those requiring experienced actors, you'll have to go beyond the radio station. Give a copy of the script to the talent you have selected.

4. **Select facility.** If a large enough studio and control room is not available at your radio station, you'll have to reserve a recording studio, one designed for radio production. If a separate producer is involved, that individual may both select and schedule the facility.

5. **Rehearse talent in the studio.** Usually, there is never enough time to go over the script before the taping. If possible, arrange to schedule the studio by itself for a couple of hours prior to the day of production. Here, you can work with the talent in the setting for the actual recording. Early hand signals—such as pointing to indicate when a person is to begin speaking or a hand across throat that means cut—are used infrequently. More modern methods like talkback through headphones, signs held up, or marks on the script are more typical.

6. **Rehearse technical people in the control room.** Once you have spent some time with the talent in the quiet of the studio, go into the control room and rehearse with all the technical people present so that microphones can be correctly set up and levels taken. Learn how to use the intercom from the control room to the studio, the **talkback.** Work with the engineer and the control room technical people so that they know your style, your directing language. Practice the agreed-upon signals with your talent. Make sure that the script person knows the material well enough to be able to cue you in time to cue the talent and technical people well ahead of the needed task. Record some of the rehearsal, and play it back to see if the levels are good.

Common Control Room Directing Commands Used in Audio Production

Command	Means
Ready to . . .	Talent or engineer prepares to receive instructions from director
Open mic	Turn it on using fader or switch
Start music cold	Start it at beginning, 100 percent VU level
Fade up music	Gradual volume increase from silence
Fade music under	Fade down so that a voice or other audio source can be heard; music is still in background
Fade out music	Gradual volume decrease to silence
Board fade	Master is faded out, causing all audio sources to fade simultaneously
Dead roll music or effect	Start audio source by pressing play button but not fading up audio
Back time	Start music so that it ends exactly when the show or spot ends; that is if music is 3:00, dead roll it three minutes before end of show

7. **Record.** Get the absolute quiet that you need in the studio and control room. Ask if all are ready. Roll the tape. Have your assistant start the clock if it is a real-time production. Using the built-in slate microphone in the console, **slate,** or put a verbal indication of the date, time, and take before the show actually begins. Record the complete show or the segments needed, and make certain that the continuity person or assistant director checks them off and notes the number of takes on the script. Stop the tape, play back and evaluate.

8. **Thank everyone.** Have the talent sign a performer release. Keep only those people needed to complete the show.

9. **Postproduction.** Do any editing, mixing, and mastering in order to get the final copy used to make duplicated copies for other stations.

10. **Distribution.** Mail or transmit by satellite the final production.

In nationally distributed productions, there is good chance that at least some of these tasks will be done for you by a producer. Most productions, however, are for limited distribution, and, for that reason, it is one individual, usually you, who will be both producer and director. No matter the scope of the production or the number of participants, as the director, the chief creative person in charge, it is your job to tell all talent and technical people what you want, who you want to do it, and when you want it done. This is the directing process for radio.

USING ADVANCED PRODUCTION TOOLS

When you are directing a production that requires a separate studio and control room, a separate engineer, several microphones, and more, the chances are good that you'll need to use the advanced production tools found in a modern facility. Specialized microphones, mounting devices, and other seldom-used equipment may have to be rented and brought into the studio. The use of modern signal-processing devices can lend valuable support to a production. Even if you rarely have access to a major facility with all these options, knowledge of them will suggest some good ideas for future productions.

Microphones for Special Applications

In the combo studio designed for quick, continuous production by a single announcer/operator, there are a few microphone designs that have distinguished themselves because of their ruggedness. Almost 90 percent of these use the dynamic operating principle, and most are designed for a single voice working at close range. Some of these popular designs may not be good enough for an advanced studio production. In the studio where much regional and national radio production is done, microphones are selected more because of quality than sturdiness.

A modern multipattern condenser microphone is used in studio production. (Courtesy of AKG Acoustics, Inc.)

Most of the microphones in a high-quality studio are of expensive capacitor or condenser design. They are manufactured with a wider frequency range to accommodate the highest fidelity from both the speaking voice and the musical instrument. Its mounting device, both the stand and the system used to isolate the sound pickup part of the microphone from the mounting, is much better than the simple shock-mounted microphone on a flexible arm found in the combo radio studio. Instead of the batteries used in the less expensive condenser microphones worn on clothing by television reporters and interviewers, the high-quality studio condenser microphone takes its power from the console, called phantom power. While the most common microphones found in the combo studio cost around $250, those in the studio may cost $1,000 or more.

Sometimes, specialized pickup patterns are used in a studio or location production where a speaker using a microphone in one area of the studio must be acoustically isolated from an activity in another part of the studio. In broadcast events such as press conferences or audience participation shows, there is often a person holding a very directional shotgun microphone aimed to pick up questions from a seated audience. The directional microphone helps to isolate the person asking the question from those around the questioner who are probably talking to each other. In a live broadcast of a variety show, the talent often will want to go into the audience and interact with guests. He or she may want to wear a wireless microphone transmitter for maximum mobility.

Signal Processing Options

Signal processing devices alter the original form of the audio by changing the length, frequency response, dynamic range, room ambience, or any characteristic of the sound. The creative production person will record a voice or musical instrument dry and on its own track and later experiment with equalization, reverberation, and other creative choices before a track is finally mixed for broadcast.

Equalization

There is no real mystery about the control of the frequency response of an audio source, called **EQ,** or **equalization.** It's just like turning up or down the bass and treble control on your home stereo system. Think about why you have used the tone controls on your own amplifier in the past. Perhaps you have used the bass control to compensate for speakers that are poorly placed, too small, or in a room that is too big. Maybe you have turned the treble control down because of an annoying **hiss** on a ten-year-old cassette or to compensate for a room that is so reflective as to sound harsh. Of course the problem with having only two tone controls is that it limits your control over the audio to one set of frequencies per control. Bass or treble control only one small range of audio. Enter the equalizer.

Bass and treble controls are common on consumer equipment.

The EQ on a production console.

The equalization settings found just above the volume level faders on most production consoles are designed to allow plenty of control over a more specific and much greater range of frequencies than possible with the home stereo amplifier. Using EQ, it is possible to **accentuate,** increase, or **attenuate,** decrease, the energy level at more than just a single selected frequency. Instead of only being able to control the bass at 100 **Hertz,** or vibrations per second of sound, the typical low-frequency equalizer permits control of frequencies at three or more positions, like 50 Hertz, 100 Hertz, and 500 Hertz. Instead of treble control at only 10,000 Hertz, a console equalizer permits control of high frequencies at 8,000 Hertz, 10,000 Hertz, and 12,000 Hertz. Consoles may also have control of middle frequencies between 500 and 5,000 Hertz.

Another form of equalizer found in a few studios, and even on some consumer level devices, has a series of level controls for the entire audible range of sound, and, when they are set, their physical pattern looks like a graph. Called *graphic equalizers,* their availability in professional studio equipment appears to be diminishing. Another related form of large equalizer often found in the equipment rack of a large studio is similar to a graphic equalizer; it is called a *parametric* equalizer. Both graphic and parametric equalizers are usually found as outboard pieces of equipment, not normalled into the console, but available using the patch panel.

Along with continuously variable control of different frequencies, some production facilities will have **notch filters.** These are designed to almost eliminate audio at selected frequencies, not just minimize it like many equalizers. Often a notch filter is designed, for example, to eliminate a measured amount of audio between, for example, 50 Hertz and 100 Hertz. An example of a practical use for such a filter would be to eliminate a 60-Hertz power supply hum that inadvertently made its way into a piece of narration audio that can't be redone. Notch filters are costly and specialized pieces of production equipment that will not be included as part of the console. These devices will be located in the equipment rack and need to be patched into the effects return pot on the console.

Most of the time, equalizers and notch filters are used to correct problems in recordings. For those recordings made on location in a noisy area, the low frequency EQ or a notch filter can be used to minimize the rumble of a too-close air conditioner or a nearby freeway, audio that would interfere with the desired voice in a recording. Recordings made using an analog compact cassette will often have unacceptable high-frequency tape hiss. A notch filter or an equalizer can remove the hiss without interfering with too much of the important high-frequency content of the tape. Conversely, a commercially recorded CD or a live recording made in an acoustically perfect studio with a good microphone may sound bad if it's equalized.

Always record every sound on every track with the EQ controls off and then experiment later. After recording, most producers listen to each track of a production and painstakingly equalize each one before mixing the final program. During a trial mix, the solo button serving a selected channel can be pressed and equalization can be added or modified. High-frequency equalization might be used to soften a strident-sounding or overly sibilant voice. The *s* sound made by some voices can irritate, and an EQ control that reduces the amount of high-frequency content in a sound can make that sound more pleasing. Mid-range EQ can be used to add warmth, or *presence,* to a voice so that it will appear to stand apart from the music and sound effects. Low-frequency equalization is sometimes used to correct mistakes in microphone selection or placement, errors that cause the room to make a voice sound too *boomy,* certainly unnatural. A combination of low- and mid-frequency EQ can yield a filtered voice like that of a telephone.

Almost everybody who has done production for radio in the studio has strong opinions on the use of EQ in a program or short announcement designed to be broadcast. Some believe that if commercially purchased music and effects libraries on high-quality CD are used in the production, no EQ can make those sources sound better. If a good-quality voice is recorded using a good and well-placed microphone in a quiet, well-designed studio, some believe that EQ is also not needed. Others bemoan the fact that studios always have massive monitor speakers that are used as the reference for how the final project should sound. On the other hand, the average listener will hear the same production broadcast by a highly compressed and processed FM station on a very average car radio, all while driving on a crowded freeway at 55 mph where there is an ambient noise level of 60db. Go figure.

Compression

Often it is desirable to alter the **dynamic range,** the range between the softest and the loudest sound of an audio source. Why is this desirable? Consider the piano. Here is an instrument that, when properly recorded, has a dynamic range much too great for any broadcast medium. What about the drama, where the voices are either

Production tools: a collection of filters, EQ devices, and harmonizers used in the production studio.

too soft or too loud and putting them into a final program would cause an engineer to constantly adjust the volume level during the mix? When the dynamic range is too great to obtain an acceptable recording level, volume compression may be required. A *compressor* can be added to electronically bring up the level when it is too low, and a *peak limiter* can be used to keep high-level audio from distorting the recording. A device called a **compander** is a combination of a compressor and volume expander, designed to give you complete control over the dynamic range of your audio.

Digital time compression is used when a commercial announcement is a second or two longer or shorter than the exact time paid for by the advertiser. Often, it is impossible to redo a spot for exact timing because an announcer's performance might not be as good, or it may sound rushed and unnatural. If you vary the speed of the open-reel recorder to change the length of a production, it causes the audio to sound different because it changes the pitch of the audio. With digital time compression, a commercial can actually be varied up to several seconds without changing the quality of the audio or the performance.

Reverberation and Echo

Spacial characteristics of sound can be changed using a variety of analog and digital devices. The most common of these devices is **reverberation,** or **reverb,** an effect that places a voice or instrument in a space relationship within a room. In a dry recording, the microphone only picks up the direct sound of the voice or instrument.

Reverberation is the reflected sound from the walls and furniture in a room. The more reverb, the larger the room appears to the listener. Since most recordings cannot be made in the ideal room using the ideal microphone placement, reverb is usually added after a track is recorded and before it is mixed to the final version.

Although most reverberation effects today are created digitally in a tiny rack-mounted unit in the studio, it wasn't always that way. In the past, reverb devices filled a small room and used the mechanical vibration of metal plates or vibrating springs, acoustically coupled to tiny microphones and loudspeakers, to get a reverberating effect. The very early users of reverb for live, on-air productions simply placed a monitor speaker at one end of a bathroom, with its hard walls and lack of carpet or other sound-absorbing surfaces, and a microphone at the opposite end of the room. The sound, after bouncing around the room, was picked up by the microphone, and a measured amount was mixed in with the nonreverb version.

Natural-sounding reverb is usually preferred to the older **echo,** gradually diminishing exact repeats of the audio, just like when you yell "Hello" across a canyon and your voice comes back, "Hello, Hello, Hello," and fades out. Starting in the 1950s after the invention of magnetic tape, echo was obtained by sending the signal that echo was to be added to into a reel-to-reel recorder during an actual recording. The output of the playback head was then rerouted back to the console and mixed into the recording, or back to the record head. The physical distance between the two heads results in a slight delay, thus causing the echo. As a radio production person, you will get this effect at least several times in your production lifetime, a result of inadvertently leaving up the volume level fader on the cart or reel-to-reel during recording.

Digital Effects

Popular digital effects are **flanging** and **chorusing.** Flanging and chorusing occur when two identical versions of the same sound are played simultaneously. Flanging occurs when the two identical sounds are played at exactly the same time, causing an out-of-phase cancellation effect that sounds like the audio is fading in and out. Chorusing happens when the two sounds are separated by a fraction of a second. The effect of two people with identical voices saying the same thing at the same time results. Before the simple digital devices now in common use, flanging and chorusing effects had to be accomplished by having the two identical sources played back on two reel-to-reel decks. By grabbing the **flange,** the name of the supply reel hold-down on one of the decks, the speed could be mechanically varied until the effect just happened. It was hit or miss. It was fun.

There are now literally hundreds of ways to change the **envelope,** or the parameters, of an audio source. From simple adjustments to the frequency response to alteration of the time and space of a voice to effects that completely mask the identity of a sound, special effects for audio production are easily available. And, as with

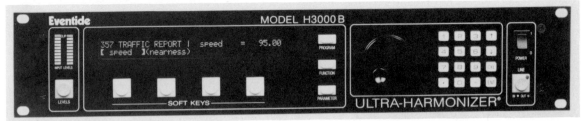

A harmonizer. (Courtesy of Eventide)

any creative process, look to the script and the goals of the production and use them when they are needed to guide the listener to a better understanding of your content. The medium should not be the message.

Other Specialized Equipment

There are some audio devices that are so special that they are found in few studios designed for radio production. Some of these devices can be rented, some are found only in the largest studios. One device that until recently could only be found in the largest studios is the digital audio workstation and editor. Today, even medium-size radio stations have such a device, but in the university and college radio environment, a major project may require that you take recorded audio sources to a large-city studio and transfer them to a digital workstation for final editing.

Other devices that a producer will have to rent for a production will be equipment that is considered musical instruments. The most expensive keyboards, sequencers, and samplers for music production will not be found in most radio studios or owned by most students and struggling musicians. Most of this equipment can be rented from a music store, along with special guitar amplifiers that have just the "right" sound for a sound track.

ADVANCED PRODUCTION TECHNIQUES

The use of multiple tracks for later mixing gives the producer many options for experimenting with all the possible signal processing, reverberation and echo, and other digital effects. In advanced productions where a variety of voice, music, and effects is needed to create a final product, each discrete sound will be recorded and stored in its own location, whether on an actual track using a reel-to-reel, or on the hard disk of a digital workstation. Using four or more tracks gives you, as the creator-producer-director, more options for getting the result, the final show that is your goal.

 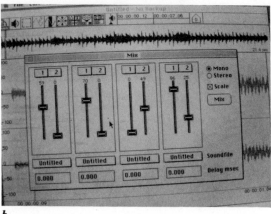

a   *b*

Multitrack the way it was: (a) four tracks recorded on reel-to-reel tape versus the way it is going to be, (b) four tracks recorded on a hard disk in a computer memory, appearing on the screen, controlled using a mouse.

Multitrack Recording

What is meant by multitrack recording? Why would you use it? First, **multitrack recording** is simply the process of putting each audio source onto a separate track of tape or location in a hard disk storage device medium. The advantage of having every audio source on its own discrete track or disk location is that each source can be separately evaluated, edited, equalized, deleted, and even moved, before it is mixed or combined into a final version. Rather than starting audio sources and mixing them in real-time, multitrack allows the producer to try different combinations and levels before the shape of the master version is finally decided.

The crude precursor to real multitrack recording was developed in the 1950s as an experimental studio device; it was a method that allowed a vocalist to sing both lead and accompaniment without the need for a second singer. Multitrack pioneers, the recording duo of Les Paul and Mary Ford, were able to create an entire chorus of female singers backed by a large instrumental group by using the then-new technology of the two-track reel-to-reel recorder. Their process was simple: They would record one instrument and the lead vocal on one of the tracks. Next, they would play the track back and, while listening, sing and play along with it. The combined result, now two voices and two instruments, was recorded on the other track. Then, the second track, with both the first track and the sing-along combination, would be played back again, and they would add still another vocal and instrument. On and on, over and over, until the final product was realized. Part multitrack, part **overdubbing.**

Of course, each time track one was **dubbed** or copied to track two and back, the noise, in the form of high-frequency tape hiss, increased. This was not a big problem for AM radio and its restricted bandwidth. But the 1960s and 1970s brought improvements in radios and consumer playback equipment. Better techniques had to

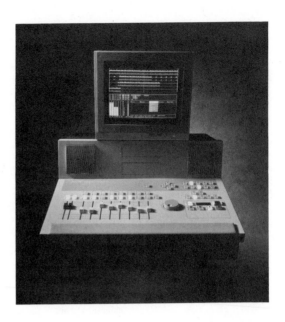

A digital audio workstation.
(Courtesy of AKG Acoustics, Inc.)

evolve. Rather than bouncing the audio between two tracks of a recorder, tape formats were developed employing four, eight, sixteen, twenty-four, and forty-eight tracks using tape widths of one-half inch, one inch, and two inches. Finally a musician or producer of commercials could put every instrument and every voice on a separate track. Simple technology was developed so that a producer could play back already recorded tracks while recording new ones. Called **sel-sync, sel-rep,** or **simul-sync,** a switch was added to allow the already recorded tracks to be played back through the record head, and thus in sync with any new recording.

While multitrack open-reel digital and analog recorders are still used in studios, digital systems are quickly replacing them. Called **samplers,** or **DAWS**—for digital audio workstations—they sample analog audio and convert it to the 1's and 0's of computer language and store it on a high-capacity magnetic or optical hard disk. There are a number of advantages of these *tapeless,* or digital, formats. One is instant access time, as compared with a linear device involving mechanical rewinding and fast forwarding of tape to find the correct spot on a track. With a hard disk, or **RAM**—random access memory—retrieval is almost instant. Plus, tracks can be deleted and replaced, or their position relative to other tracks can be changed with the click of a mouse. Instead of cumbersome reels and recording technology, the entire multitrack process can be contained in a rack-mounted device in a few inches of space. For the producer, it all means less tinkering with technology and waiting for it to catch up with the creative process.

TABLE 7.4	*Organization Steps for Multitrack Using Reel-to-Reel*

Input selectors and level controls show record selector and sel-rep for each channel.

The pan pots are the round knobs at the top of these faders.

1. Identify each audio source and its location. Is the music on cassette, cart, open-reel, DAT, record, or CD? Is the voice live or on tape? Are the effects on CD, record, tape, or live?

2. Determine the tape track location on which you will record each audio source. Will each voice be on its own track? Will music and sound effects sources occupy a separate track or be combined in real-time with a voice?

3. Record each track. The audio source will have to be played back through the console at the proper level and assigned to the selected track of the tape deck or computer. When recording a track, make certain that all other tracks are in play or "safety" so they cannot be inadvertently erased. Always turn off the tracks record selector after the recording is complete.

4. Play back selected tracks for synchronization with live voices. If a new track must be precisely synchronized with an existing one, the existing one must be played back in its sync position through an isolated monitor or headphone system in a way that the live voice can hear it while he or she is recording a new track to be in sync with the track playing.

5. Check each track separately. If technical problems exist, redo just that track.

6. Assign the playback of each tape track to its own level fader module. While playing the tape, select **solo** in order to hear each track by itself, then set the level, equalize, and add the desired effects to the track. Write down the settings on your cue sheet.

7. Assign the output of each playback module to get a stereo master for broadcast. Usually, each module has a pan control, allowing the track to go to left, right, or center. The center position sends the output of the track to both channels at an equal level. This is **mono,** or monaural.

8. Mix. While the tape is playing, follow the instructions on the cue sheet. Do it until you have an acceptable production.

When doing multitrack production, a new organization process must be learned. Compare it with the familiar real-time combo method of production where, script in hand, you start the music, fade it under, and announce to record a spot or program. It's still an adequate method for the basic production. However, if the production is complex enough to require a number of separate tracks added one at a time, then multitrack recording may be necessary. Compared with the real-time production, a different form of organization is required. From original audio to its place on the selected track or location in the recording media to the final mix, there is a logical process for multitrack recording using a reel-to-reel format, shown in Table 7.4.

Whether you have selected audio sources ahead of time or as the tracks are assembled, each source and its location must be kept track of for later mixing. A written cue sheet will have to be changed each time an audio source is added or deleted. On the sheet, the volume level for the final mix can be noted, and any signal processing settings should be written down. When the tracks are finally combined, the cue sheet guides the producer and engineer. This is the traditional way to mix a multitrack recording from a reel-to-reel format, using the console.

The ADX digital audio production system is located to the right of the production console. (ADX, courtesy of Pacific Recorders & Engineering Corporation)

Digital Audio Workstations

Digital systems are a bit different. While a similar production organization process can be followed, the digital sampling workstation often allows you to enter track descriptions right on the computer screen. It will allow you to actually perform most signal processing, volume level, and equalization tasks on the screen for a final mix without using the separate faders of an audio console. One of the real advantages of the digital workstation over multitrack tape formats is the ability to move the location of an already recorded track into a different location relative to other tracks. With reel-to-reel, a track cannot be moved, only re-recorded. When using a digital device, follow the on-screen instructions and the dialogue boxes. Digital systems have been designed to replace many of the familiar devices and processes found in the production facility.

Whether you are performing multitrack production in the digital or analog domain, the final production is mixed down to a two-track master from which copies are made for distribution to radio stations. The master could be in a digital format, like DAT, or it could be a reel-to-reel format. Until a digital distribution and playback format is finally agreed upon by broadcasters, the reel-to-reel two-track recorder remains a standard format at the majority of stations. More details on how to use a digital audio workstation will be presented in the chapter on editing.

PRODUCTION SITE OPTIONS

As a beginning producer of audio for radio, most of what you'll do will occur in your institution's facility. But what if the facility available to you is not good enough? What if you have a production budget? What if the audio that you need cannot be recorded without going to a nonstudio location? Now, and in your professional future, there will be a time when you will have to find equipment or a facility for a production.

Going on Location

The reason that you go on location to record audio for a production is simple. You have decided that the goals of your production cannot be accomplished in any other way, certainly not in a studio. You go on location for the ambience—the background excitement that an on-location recording can convey to the listener. You might even go on location to record a complete program, audience and all. In news and documentary production, you go on location because that is where you can find the content people needed to reinforce your story. Sure, for non-news productions it's possible to re-create the ambience of a simple location in the studio using sound effects, but if you need the voices of real people at a real event, it may be easier to record it live than to find and rehearse actors to perform in a studio. You decide to go on location when you need to record a unique piece of audio to bring back to the studio to combine with other audio into a final production.

A popular battery-operated cassette recorder for remote recording.

Going on location to record audio requires equipment that is easily portable, plus a way of monitoring and playing back that audio before you leave the location. On-site recording equipment can be a simple cassette deck, microphone, and headset, or it can be a complete portable studio consisting of a small console, a dozen microphones, a DAT or open-reel, and monitor speakers. Going on location means that you will have to be prepared to get audio at a place that is often many miles from engineering help.

Going on location also means that, unlike the quiet studio, there will be many unwanted sounds, all trying to become a part of your recording. A nonstudio location is a hostile place. The major thing to remember is this: Always play back the audio you have recorded in a quiet place using a good pair of headphones before you leave the location. If there is wind or other unacceptable background noise, correct the problem and try it again.

When to Go into a Major Facility

There are times when it is absolutely necessary to rent time at a major recording studio. Whether by the hour or day, a studio may be the only place where the desired combination of space, equipment, and needed technical personnel can be found. Most studios can be rented with or without engineers, but a knowledgeable house engineer in a strange facility can really save you time. While you pay more for added people, they can help you get the best sound in less time.

SUMMARY

Knowledge of creative options allows you to match the tools and techniques available to complete any production. You began with a simple knowledge of the production process and a combo production facility. It was simple. Start the music, open the microphone, read the script, transfer it to a cart, and put it in the on-air room for broadcast. Those are the methods that will serve 90 percent of the production needs of the local radio station. The process of combo production is adequate for most of what radio stations require in the way of local production for their own air.

But what about the major national spots for the big products, the ones you really admire when you hear them on the local radio station? What about the drama and comedy production that your station has purchased for the morning show? Or what about the full-length dramas that seem to be making a comeback on public radio? These are advanced productions, and they require greater organization and direction, more talent and technical people, and a larger, more fully equipped studio and control room. They have to be done in a major recording studio, one with all possible control over the audio.

ACTIVITIES

1. Arrange to tour a local recording studio during the production of a commercial. Notice the number of people required to complete this production.

2. Does your local public radio station record for broadcast a variety show or a musical event? Try to observe the planning process necessary to get the broadcast onto tape for air.

3. Ask a local recording studio that does production for radio to send you a catalog and rate sheet. Look in the yellow pages under *audio* or *radio production.*

4. Arrange to get a demonstration of multitrack recording at a local recording studio. Ask to sit at the screen of a digital sampling workstation.

5. Direct a short radio drama. Work with actors and use prerecorded sound effects and music for the production of a simple two- or three-minute dramatic vignette. You can always find scripts at your college library.

Using Music and Sound Effects

Up to now, the radio production experience has centered on understanding the tools and techniques of production. You know why a radio station uses production, and you understand where production takes place. You've actually operated the equipment, may have already completed a basic production assignment, and have at least learned about a few of the advanced tasks necessary in radio production. You know the technology, terminology, and the process of production. Now consider two of the elements in a production over which you can have some creative control: music and sound effects. Even if you never intend to use any music or sound other than what is found in the station library, some familiarity with how professionals look at music and sound effects creation, selection, and use will demonstrate how you can have more control over the creative process.

Of all the individual parts that can be put together to create radio production, music is the most common. Listen to any hour of any radio station. When a commercial, PSA, or station promo is aired, the chances are good that some form of music is heard in the background. Where does this music come from? It might be prerecorded, supplied by one of several dozen production music libraries, or it might be original music, written, arranged, and performed specifically for a single commercial or program. And more important, how is the music used? Is it simply there to be in the background while an announcer speaks, or has it been specifically selected to motivate or create a mood in the mind of the listener? As a radio producer, you'll want to know how to use music to best serve your creative ideas and goals.

Sound effects are another element found in a creative production. If radio is the theater of the mind, it is often a sound effect that helps to create this theater, the *picture* or image, we have of what we hear when we listen to the radio. In early radio, sound effects were created live by "sound designers," real artists using all manner of mechanical devices. Today, you can create original sounds, record them on location, or use a prerecorded sound effects library. As a creative radio producer, you may have ideas for producing short announcements or complete programs that will need just the right sound effect to communicate a message. Music and sound effects are two important parts of the creative radio production process.

USING MUSIC CREATIVELY

Creative radio production is defined as the perfect balance of idea, script, talent, music, and sound effects all working together to create a mood that promotes an idea, a product, or a feeling. The idea may be a simple one—to try a new product, to work for or support a nonprofit community organization, or even to listen to a particular show on a radio station. Music can be an important part of this creative process. When used as a background for a brief scripted spot, promo, or PSA, music can be used to reinforce the content or message, the goal of the production. As a producer, it's important to know when to use a certain style of music and when to avoid music altogether. You'll want to know when to use music to get attention and when to use it to reinforce a character or an event. You'll want to use music to help create theater.

Determining Your Needs

The perfect script, the best announcer, a great production facility with plenty of audio effects. Sound familiar? What about the music? What will you need, and when will you need it? Some music needs may have been determined before the production. Perhaps while you were writing the script, an idea for using music even occurred to you. Now, it will have to be selected from a library or planned and recorded in a studio. Some music needs may only be obvious after reading the script or hearing the announcer read it aloud a number of times. You begin to think, "maybe some music needs to go here," or "this transition could sure benefit from a certain type of music. . . ."

There may be specific reasons why you'll use a certain piece of music in a production. Often, you'll have some creative choice, but other times a sponsor may hand you a piece of music. It may be that a particular product has long been identified with a style of music or an advertising agency has contracted with a musician to record music for all of a company's commercials. Perhaps the sponsor will indicate that *jazz* or *rock* music should be used, and you'll select the specific cut from a production music library. What about a PSA for a folk music benefit? Here, you would want to use the music that best describes what an audience member would hear at the event. Another practical consideration is the station format. Promos and PSAs that must be integrated into an overall air sound will require music similar to that played by the station. Whether it's your choice or that of a sponsor, the music that you finally use for a production will always be determined by a combination of the aesthetic and the practical.

If you have complete creative control of the finished product, your reasons for selecting music will depend mostly on the goals and content of the production. Do you need simple theme music for a half-hour community affairs program? For this, you'll want music that both fits the format of the station and, at the same time, adds no particular meaning of its own. Music that is completely instrumental is ideal for theme purposes. You wouldn't want to use a song that is identified with youth gangs as the theme song for the chamber of commerce interview. Because theme music for a public affairs show will be heard every week, it will eventually be identified with the show in the mind of the listener. It will have to be music that can be established for a few seconds, then faded under while an announcer or host introduces the show.

Sometimes, music will be selected because it helps to communicate a message to the audience. Background music, when used for the comedic spot, the short dramatic vignette for the morning disc jockey show, or the clever station promotion can help reinforce the content of the message. Perhaps music can be used to help the audience believe that it is at a particular location or attending a particular event associated with a type of music. Maybe you'll need music that helps the listener know or believe something about a character in a drama. Does the production contrast a happy person with one who is not? Along with the dialogue spoken, music can be used to create the character's image for the audience.

And finally, music may be selected only because it will help one particular production stand out during the typical format radio hour of music, talk, and recorded announcements. What about the simple fanfare? While probably overused, a loud, brassy trumpet fanfare has long been used to grab the attention of the listener. What about a simple electronic *sig,* a familiar music signature that is used to precede the station contest or promotion for the contest? When used effectively, sigs may draw desired attention to what follows. Consider using no music at all. Many stations are *overproduced,* that is, all you hear is nonstop music and production with music. Here, a production without music may be very effective, the perfect way to get the listener's attention. An effective voice or voices reading a well-written script could be all the production that is needed.

Developing a Plan

Once you have considered the content, the needs of the sponsor, and your own creative goals for the production, it's time to develop a plan for obtaining and using the music you are about to select. Unless the production is a simple one or one where the music already has been selected, you'll have to decide where in the production music is needed, how much is necessary, where to find it, and by when. A written plan, including comments about the content goals of the production, can help to make logical sense of all of the discrete elements that make up all productions. For now, the logical place for these written ideas is on the script.

What you need will depend on your creative vision and the goals of the radio station, public service organization, or sponsor. Suppose the goal of a commercial is to convince the listener that he or she needs a vacation in Hawaii. Relaxing music, even music that is native to the islands, would certainly be appropriate. Is it the goal of a station promotion or contest to build an audience by giving away a new car? Music for this promotion should be *up-tempo,* or fast and exciting. Are you creating a PSA designed to convince listeners to feel a certain way about the environment? Music for this production should be light and hopeful, not somber. Write down all your music ideas on a copy of the script.

TABLE 8.1   *Music Needs for a 30-Second PSA*

What You Need	Where Located	Needed By
Background music, light rock, open	Station library	Day of production
Headliner group featured at concert	CD at record store	Day of production
Backup local band at concert	Local band has tape	Early enough to dub to open-reel
Closing music	Station library	Day of production

How much music will be needed to complete the production? Where will it go? Look at the narration script. Since there is no standard format for a commercial or PSA script, it is up to the producer or director of the production to mark the places where the music and other effects might go. Some radio production people are able to look at a script and actually hear a finished production in their heads. Other producers will actually go into the production facility and experiment with music placement or where in the production the music might fit. Whatever your preference, you'll have to have some idea of how many different pieces of music are required and the approximate length of each. You'll also have to know where in the script music will be most aesthetically useful. You'll have some creative choices.

Where will you find the music you need? In professional radio production designed for regional and national distribution, music either comes from a cleared production music library or musicians are hired to write and perform original music. If you are fortunate enough to know any musicians, you'll be able to have more control over that part of your production. Even in a school environment, music classes are a good place to find a talented group or an individual more than willing to provide the music for a PSA campaign that will run on the campus radio station. Some campuses even have a recording class, complete with studio. Otherwise, you'll have to find out if your school radio/television department or radio station has a production music library. If one exists, make arrangements to go through the catalog and audition those cuts that seem close to what you have in mind. If you are producing for an instructor or classroom only and your production will never be aired, you can probably get away with using your own personal records and CDs.

You will need the music, along with everything else used in the production, on the day of the production. If you are unsure as to what you might end up using, it may be possible to first record the voices, and later return to the facility to add the music. The typical music needs for a thirty-second PSA for a benefit concert to aid the homeless are shown in Table 8.1.

USING PRERECORDED MUSIC IN PRODUCTION

Once you have determined that some form of recorded opening, closing, or transition music will be important to the production, where will you find it? There are really only two practical choices: cleared library music and original music. A third and more difficult option is to attempt to get permission to use a piece of copyrighted commercially recorded music. Consider the options that you'll have, both as a college student in radio production, and as a future radio production professional.

Copyrighted Music

The easiest way to find a piece of music is to just take it off one of the records or CDs played by the station. Indeed, most production people at local stations in small and medium markets rarely consider the legalities of using copyrighted, recorded music as background for a commercial, promo, or PSA. Technically, what they are doing is not legal. Ask a radio production person or a disc jockey about the station's license to play music and chances are you'll be told that it pays thousands per year in music fees to both **BMI,** Broadcast Music Incorporated, and **ASCAP,** American Society of Composers, Authors, and Publishers. The problem is, this license is only for the privilege of playing the complete record as part of a station's format. The license fees that all radio stations pay do not include what is termed its **synchronization** with a prerecorded announcement. That use requires a separate license.

Students may also wrongly believe that their educational status allows them to use copyrighted music. Recently, the laws were further tightened to control the use of artistic work. Prior to the change in the laws, educational institutions and their students believed they could use any music they desired because their productions were not making a profit. Then, like now, it was against the law. The newest law states that if you use a copyrighted work without permission, its owner can actually sue the university president, the board of trustees, and even you. While the chance of this extreme legal action is small, the indiscriminate use of copyrighted music without permission is a poor precedent to set for a professional future. Nevertheless, as a practical matter, the use of copyrighted music from your favorite cassettes and CDs for classroom-only assignments will not cause economic harm to any recording artist.

Sometimes a production can really benefit from the use of a copyrighted piece of music. Although difficult, it is sometimes possible to obtain partial rights to a piece of music. Every phonograph record, cassette, or CD made here or abroad is copyrighted. Once you determine who wrote the song, who performed it, who published it, and who licensed it, you can consider writing to each separate entity for written permission to use the music for free. This is next to impossible. The experience of most students is that no one will even answer their letters. Even if they do, they always refuse. After all, professional producers always pay for the music they use and the artists and writers will treat you the same.

If you really must have a piece of music, you may decide that even though you cannot use an existing record of a performance, you are willing and able to pay for the rights to use the song and have a musician friend perform it. By contacting BMI or ASCAP in Hollywood, you can find out which publisher owns the rights to the song and how much it will cost for permission to use it in a production. This is called a synchronization license, and it is very specific; for example, worldwide rights for five years on local radio only. The fee does not include anything except the rights to use the sheet music. You also need musicians.

Legalities aside, from a creative perspective, limiting yourself to music from those familiar sources heard everyday on radio is not all that original. With the exception of copyrighted music used in a record store commercial for a new CD, or a spot to announce the appearance of a group at a concert, there are better ways to obtain music for your productions. Good experience can be gained by working with cleared music libraries and original music that you design specifically for a single production.

Cleared Libraries

The easiest way to get "legal" music is to use the prerecorded production music library owned by radio stations and schools. A *cleared music library* is purchased on record or CD from a specialty company by paying a one-time fee and perhaps a yearly renewal fee. Some are licensed for so-called educational use only, but most are licensed for all educational and commercial purposes, radio and television. If your institution lacks a library, you can go to a large recording studio and buy the rights to use a single piece of music from its more extensive, up-to-date library. For this you will pay a one-time **needle drop** or **needle down** charge, perhaps less than fifty dollars for a single piece of music. Now you have a much greater choice because professional studios have many clients using library music, and, for competitive reasons, they must have the best. This is a good option if you only need a small bit of high-quality cleared music.

How is a production music library organized? First, all of them have what are called **cue sheets,** or listings of the individual **cuts** or selections on each disk. Listed on each sheet is a category of music that may include a generic description like "small group rock with guitar, bass, and drums." Under each category, there will be a variety of **tempos,** or the speed of the music, like slow, medium, fast. The more extensive libraries will contain all possible standard lengths from several minutes to be used as themes for long-form shows like documentaries, to ten-, twenty-, thirty-, and sixty-second lengths for commercials, PSAs, and promos. Depending on the type of music, most of the cuts will be complete versions of the same melody and instrumental group. For example, rather than just including ten seconds of a longer cut and then fading out, the ten-second version may actually be a condensed, edited version of the longer cut.

Is library music for you? Perhaps not, as most of it is very generic and may not fit every purpose. It is typically performed by lesser-known, nonunion musicians, and since musical styles change, a music library can be out-of-date in a few years. Some will even send yearly updates, but because the library must be good for at least five years, even the updates tend toward bland. If you are planning on using a music library, spend some time listening to the various cuts before you decide for sure. It may be that there is nothing there that fits the content or style of your production.

CREATING ORIGINAL MUSIC FOR PRODUCTION

If music is to be a vital, integral part of an overall production, you cannot always depend on finding it in a library. After all, you had an original idea, wrote the script, and directed or performed the dialogue. Are you going to leave the choice of music up to a library service? Probably not. For you, the most creative and satisfying method of obtaining music is to seek out original music. This means finding a struggling musician to perform original music that the two of you have agreed upon, before or after the production is written, produced, and edited. You may already know several musicians with guitar, keyboard, or drum machine eager to do a commercial or PSA score just for the experience and a copy of the finished show. Using the modern technology of the synthesizer, sampler, and sequencer, it is possible to get a complete band from a single musician. With original music, it is possible to get exactly the style, tempo, and timings needed.

Finding a Musician

Musicians are everywhere. Just look at the people you know who play some sort of instrument. Think about the number of times you've heard an interesting piece of music performed. Perhaps you've even thought of how this music might sound as a background for the PSA campaign you've been thinking about producing. Where do you find a musician willing to perform original production in a studio and give it to you to be used in a production for radio? From the friends and neighbors who have simple keyboards and computers to music classes at your school to the connections you have made through the college radio station, there is a tremendous variety of people who compose and play music. Depending on the scope of the production, the supply of musicians is always greater than the demand.

You may have some familiarity with the technology of the modern keyboard. Maybe you've experimented with music yourself or spent some time with a friend or neighbor who is musically inclined. Fine. As a student, the best way to get a simple piece of music for a production is to either play it yourself or get a good friend to perform gratis. This is often the best option when a very simple background is required but nothing in the cleared music library appeals to you. Lacking musically inclined friends, the next step might be to contact an instructor in the music department. Post a notice on the appropriate bulletin board stating your needs or visit labs where students are practicing, and the chances are good that you'll find several dozen willing participants, some with the technology to actually record your production music. It doesn't have to be a major score either; a single piano or guitar recorded in a simple studio using a single microphone will suffice for the majority of productions.

If you have the time, the interest, and the budget, you may find very good professionals at a local recording studio who are willing to supply music for your production. Perhaps it's a group struggling to get a hit record that will welcome the chance for additional exposure. Maybe the group plays primarily at local clubs and even gets some airplay on the local college station, but because it's not made the larger station playlists yet, it will still be willing to do a favor for your production. There are thousands of very good local bands that have not yet made the *big time*. Another obvious advantage of a lesser-known group could be its nonunion status. The major, established groups will rarely be able to perform and be recorded by you without some cost involved. They may even want to cooperate but because of myriad agents, recording contracts, and lawyers surrounding them, their hands are tied. While working with original music at this level is not common in local radio, it is nevertheless good experience to know about options and techniques used by production professionals.

Finding the Music

In addition to the creative choice realized by producing an original music score for a production for radio, it also will be much easier to negotiate the rights to use the music. Even if you find a friend to perform the music, who will write it? On one level, you may have a certain *sound* in your head, perhaps one that can be picked out on a piano using a simple chord progression or two or three notes played in a certain order. Some commercials have used only a simple bass run as music background for the narration. Using the resources available on the most basic keyboard, those simple chords or bass notes can sound like a professional group. By working with a single musician or actually doing it yourself using basic keyboard technology, you can design a simple music theme or logo that is perfectly satisfactory as the background for a PSA or commercial. You own the music free and clear. Even if you are not musically talented, every keyboard owner has at least one original piece of music developed by trial and error.

Another option for a musician is the use of so-called **public domain music.** Music in the public domain includes, but is not limited to, folk music and music you sang at camp, often referred to as traditional. Usually, a piece of music is in the public domain either because it is extremely old or it might have been written and copyrighted fifty or more years ago but the rights expired before the recent copyright laws were enacted. Public domain probably includes most material where the authorship has been forgotten or much of what was written before the beginning of the twentieth century. If you have questions about music in the public domain, you can get a list of popular public domain tunes from your local library.

TABLE 8.2   *A Music Rundown Sheet*

Theme	Instruments Used	Timing	Tempo
"A" version 1	Piano, flute, drum	30 seconds	Fast
"A" version 2	Same	10 seconds	Fast
"A" version 3	Same	10 seconds	Slow
"A" version 4	Piano, flute	30 seconds	Medium
"A" version 5	Flute	10 seconds	Slow
"B" version 1	Piano, flute	30 seconds	Fast
"B" version 2	Piano	10 seconds	Medium
"B" version 3	Flute	10 seconds	Slow

Consider eighteenth- and nineteenth-century classical music. If you want to use, for example, a Beethoven piano sonata or a Bach fugue, the actual music is probably in the public domain. This does not mean you have the rights to a particular written arrangement or a recording of a performance, though. You still have to get your own musician to play the actual music for the production, and this music must be from an original score of the composer and not from a newer, copyrighted arrangement. The easiest way to get access to this form of *free* music is to visit the office of a music professor on your campus. Many have pianos right there in the office, and their benches are usually crammed with sheet music. They will be able to tell you if what you like is in the public domain.

Scoring and Timing

Once the basic musical theme has been decided on, the actual arranging and scoring can be done. In concert with the musician, try to focus in on a maximum of two simple themes or melodies, perhaps the basic progression of chords. Next, have the musician play slow, medium, and fast versions of these themes. Try them with different instrument combinations, ranging from a simple guitar to a keyboard, with and without percussion. Record these, and listen to them with the musician and note what you like or think will work. Remember, as the creative person, only you can decide what works best. Pick the theme that you feel best typifies your vision of the final production. Also, by having a variety of instrument choices for your selected theme, you can try several possible mixes to hear how it sounds when combined with voices and other effects.

Now there are at least two different themes, identifiable music signatures for use at the open, close, and transition points of the production. And with several different versions and tempos of the same original theme or themes, editing will be

TABLE 8.3	**30-Second "Protect the Environment" PSA with Music Cues**

MUSIC UP, VER 3B, AND UNDER:

ANNCR: (very slowly) Consider what will happen to our way of life if we don't take care of the earth. . .

CUT TO MUSIC UP, VER 1B, AND UNDER:

ANNCR: (reading rapidly) Every day millions of gallons of toxic wastes from residences and factories pour into the Pacific Ocean, continuously, nonstop, all the time, never stopping. . . How much more can the oceans take?

CUT TO MUSIC, VER 2A, AND UNDER:

ANNCR: Only you can save the earth. Send for a list of environmental groups in California that need your help. Save the earth.

MUSIC ENDS

so much easier. In fact, to make it extremely simple, use the slow tempo version, such as 3 of "B" in Table 8.2, for the opening ten seconds of the following thirty-second public service announcement for the environment. After the announcer completes the first sentence, change the tempo by using the fast tempo, version 1 of "B," because the content of the PSA changes. Finally, change the music altogether to version 2 of "A" for the final ten seconds. In addition to the different tempos and orchestrations, all the music will be in the same key, making it possible to edit the themes together to sound like one continuous one. This is how the pros do it.

Now see how the music that you have arranged might be used in the PSA example shown in Table 8.3.

Recording Live Music for a Production

There are several ways to record a musician for your production. Consider the type of music and the instruments used. Are they acoustical, like a piano, horns, saxophone, and drums? Or are all the instruments electronic? A combination of both? The way that you record them will be very different. Are you going to use a group or a single musician? Where will the recording take place? These are important considerations if you want the music to sound professional. And while it is easy enough to plug the output of a synthesizer into a mixing console to be recorded onto tape, recording even the most simple acoustical instrument or a group of musicians requires some careful preplanning. It also requires an ear for how music should sound.

Using keyboard, a drum machine, and even an electric guitar singly or together can be as simple as mixing several tape sources. If a single musician is using all digital sources, the **mixing,** or assembly, of the program can be done using a computer and a sampler/sequencer program. This technology is found in the music department rather than in a radio studio. With most modern systems, the music from the keyboard or music sampling device is put into the computer program a track at

A computer is used in music production.

a time. After all the "voices" are added, the tracks can be played back together, edited, changed, and processed for use in your production. The computer controls the playback of several synthesizer voices and the results are fed into a console to be recorded on tape for use in the radio studio. If an actual group is playing in real-time, keyboards, electric guitars, and other instruments with an electronic signal for an output can be individually patched into the faders on a production console. They can be either put onto separate tracks of a multitrack tape format or mixed into a basic two-track stereo master to be used later in the production.

Acoustical instruments require different techniques. Consider the piano. Professional recording engineers have long debated the best way to get a good sounding recording from this popular acoustical percussion instrument. It is not as simple as it appears. There are too many choices. Never mind that its **dynamic range,** the variation of loudness and softness possible with the piano, is too great for almost any recording format to capture, let alone the compressed audio broadcast by a radio station. At least dynamic range can be controlled by the musician. What about the relationship of the instrument to the room where it is located? As with all acoustic instruments, the amount of reflected sound, or room reverberation, in a recording is related to the distance of the microphone from the direct sound of the instrument itself. Some producers like an echo-free, or *dry,* piano sound so they put the microphone a few inches away from the strings and sounding board. Others like a lot of room reverberation, so they place the microphone several feet away from the piano. Of course, when the recording takes place in a studio lacking any echo, it can always be added later.

Small groups, which are combinations of acoustic and electronically amplified instruments, may require complex microphone placements. The techniques used will also differ depending on whether you are recording in a studio, a music practice lab, or a performance hall. In most studios used for music recording, there are standard microphone setups for every instrument and combination of instruments. For the drums, for example, there are often a half-dozen different microphones, whose placement is usually worked out by trial and error during hundreds of recording sessions. In fact, if you go into a dozen different recording studios and ask which microphone sounds best for placing in front of a Fender guitar amplifier or recording a saxophone, you will get a dozen different answers.

While a studio recording session is best left to those with experience, there are a couple of simple ways that you can make a decent recording of a small group at a nonstudio location. Find out if someone with recording experience and basic technology can accompany you to where the musicians are performing. Sometimes, if you are recording at a practice or performance venue at a school music department, microphones and recording equipment are already present, with a technician responsible for operation and maintenance. This will solve your problem. Like your radio and television studio complex, there is probably a way to sign up for and reserve the equipment needed for a school recording session.

If that is not possible, a good recording of a well-balanced group in a small hall can be made with one microphone, variously called a stereo microphone, a point-source microphone, a coincident pair, or a figure-eight design. While the group is playing, find the spot in an area a dozen feet in front of the group where the music sounds most balanced. Place the single-point stereo microphone on a stand and aim it at the group. Because the volume level of a live group will vary more than a prerecorded audio source like a CD, have the group play the entire music through while you set the VU meter to read 100 percent or less during the loudest sound. Leave the level control(s) set at this point and make a recording. Play it back and check for quality.

Finally, when working with musicians, there are always two tasks that must be done to ensure that the use of the resulting music will be possible. First, the music must be free of copyright. This should have already been determined ahead of the recording. And second, have the musicians sign a performance release, such as that shown in Box 8.1. This gives you permission to use the music in your production, even to have it broadcast on the air. Always complete these two tasks when you are working with any group or individual musician.

A music recording session is mixed at San Jose State.

A high-quality stereo microphone. (Courtesy of Shure Brothers, Inc.)

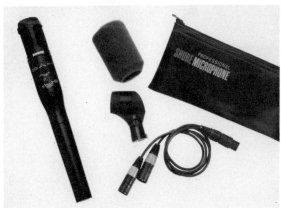

BOX 8.1   *Performance Release*

San Jose State University
Department of Theatre Arts
Radio—Television and Film Program

In consideration of my appearance on the program entitled _____
and for no subsequent remuneration, I _____ , on behalf of myself,
my heirs, executors, administrators, and assignors, do hereby authorize in perpetuity, San
Jose State University, to use live or recorded on tape, film, or other media, my name, voice,
performance, musical composition, and/or written material therein for television and/or radio
broadcasting, over stations and cable systems worldwide for audiovisual and/or education
purposes.

   I further agree that San Jose State University may also use my name, likeness, and biography for publishing and promoting broadcast and other associated uses.

   I warrant and represent that all material furnished and used by me on any such programs
is my own original material, or material for which I have full authority to use for such programs. Furthermore, I agree to idemnify, defend, and hold harmless the State of California,
the Trustees of the California State University and Colleges, and San Jose State University
and its employees, officers, directors, and/or agents for any and all claims, suits, or liabilities
arising from my appearance and the use of any of my materials, name, likeness, and/or
biography.

CONDITIONS: _____
_____

SIGNATURE: _____	WITNESS: _____
NAME: _____	NAME: _____
ADDRESS: _____	ADDRESS: _____
CITY: _____	CITY: _____
STATE: _____	STATE: _____
ZIP CODE: _____	ZIP CODE: _____
PHONE: _____	PHONE: _____
DATE: _____	DATE: _____

USING SOUND EFFECTS CREATIVELY

Perhaps you have decided that the use of music in a thirty-second spot will be a real
distraction. Perhaps you are planning to use music in part of the production and
just a voice in another. Even a single PSA or commercial that will be primarily
narration by an announcer may benefit from some environmental or background

sound, usually called **sound effects.** Listen to an hour or so of radio, and try to notice when sound effects are used. Chances are, they occur in more productions than you are aware of—in the background to suggest location, in the foreground to draw your attention to a car by making you believe that you're riding in it, or to help you believe that you are attending a sporting event or recreational opportunity.

Like music, sound effects have been used in radio since the beginning to create the illusion of place, to draw pictures in the mind of the listener, to create the theater of the mind. Variety and comedy shows? Like the television sitcoms of today, early radio often added audience sounds to make you feel a part of the performance. What about those laughs that occurred at just the right time? Or the applause? The big national shows actually performed live before an adoring audience, but sound effect records of audiences often were used in smaller towns. Big sporting events? Small-town radio stations, unable to afford the line and talent charges of big-time baseball, actually had their announcers *read* information about the game from a continuous teletype, and re-create the play-by-play. Often the sounds of the bat hitting the ball and the cheering crowds were all done with sound effects devices. But it was the plays, the major dramas, that really made creative use of sound effects in early radio. Try to imagine the opening sequence from a dramatic 60-second commercial, shown in Box 8.2, without any sound effects.

BOX 8.2   *Script without Sound Effects*

A man drives up, gets out of his car, walks to the front door of a house, and rings the bell. The girl comes to the door and the dialogue about the product begins.

Now add the sound effects, as in Box 8.3.

BOX 8.3   *Same Script with Effects*

(sound of car engine) A man drives up, (car engine stops) gets out of his car, (door slams) walks (walking sounds) to the front door of a house, and rings the bell. (bell) The girl comes (walking) to the door and the dialogue about the product begins.

Drama requires sound effects to give it a realism demanded by listeners. It needs sound effects to establish location, distance, the use of a car, and so on. In early radio, there were at least one or two sound effects artists for every show. One of the sound effects people would be operating a **sound effects truck,** a device with three or four turntables and a mixer for controlling those sounds that were on record like cars, trains, and other sounds impossible to create realistically in a studio. Another sound effects person was very much like today's **foley artist,** the person who adds environmental sounds to a movie or television audio track. This individual had at his or her disposal a variety of surfaces to walk on, doors to open and close, bells, buzzers, and a whole variety of mechanical devices that were picked up by microphones and mixed in with the show.

Because audiences were long used to the sound effects that accompanied live plays and motion pictures, it was only natural that part of the language of radio included the use of these sounds. And in radio, unlike visual media, sound effects provide an integral part of a listener's understanding of the content of a PSA, drama, commercial, or promotion. Your production, just like those of the golden age of radio, may benefit from sound effects that you create, record live, or copy from a CD.

Selecting Sound Effects for Your Production

The most common source of sound effects is the commercial library like the one that your institution purchased along with its music library. Perhaps the school library or campus radio station also has a collection of sound effects records or CDs, cleared for production and broadcast. Still, sounds that you make or record are sometimes better than the canned variety. A forest fire? In early radio, cellophane was crinkled close to the microphone. Horses? Coconut shells on a table or a bed of gravel were used. And, you can actually take a good-quality microphone and field recorder to a location where the sound that you need occurs. You can also manufacture entirely unique sounds by using a sampler and an audio facility. The creation and use of nonmusic, nondialogue sound is often an important element of a radio production.

The easiest way to get sound effects is from your library. Most radio producers will have access to a cleared **SFX,** or sound effects, library, perhaps as part of a total package containing both production music and the sounds. Like the cleared music, these libraries are on CD and are organized so the producer can find the needed effect in a hurry. And while cleared music cuts are grouped by genre of music, orchestration and tempo, sound effects may be categorized by the location where the sounds are recorded. Some libraries have one disk devoted to, for example, "transportation." Under a subcategory of *aircraft* will be all airport and airplane sounds, such as passenger terminal crowd ambience, all types of planes taking off and landing, all the sounds you are likely to ever hear in an airport. The more extensive libraries will have thousands of familiar sounds, all recorded on location.

But what about those sounds that are so associated with a location familiar to the listener that their use cannot be *faked* using prerecorded sound effects? Is there a local amusement park boardwalk, next to the ocean? Does it want to advertise? In this case, the sound of the 1880s-vintage band organ at the carousel and the accompanying sounds of beach goers may not be found on a CD. Even if something close exists, it may not be realistic enough to convince your local listeners. For this reason, there will be times when you must go on location with tape recorder and microphone.

For on-location recording of sound effects, professionals will use a DAT recorder and stereo coincident pair microphone. At the very minimum, a high-quality cassette recorder and microphone should be used. Most good cassette recorders will

A sound effects library on CD.

A portable cassette deck has a vu meter and a XLR microphone input.

have provisions for monitoring using a headset, and some will even have **Dolby noise reduction** circuitry to eliminate the *hiss* or tape noise inherent in the analog cassette system. When recording any ambient sound on location, remember that a microphone cannot discriminate between wanted and unwanted audio like the human brain. If the location is too noisy, experiment with different microphone placement; the closer the microphone to the wanted sound, the less noticeable the unwanted or interfering audio will be. Finally, always try to go to a quiet room, perhaps your car, and listen to the playback of the sound using a headset. It is here that any unwanted sounds will be heard.

TABLE 8.4   *30-Second "Protect the Environment" PSA with SFX Cues*

SFX: people having fun, laughing

ANNCR: (very slowly) Consider what will happen to our way of life if we don't take care of the earth . . .

CUT TO SFX: factory sounds

ANNCR: (reading rapidly) Every day millions of gallons of toxic wastes from residences and factories pour into the Pacific Ocean, continuously, nonstop, all the time, never stopping . . . How much more can the oceans take?

CUT TO SFX: ocean waves, seagulls

ANNCR: Only you can save the earth. Send for a list of environmental groups in California that need your help. Save the earth.

SFX ENDS

Using Sound Effects in a Production

How will you incorporate sound effects into a production? As with music, the first place to look is the script. Perhaps there are no obvious clues to any possible places where sound effects might be used. Look again. Practically every location has some **environmental,** or ambient, sound that, if heard by the listener, might create a desirable visual image. A quiet forest? The crashing of waves on the beach? Inside a car on the freeway? A crowded supermarket? Every place has some recognizable audio background associated with being at that place. Every PSA and every commercial that attempts to motivate the listener to visit a specific location might benefit from a sound effect, however subtle. The seasons of the year? All have a group of sounds associated with them. Products? Many make sounds that, when recorded and used in the background, can elicit a positive feeling from the audience. Consider the environment PSA used earlier to demonstrate the use of music. Table 8.4 shows the same PSA, but with sound effects instead of music.

Now you have made another creative choice. You have decided to use sound effects instead of music to enhance the meaning, the urgency of your message. Believe it or not, you have even more creative choices. You can decide to combine both the music and the sound effects, using the same announcer reading the same script. Or you can use sound effects in the beginning, then cut to music for the middle section of narration, and then go back to sound effects only for the conclusion. In just thirty seconds, you have taken a listener from the happy sounds of people living to the frantic music of busy life and industry to the peaceful sounds of the ocean. Using audio only, you have created images to move the listener from the ideal to the real and back to the ideal.

Look at your script or idea and make a list of possible sound effects to be used.

TABLE 8.5	*Sound Effects Needs for a 30-Second PSA*		
	What You Need	**Where Located**	**Needed By**
	Busy factory	SFX library, disc 5, cut 27	Day of production
	Crowds at mall	SFX library, disc 1, cut 4	Same
	Crowds at beach	To be recorded on location	2 days before production
	Ocean	As above	As above

Now you can go into the production facility prepared to add either sound effects or music to the PSA on saving the environment. You can make a version with narration only, music and narration only, sound effects and narration only, or any combination. You may even make two versions. You have taken one simple idea and looked at it a number of ways, all designed to *sell,* to convince the listener of your point of view, in this case, saving the planet. You have done it all using audio.

SUMMARY

Creativity in radio production always involves options. As a producer, you will want to have as much choice as possible when selecting an idea and writing the script. Sure, the needs of a sponsor or the format of a station may limit your choice in some productions. And while the idea and script could be predetermined, the way that the production is treated will probably be left up to you, the producer. This is where the selection of background music and sound effects becomes important. Whether your idea or that of the sponsor, the effectiveness of the production can be in your control.

Now that you know how to organize a production and select and operate some of the equipment, and now that you are beginning to see some of the options possible for finding and using music and sound effects creatively, more creative and satisfying productions are possible. Do you have some ideas? Good, because now you can go into a production facility with more than just your voice and a favorite CD. Soon, you are going to see how radio programming ideas can be turned into the production of commercials, PSAs, news, drama, and comedy. The more you know about creative options in radio production, the more you'll realize your creative self.

ACTIVITIES

1. Listen to an hour of your favorite format radio station. Note the type of music and sound effects used. Are they effectively used? Are they used for meaning?

2. Audition the music and sound effects library of your radio station or institution.

3. Arrange to attend a recording session at a local studio where music is being recorded to accompany a commercial.

4. Go to a variety of locations and just listen to the variety of environmental sounds. Close your eyes, and try to imagine pictures to go with those sounds.

Editing

It is physically impossible for you to fit an orchestra to play your musical background, a city bus for a bus-stopping sound effect, and your cast of characters or narrator all inside your studio at one time for a radio production. Instead, you would find recordings of all these sounds and music and take them with you into the studio to later add them in the production process. In a real-time production, when you want to use several voices, background music, sound effects, or a jingle, all you have to do is have the audio sources cued and ready to start them with split-second accuracy so the entire production comes together as a whole, without stopping. Ideally, this procedure will not require any changes once you get it right. Since you record the audio segments in real-time as they happen, this is usually called **live-on-tape** recording. Keep in mind that you can repeat this recording procedure over and over until you hit all of your cues on time and get it right.

Carts are especially valuable during live-on-tape productions because you don't have to thread the tape; they cue themselves, which gives you one less thing to think about. For example, if you have several short sound effects you want to use in a production, simply record them in order onto a cart. As soon as you play one, the cart will automatically cue to the next recorded sound effect. All you have to do is hit the play button again at the appropriate time.

WHAT IS EDITING AND WHY EDIT?

But what if you want to change a part of the production without having to record the whole thing over again? Perhaps you make only a slight mistake that needs to be removed. Or maybe your client wants some words changed in the script. What if you want to first concentrate on recording the voice and later add the sound effects? You could edit. **Editing** is the process by which you can add to or delete from previously recorded material without having to re-record the entire project. Editing allows you to create elaborate productions from simple or limited equipment. With editing, you can:

1. Delete unwanted sounds such as a speaker's cough or mistake sounds such as a dropped microphone or unwanted copy.
2. Combine several segments that may have been recorded at different times and locations into one whole production.
3. Record multiple sources at the same time onto a multitrack tape.
4. Shorten or lengthen a project to fit within specific time constraints.
5. Add music or sound effects later.
6. Repair damaged tape.
7. Make changes or redo the production over and over until you achieve your desired results.

Editing can be done in three basic ways: manual editing, electronic editing, and computer-assisted editing on what is commonly known as the digital audio workstation.

Manual Editing

Manual editing requires you to physically cut the tape, discard unwanted segments, and **splice,** or connect, together remaining portions in the desired order using **pressure sensitive splicing tape.** This process requires a few tools:

1. Empty take-up reels are needed to store spliced tape, which can be degaussed and used again. Final productions can also be stored on empty take-up reels. Always be sure and label your reels carefully to avoid confusion and time finding out what is on your various reels.

The three most common reel sizes are 10½ inches, 7 inches, and 5 inches.

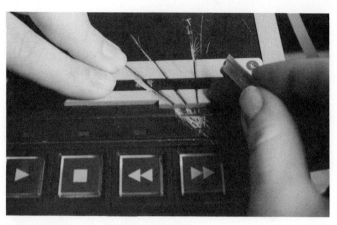

This edit block is part of the tape deck.

2. An **edit block,** also called a cutting, splicing, or chopping block, for 1/4-inch audiotape has cutting guides to enable you to precisely cut the tape at angles of 90 degrees, 45 degrees, or 30 degrees. Ninety-degree **butt** joints tend to cause an audible sound when it passes over the playback head, so typically the 45-degree angle joint is recommended. It tends to sound smoother since the two sounds are more blended as the tape is played. Also, a worn cutting block can cause messy splices, resulting in distorted sound.

3. A wax marking pen, sometimes called a **china marker** or **grease pencil,** is used to mark the editing points without damaging the tape. The grease pencil must be white or some other light color in order for marks to contrast with the dark color of the audiotape. If you are not careful, you might get some grease marks on the tape machine heads as you edit. If it does happen, clean the heads when you have finished editing. It will prolong the life of your equipment and prevent problems for the next person using the machine.

4. A single-edged razor blade is needed to actually cut the audiotape. Razors become dull with use so make sure to change blades often. The sharper the blade, the cleaner the splice.

5. Connecting magnetic tape requires a special kind of adhesive on a special kind of tape. Splicing tape comes in various widths to coordinate with different tape sizes. For splicing 1/4-inch tape, use the slightly narrower 7/32-inch width. This is easier to use because it doesn't require trimming. Special pressure-sensitive splicing tape comes in rolls or in precut splicing tabs. Though the individual tabs are more convenient, they are also more expensive.

Editing tools include a razor blade, china marker, and splicing tabs.

6. **Leader tape** is placed at the beginning of a taped production to absorb the abuse of tape threading and to mark cue points. Some find timing leader tape most useful because its plaid markings are exactly 7 1/2 inches apart, which makes it perfect for establishing precise timing between tape segments.

7. Cotton swabs and alcohol are needed to clean tape heads. Dust and magnetic particles collect on the tape heads. In order to avoid damage to the audiotape caused by the abrasion as the tape moves across the dirty heads, simply swab the heads with alcohol on a cotton swab. Use a new, clean swab on each head. It is best to clean heads every time you use the machine.

The Manual Editing Process

To make an edit, first play the tape to find the edit point. Stop the tape machine. When the machine is stopped or in fast forward or rewind, the tape will be lifted away from the tape heads by arms called *tape lifters*. In order for you to be able to find the exact edit point, you must place the machine into the *cue mode* (some machines utilize pause or play-pause), which disengages the tape lifters. You may now turn up the volume and rotate the reels back and forth by hand until you locate the last sound you do want and the next unwanted sound. That point is now centered over the **playback** head. Mark this spot with your marking pen. It is not possible to make an accurate edit mark without knowing which head is the playback head. Never mark *completely* across the width of the tape—this is how you get grease marks on the machine heads, which should *never* happen. Mark only the center of the audiotape. Make sure you are familiar with the tape machine's heads; if you happen to mark the tape over the wrong head, the splice will be in the wrong place.

Continue playing the tape until you have reached the end of the unwanted section. Again, stop the machine, place it into cue mode, and manually move the tape back and forth until you find the next exact edit point. Mark this spot with your marking pen. Now you are ready to edit.

Search for the edit point by moving the reels manually with both hands.

a

b

Mark the edit point over the playback head (a); and the tape, showing the mark (b).

Go back to the first point. Place the tape securely into the editing block with the mark on the diagonal cutting groove. Cut the tape with the razor blade by applying a steady motion. Do not use a forceful, sawing motion as you might stretch or otherwise damage the tape. Find the second editing point and make that cut. Do not discard this **out take,** the edited piece of tape. Instead, label it and set it aside. You may need it later, especially if you have made a mistake in editing.

To splice the tape, place the two ends to be joined in the channel of the cutting block, emulsion side down. Be sure the ends fit snugly together but do not overlap or leave a gap. On the base of the tape, often the shiny plastic side, apply a piece of the splicing tape approximately 3/4 of an inch long, covering each side of the splice equally. Press the tape firmly into place and gently rub out all air bubbles.

Check your editing by replaying that portion of the tape. If you have made a mistake, find the portion you cut out, splice it back in, and redo your edit points.

When you have finished editing, add leader tape at the beginning and end of your production. If you have recorded several separate sound segments, place leader tape between them so they will be easy to find and cue.

Carefully use the razor blade to cut the tape.

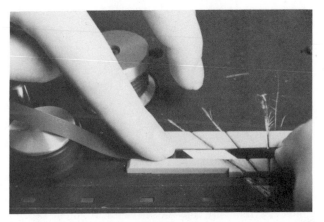

Press the splicing tab onto tape.

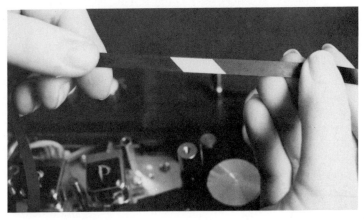

The complete splice.

BOX 9.1   ### *Summary of Manual Editing Steps*

1. Play the tape until you reach your first edit point.
2. Manually move the reels to find the blank spot between the sounds.
3. Mark the edit point centered over the playback head.
4. Find the second edit point.
5. Manually move the reels to find the blank spot between the sounds.
6. Mark the second point over the playback head.
7. Rewind the tape to the first mark.
8. Lay the tape in the cutting block.
9. Cut the tape at a 45-degree angle.
10. Repeat the same procedure at the second edit point.
11. Put the two ends in the cutting block channel. Make sure they touch but do not overlap.
12. Apply the splicing tape. Smooth out the bubbles.
13. Listen to the edit.

Try several splicing exercises until you get it right. Try recording a paragraph but intentionally make several mistakes while reading. Edit out the mistakes using the techniques above.

Electronic Editing

Electronic editing eliminates the need for manually splicing tape. With this method, you **dub,** electronically copy, or re-record, from one tape to another, which enables you to re-record the sound segments you want in the order that you want them. Obviously, this procedure requires that you have at least two tape machines, one to record and the other to play back. Many reel-to-reel machines allow you to **punch in,** or turn on, the record mode of a tape machine while already rolling in play mode. This makes adding sound information to the end of a segment very easy. Be careful! If you punch in too soon, you risk recording over the original production and you might have to re-create it. This is a technique used by radio production people when speed is more important than quality and accuracy.

Computer-Assisted Editing

Once again, knowing computer technology is a must as you set out into the world of radio and audio production. Production is changing drastically, as analog systems are replaced by new digital applications. This process seems to answer previous analog recording and editing problems: generation loss, storage, the perfect re-creation of the original recording with much less noise, absolute edit accuracy, speed of process, and more. In earlier chapters you were introduced to audio with discussions of CDs and DAT. Most broadcast stations currently operate using CDs, which are especially useful for storing musical beds and sound effects because of their versatility. The big breakthrough may be when recordable CDs are low enough in cost. Many think that when that happens CD technology will completely replace magnetic tape as a storage medium. Others predict that computer hard-drive technology will replace tape as a primary storage option.

Computer-assisted editing, obviously, utilizes computer technology to function. Basically, audio signals are *sampled,* or changed, into information that is interpreted by computers as bits of information. This information is presented visually, on screen, for audio production. Elaborate and sophisticated systems are available to broadcast stations but can be somewhat expensive. Recently, however, smaller editing programs are emerging that are compatible with home computer systems. They sample smaller amounts of sound information, from one to a few minutes long, depending on the amount of computer memory available on the computer system.

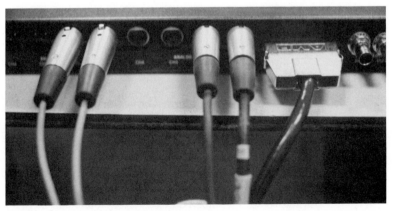

The back of a digital workstation shows connections for audio to and from the audio console and connections to the computer.

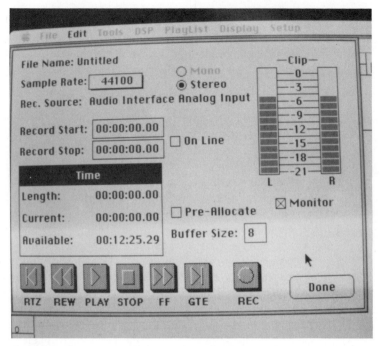

One of the first screens shows a "0" VU level sent to a computer from the audio console. The on-screen icons are designed like the familiar transport controls on a reel-to-reel recorder.

Utilizing on-screen operating characteristics and mouse functions already familiar to the computer user, computer editing can be quite easy. You simply select the record function and type in a name for the recording. You are then recording direct-to-disk. That is, your analog or signal is being recorded onto the computer's hard disk. When you stop the recording, the waveform of your production will appear on a video monitor, the computer screen.

Watching the monitor, you then use your mouse or keyboard to select portions of the waveform and apply various editing techniques such as deleting, copying, moving, mixing, or adding segments. Basically, anything you can do with manual editing, you can do much quicker, cleaner, and easier. In addition, computer editing offers other time-saving conveniences not found in manual or electronic editing. An *undo* feature instantly reverses your last edit operation. A zoom function enables you to see the waveform in any level of detail so you can locate the exact start and finish of a particular sound. And a catalog feature lets you build collections of sounds that you can play by hitting single keys on the keyboard. Hard-disk editing also allows you to adjust waveform levels by increasing or decreasing amplitude and frequency. Once edits are complete, an audition feature plays your production in order for you to fine-tune your edit points. And finally, on-line help is available at any step of the editing process.

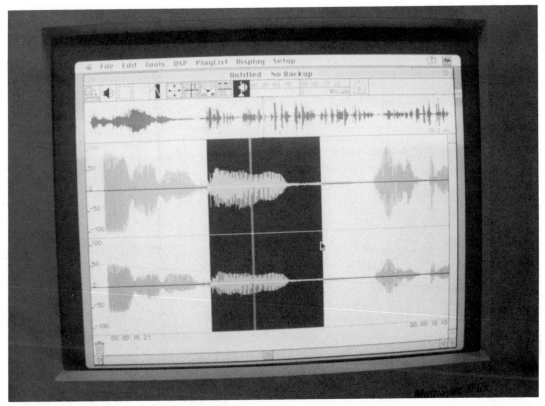

The waveform of the audio is depicted visually on the screen. The dark area shows the part that has been marked for editing, mixing, or processing.

More elaborate systems are engineered specifically for radio broadcast applications and are designed to replace cassette recorders, cart machines, reel-to-reel decks, and any other tape-based audio recorder-players now found in a radio studio. However, when necessary, once your production has been edited you can still feed the completed production out to an audio tape recorder for storage and distribution on tape.

Manual, razor-blade editing used to be the most prevalent editing technique used by the broadcasting and audio industry. However, more and more organizations are opting for the convenience and accuracy of DAWS editing, making it the preferred editing method of the future.

Checking Your Edits

Once you have finished editing your production either manually, electronically, or using a DAWS, ask your classmates to listen to it in case you have become so involved with the project that you cannot objectively judge it. Be sure to check your work thoroughly before your boss, instructor, or client hears it.

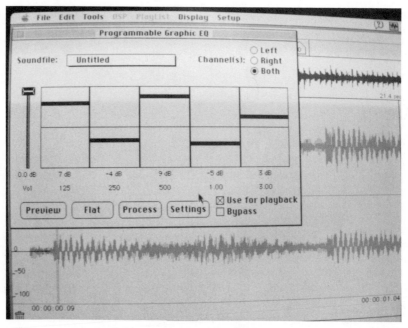

One of the many signal processing options is this programmable graphic equalizer.

All audio editing will soon be performed using a computer.

SUMMARY

Editing is the process by which you can add to or delete from previously recorded material without having to re-record the entire project.

Manual editing requires you to physically cut the tape, discard unwanted segments, and splice remaining portions in the desired order. Special splicing tape is used for this procedure since a particular type of adhesive is necessary to connect the tape without damaging the oxide emulsion. Other tools that are necessary to manually edit are an editing block, a grease pencil, a single-edged razor blade, and leader tape. Manual editing is accurate, if slow, and it is still popular in the broadcasting and audio industry.

Electronic editing eliminates the need for manual tape splicing. You simply dub information in sequential order from a source machine to a recording unit. Electronic editing is faster, but less accurate.

Very soon, however, the speed, the convenience, and accuracy of digital editing will probably make it the sure standard of the industry. One reason is that is relies on familiar computer technology, language, and equipment. Using a monitor, mouse, and keyboard, you can perform the same procedures that are available in manual editing, only faster, cleaner and easier. In addition, computer-assisted editing offers other time-saving conveniences not found in manual or electronic editing such as the redo, zoom, audition, and on-line help functions.

ACTIVITIES

1. Record a line of copy, and select a word to edit from it.
2. Take the same line, and switch the position of two words.
3. Add a musical intro to the beginning and middle of your copy.
4. Insert edit a sound effect over the music in the middle of your copy by using the edit button on the tape machine. In other words, do not manually insert this effect. Instead, edit electronically.

   Here is an example of an editing exercise.

   Record this line of copy:
   Oh yes, we have no bananas (pause)
   We have no bananas today.

   Select the two "no" words and edit them from the recording.
   Your production should now say:
   Oh, yes, we have bananas (pause)
   We have bananas today.

   Move the word "today" from the end of the copy to the very beginning.
   Your production should now say:
   Today, Oh, yes, we have bananas (pause)
   We have bananas.

   Insert edit a sound effect **over** the pause using the edit button on your
   recorder (don't manually splice this one).
   Your production should now say:
   Today, Oh, yes, we have bananas (SFX)
   We have bananas.

Turning Radio Programming into Production

All this audio production does not exist in a vacuum. Sure, creative radio programming and production is about audio production, about learning about the equipment, how it works, and what it can do. But it's also about the radio station, that 24-hour-a-day distributor of nonstop produced audio. Whether prerecorded in a fancy studio using several actors and plenty of music and sound effects and edited on a DAWS, or the live, real-time on-air production done by the DJ, it is only because of the existence of the radio station that all this discussion, this learning about equipment and production techniques, makes any sense. No radio stations, no radio productions.

Now it's time to get practical. It's time to apply all the generic production information you have been reading about and hopefully experiencing to the service of radio programming. Now you are going to go behind the scenes of the radio station and find out what goes on behind the production, behind the sound that you listen to daily. Why do stations program the type of music that they do? Why do they suddenly change that programming? What influence do sponsors have? What do ratings tell station management? Who are the people who work in the radio station in the service of programming and production? What is the difference between the formats called CHR and MOR? In what ways do the people who determine a station's programming influence its production?

Next you'll learn about programming styles or formats. Then you'll be presented with examples of every type of production done to support every format, music or talk, commercial or community. Learn all about the production of commercials and public service announcements. How does the radio programmer communicate his or her promotional needs to the production staff? How does a production person work with a sponsor in the production of a commercial? How do you produce an underwritten message that legally can be aired on a noncommercial station? News and information formats will be detailed, and production strategies for both spot news and feature-length documentaries will be described. Soon you'll be thinking about production the way people at a radio station do. Soon, the connection between programming and production will be apparent.

Finally, you'll learn all about the role of the modern-day disc jockey and why and how this staple of radio programming has changed yet still survived for more than half a century. You'll be in the seat during an air shift. See what the DJ does and what he or she says and learn how to construct an audition tape before you look for an entry-level position at a small radio station. In the last chapter of this section, there is a perspective on radio—its business, its programming, and its technology. Learn where it has been, where it is now, and where it is headed. In this section, it all comes together: radio programming and production.

▲

Understanding the Radio Station

In this chapter, you will be introduced to the structure of radio and its potential as an audio production outlet. The radio station is probably the most famous of outlets for audio production, employing some sixty thousand people full time. Radio is a popular mass medium. Broadcasting allows the transmission of messages to thousands and sometimes millions of people simultaneously. This is a very powerful and important ability.

THE RADIO STATION

You've probably noticed that your radio dial numbers are limited to a specific number of frequencies that it can receive, like **AM**—from 535 to 1700 kHz—and **FM**—from 88 to 108 mHz. These are the frequencies within the electromagnetic spectrum that have been allocated by the government for radio stations that program entertainment and information for a mass audience. Since there are a limited number of frequencies available and each channel has the potential to reach such large numbers of people, only certain individuals are licensed by the government to use the mass medium. The traffic cop that watches over these airwaves is the **Federal Communications Commission,** or **FCC.**

The FCC

The government hasn't always been involved with broadcasting. When broadcasting first began, people did not know quite what to do with this exciting and new technology. Radio receivers were being sold by the thousands, and anybody who wanted to transmit could do so from any frequency and at any power level. Early broadcasting efforts were riddled with poor-quality programming, nonexistent scheduling, undependable equipment, and constant signal interference. Aside from implementing temporary restrictions on radio during World War I, the government did not become officially involved in broadcasting until it was obvious that interference problems would not be solved without government regulatory intervention. In other words, it was broadcasters themselves who pleaded with the government

An announcer on the air at KSJS San Jose.

to step in and do something. Regulation didn't actually come to radio until the **Radio Act of 1927,** which established licensing provisions and, for the first time, created and empowered a government entity specifically in charge of radio matters, the **Federal Radio Commission,** or **FRC.** Before the FRC, radio licensing had been under the jurisdiction of the secretary of Commerce.

With the advent of new technologies, it became obvious that radio would not be the sole user of communication electromagnetic waves. A few years later, a more concrete piece of legislation was passed, which we still abide by today, the **Communications Act of 1934.** This act canceled the FRC and established a new **Federal Communications Commission,** which was given jurisdiction over the use of all airwaves in the United States, intending that they be used in the **public interest, convenience, or/and necessity** (PICON). The idea behind this "public interest" provision is that since the airwaves in theory belong to the public, those who are granted the privilege, or **license,** to transmit on those public airwaves should give something back to the public. The Communications Act of 1934 provides the general guidelines regarding what is expected of licensed broadcasters. The FCC sets rules and bases decisions upon these guidelines.

For example, at one time, the FCC was very concerned with programming that would serve local needs and address local issues. However, these guidelines were changed in the 1980s with the proposition of government deregulation. The idea was to ease the government out of the business of broadcasting and simply let the marketplace decide. This deregulation trend altered the definition of the public interest standard.

An operator license like this one was once required for all on-air operators.

At the top of the chain of command at the FCC are five commissioners who are appointed by the president of the United States and confirmed by the Senate. Of course, these five commissioners can't possibly handle all of the work that is involved with overseeing all communication entities such as radio, television, cable, satellite, and telephone. Therefore, the FCC employs a support staff of approximately fifteen hundred people spread across the nation in regional offices. The five commissioners and their staffs handle all the complaints filed by listeners against the twelve thousand radio stations, both technical, such as interference between stations, and programming, such as complaints about the lyrics of songs.

What if you as a DJ or station owner do something against the policies set by the FCC? Depending on the type of violation, the commission may take one of the following actions:

1. When it isn't a serious matter or the commission accepts an assurance that the violation won't happen again, the FCC sends a simple **letter of admonition** as a mild reprimand.

2. The FCC imposes a **forfeiture,** a fine, as the most common sanction on a station. The amount of the fine varies with the severity of the violation and by the station's ability to pay. It can be as high as $20,000 for more serious violations.

3. A more severe sanction occurs when the FCC imposes a *denial to renew a license.*

4. The most severe sanction is the outright **revocation** of a license. This rarely ever happens. From the time the FCC was created in 1934 through 1987, only 141 stations lost their licenses.

It is important that you as a radio producer, especially if you are going to be an announcer as well, become familiar with and follow the rules and guidelines set by the FCC. These rules take up hundreds of pages worth of text, including basic rules such as maintaining proper transmission levels; giving a station **ID,** its call letters and location; keeping an accurate log; and implementing an emergency broadcasting service, **EBS,** test. The best rule of thumb for adhering to FCC rules and avoiding trouble is: When in doubt, look it up in the FCC rule book or ask the station manager.

The Community

Since the FCC licenses broadcast stations to serve the public interest, broadcasters are responsible for getting to know their community and finding out about issues and needs in order to be able to serve better. This process is called **ascertainment.**

Radio is normally considered a local communication entity. If a station is not in touch with its listeners, it will eventually lose those listeners to other stations. As an audio producer, you, too, must be in tune with your audience in order to determine how you can communicate both yours and the station's message most effectively.

The Business

Public service isn't the only reason broadcasters must know about their audience. The existence of stations, formats, programs, and air personalities are all dependent upon revenues determined by the ratings process that monitors who is listening. It is simple business economic practice involving a seller, a product, and a buyer. For example, you want to purchase a car. The buyer would be you, the seller would be the dealership, and the product would be the car. But when applying the same categories to the broadcasting economic system, who would be the seller? The buyer? And what would be the product?

Many people would say broadcasters sell commercials/air-time to advertisers. However, this is not correct. In fact, this is the way it actually works: broadcasters sell *you,* the audience, to advertisers.

Commercial broadcast stations are funded by advertising revenue. The amount of money an advertiser will pay for commercial time is based solely on how many individual audience members the station can deliver. The quality of the program is almost incidental. Advertisers are only interested in the program's ability to draw an audience. And though it is true that a station that cannot make money will not stay in business for very long, many interesting and diverse programs are lost because they are not viable economically. That is, a program might generate an interested audience, but if that audience isn't large enough or can't be sold to an interested advertiser, that program becomes worthless to the station. The business of broadcasting can at times present harsh realities that you must recognize and work with as you proceed with your audio production.

There are noncommercial alternatives found in community radio, cable, or public radio. These stations rely on subscribers, program underwriting, and government support to fund their operations so that the need to achieve large ratings isn't as crucial to survival. Consequently, many productions that are targeted for a very specific, even small, audience are broadcast on noncommercial radio when they wouldn't even be considered on a commercial station. These stations still have to sell their programming to a community willing to donate, subscribe, or otherwise pay to listen.

The Structure of the Station

Stations are all structured differently. Depending on the type of station and the size of its market, the specifics of jobs and the number of responsibilities assigned to each person vary. For example, in smaller stations one person may perform the duties of more than one of the following positions. Still, certain basic functions need to be served regardless of station size or how many people are assigned to these tasks.

Management and Administrative

The management and administrative people are responsible for monitoring the actual work flow within the station. They are concerned with getting the job done, whether it is hiring or firing personnel, issuing paychecks, meeting FCC requirements, accounting, printing stationery, buying office supplies and equipment, or organizing correspondence. Typically when people think about how it is to work in the broadcast industry, they forget about the numerous employment opportunities available in this area of the business, which include: clerical workers, bookkeepers, receptionists, and accountants, as well as the general manager of the station.

Programming

The people in the programming department are responsible for putting together a coherent and profitable program schedule. Since advertising rates are directly determined by the number of listeners, program choice and scheduling is crucial in acquiring and maintaining revenue. In this department are found the program director, music director, promotions director, news director, and the announcing staff.

Sales

The people in the sales department actually produce the station's revenue by selling the audience acquired by programs provided by the programming department. There is more potential to make money in sales than in any other station department. Those in this department, in addition to salespeople and their managers, include support staff in traffic and marketing.

Technical

This department is made up almost exclusively of engineers. These people are responsible for the operation, maintenance, and repair of all station equipment. They are concerned with the quality of the audio and the operation of the transmitter. In the small- and medium-size modern radio stations, engineers may be contract employees belonging to an outside company.

▼

| BOX 10.1 | *The Four Station Areas with Job Titles* |

Management and administrative:
> General manager
> Continuity director
> Personnel
> Traffic department
> Payroll
> Reception

Programming:
> Programming director (also management function)
> Promotions director
> Production director
> Announcers
> Music librarian
> Production staff
> News

Sales:
(The structure of the sales department varies from market to market)
> Sales manager
> Marketing and research
> National sales
> Local sales
> Co-op

Technical:
> Chief Engineer

Keep in mind that even though the exact departmental structure will vary between stations and markets, the functions of the departments remain the same. Descriptions of specific station personnel will be highlighted later in this chapter.

WHY PRODUCTION?

It is said that TV must be seen to be believed, but radio must be believed to be seen. As a production person, your mission is to enclose your listeners in a *sound environment* that helps them create a mental experience of what you want them to experience. You must accomplish your goal with audio production. At a radio station, yours will be one of the many productions being considered. Organization becomes especially important because you will be given strict deadlines for scheduling talent, studios, and actual production time.

A production person at KGO San Francisco threads up a tape for production.

Live or Recorded?

One of the first decisions an audio producer must make is whether the production will be done live or recorded. The basic difference between the two methods is that live on-air production is a one-shot deal. All music, sound effects, and voice-overs must be put together simultaneously, and you must get it right the first time because you won't get another chance. Using live announcers can be very effective since they can respond to audience input directly and immediately, as well as provide a personal touch to listeners who are familiar with them. Most commercials and other announcements done live will not have much in the way of music or sound effects.

Recorded productions, on the other hand, allow as many opportunities as it takes to get the production right, and, once completed, recorded messages can be reproduced or played over and over again. Consequently, very complex productions are typically recorded because all aspects of the production, like music, sound effects, and multiple voices, can be handled separately. In addition, live on-air productions necessitate that participants be available at a strict specified on-air time, while recording studio time can be reserved to work around everyone's schedules.

Getting Attention

The first five or six seconds of your message are very important. If you do not capture the attention of the audience then, your production might be wasted. Remember: people can switch to another radio station in a split second. So concentrate your creative thought on your opening. Your ability to capture an audience quickly depends upon a grabbing idea, or a *hook* as it is called in the business.

Predictability/Repeatability

When was the last time you sat glued to the radio, carefully absorbing every single syllable spoken by the announcer? You have probably not done this in the past nor will you do it in the future. Radio is the type of medium that you consume while

At KCBS San Francisco, a reel-to-reel tape's analog audio is loaded into a computer for editing digitally.

doing something else, whether it's driving, doing homework, having a picnic, or writing a book. Consequently, if you provide important information during your message, you need to repeat the major or important points more than once. Give your audience the opportunity to mentally record essential information, such as phone numbers and addresses. The rule of thumb for commercial messages is to repeat the product name at least three times in a thirty-second commercial.

Marketing the Station

Stations operate in certain areas with specific characteristics. A station only exists due to its direct ties to the community. The overall area that a station is licensed to serve and from which a station draws its income is called its **market.** It isn't enough to know how many people are out there with radios; what is important is finding out who those people are and what are they looking for from radio. A market is not stagnant nor easily defined. It is constantly changing as the environment and the people within it change. In order for a station to be successful, it must understand the market, monitor changes, and, most important, find ways to create new listeners inside the existing market. The best way to achieve this latter goal is to promote and position your station in the market.

BOX 10.2   *Examples of Underwriting Commercial Copy*

Examples of KSJS Radio Underwriting Spots

Underwriting rules limit your spot only slightly. Otherwise, the more creative you are, the better the spot will be.

Remember: If you need help writing copy for a radio spot, contact any KSJS manager or someone in the production department.

Here are some examples of BUCs
(Basic Underwriting Commercials):

This portion of KSJS is brought to you by <u>FAUX HAIR SALON</u> featuring Joi-Co hair products. <u>FAUX</u>'s services are by appointment only. <u>FAUX</u> is located at 378 Campbell Avenue in Campbell and their phone number is 378–0000. That's <u>FAUX HAIR SALON</u> featuring JOI-CO Products.

This portion of KSJS's programming is brought to you by <u>FEDERICO</u>'s . . . featuring an authentic Tex-Mex menu, that includes seafood prepared for you by Tex-Mex chefs. <u>FEDERICO</u>'s is located at 325 South First Street in San Jose. Their phone number is (408)–000–0000. <u>FEDERICO</u>'s, another proud sponsor of KSJS programming.

This portion of KSJS's programming is brought to you by <u>DIMENSIONS IN HEALTH</u> specializing in massage therapy. <u>DIMENSIONS IN HEALTH</u> offers a variety of massage therapy ranging from sports to Swedish Massage. <u>DIMENSIONS IN HEALTH</u> is located at 20 South Santa Cruz Avenue in downtown Los Gatos. The staff, directed by Bob Sanchez, can be reached at 408–000–0000 for additional information.

BOX 10.2   *continued*

When writing copy, here are some things you should include:

1. **The Sponsor's Name.**
   Mention the name **at least three times** throughout the spot. Roughly once in the beginning, middle, and end.
2. **Products or Services that the Sponsor Offers.**
   Again, according to underwriting rules, you can't describe them, just creatively list them.
3. **Sponsor's Address and Phone Number.**
   This should be included in every spot!

Positioning and Promoting the Station

Promotion is a method of getting public attention for a station. People will not listen to a station if they do not know it is there. People identify and support organizations that are familiar to them. Station promotion provides this familiarity and identification. However, since there are many radio stations, each with unique characteristics and services they can offer to the public, stations must also engage in marketing to separate themselves from their competition. This is called **positioning.** And the competition isn't just other radio stations; it is also other advertising outlets. Newspapers, magazines, television, billboards, direct mail, and cable are just a few of the businesses competing for those valuable advertising dollars and audience members. Radio stations position themselves in terms of their unique features to entice people to listen to or clients to buy from their stations instead of others in the area.

Station promotion and positioning can take many forms. Radio stations can advertise on other media such as television, newspapers, and billboards. Or stations might use merchandising devices such as contests, which are regulated by the FCC; promotions involving sponsors in planned events; participation in charity affairs; straightforward giveaways like T-shirts, Frisbees, or other free gifts that always have the stations' names on them; and competitions with community groups or trade-out deals, which swap merchandise and services. It is these "outside" station events that increase public awareness of a station's presence and separates it from its competitors.

Competition and Ratings

A station promotes itself in order to get high **ratings,** or audience share. The ratings represent how many people are listening to programs. Rating scores in points and percentages are the commodity used by broadcasters and advertisers to set the dollar price for commercial time. Advertisers buy according to cost per thousand, or **CPM.**

Three stations use their logos to position their stations.

Bumper stickers, buttons, and T-shirts are used by radio stations for name recognition.

(M is the Latin symbol for thousand.) Once salespeople identify the ratings of a program and translate listener ratings into a dollar figure, they transfer this information onto a price list called a **rate card.** Even though rate cards reflect how much each commercial spot costs, once again, it is not just the 30-second time slot that is sold to the advertiser. The rating points representing the number of listening individuals is sold to advertisers.

Underwriting Rates

KSJS 90.7 FM
1 WASHINGTON SQ.
SAN JOSE, CA
95192-0094
408-924-4548

30 seconds during music programming_____$30.00

30 seconds during sports programming_____$35.00

Sponsorship of a public service announcement campaign
(Mention of sponsor's name and address in connection with
a public service announcement)
Per public announcement_____$24.00

Sponsorship of a specialty music or public affairs program
(3 X 30 second underwriting spots, one at the beginning,
one in the middle and one at the end of the program)_____$100.00

Sponsorship of KSJS live remote
(KSJS Disc jockeys will broadcast live from sponsor's establishment
mentioning sponsor's name, location and other vital information
at every music break while also running promotional contest)
For a period of 4 hours_____$500.00

Sponsorship of KSJS bumpersticker
(Sponsor places a coupon on the peel-off back portion of the sticker)
Price depends on quantity_____Ask for rate

Program guide Advertising Rates

Back Cover_____(plus 10 radio spots FREE)_____$400.00

Full Page_____(plus 7 radio spots FREE)_____$250.00

Two Thirds Page___(plus 5 radio spots FREE)_____$180.00

Half Page_____(plus 4 radio spots FREE)_____$140.00

Third Page_____(plus 3 radio spots FREE)_____$100.00

Sixth Page_____$60.00

Twelfth Page_____$35.00

*All rates ask for "camera-ready" art.   Simple ad layouts can be designed for a small
charge.   Ask your KSJS fundraising representative for a quote.

Underwriting Rules

For Non-Commercial Station Program Sponsors

- **An Underwriting spot can identify, but cannot promote**
  A "menu list" of items that the sponsor offers can be given (e.g., list of products and services), but cannot be "hyped" by the station (e.g., "go buy these")

- **An Underwriting spot cannot be qualitative or call to action**
  Flowery qualitative and comparative adjectives (e.g. "delicious food," "best in town") are prohibited, as is urging to do something ("apply for a credit card now")

- **An Underwriting spot must be a value-neutral description**
  Do not ascribe value-imparting adjectives (e.g., "**fine** dishware") to the product or service

- **The mention of discounts or savings percentage is prohibited**
  Not only are specific numbers prohibited (e.g. "10% off") but the concept of discount (e.g., "it's on sale now") is also banned.

The only exception to the 2nd and 3rd bullet points above is if the sponsor's *logogram* (the motto which normally accompanies the sponsor's name in promotional and advertising materials) contains such a phrase. For example, "Waterford--Fine Crystal Since 1891," if that is their trademark line, could use it in an underwriting spot.
      (**Be advised that the use of a** *logogram* **must be approved in advance by KSJS management**)

__NO__	__Yes__
Best burgers in town	Charcoal broiled burgers
Delicious fine wine	French & Domestic wine
The **largest** selection of wallpapers in the valley	A large selection of wallpapers
Fly the Friendly Skies	Serving most major cities
The city's **first** bank	Serving San Jose since 1898

A college radio station rate card shows the cost of underwriting.

The main radio rating service is called Arbitron, which provides market by market information about audience listening behavior. Arbitron covers two hundred and sixty radio markets in a twelve-week rating period, known as a sweep. Since it would be impossible for a company to monitor every listener twenty-four-hours a day, it chooses a small group, called a statistical sample, from the entire population and relies on statistical data to support its predictions. The whole process hinges on the scientific statistical concept of a random sample. As long as everyone in the population has an equal chance of being chosen for a ratings survey, a small group can be statistically considered representative of the whole population.

The problem, then, becomes how the random sample can be achieved. Usually, sample members are chosen from name lists, such as the telephone book, or place lists, such as housing maps. Critics of the ratings system claim that the problem with using these resources is that they automatically leave out parts of the population who cannot participate; therefore, a random sample is not achieved. For example, if the telephone book is the source list, then all people who do not have telephones or who have unlisted numbers (some cities cite 40 percent or more are unlisted) will not have the opportunity to be chosen. If home listings are the source, then the homeless or people in transient living situations, such as college students moving in and out of dorms, will be left out of the mix. Since nearly all broadcasting decisions hinge on ratings, it is important to consider the ramifications of disenfranchising those who cannot participate in the ratings game. According to the ratings, a part of the population does not exist and yet it is still a part of the public that broadcasters are licensed to serve. Of course, the cynical broadcaster will tell you that disenfranchised people, or people without places to live or phones, don't buy many products either.

Once participants are chosen, a variety of methods are used to acquire listening behavior and **demographic** information pertaining to vital statistics of a population, such as age, gender, geographic location, and marital status. The Arbitron uses a diary in which people are asked to keep a written record of their media use. Careful screening of these diaries is necessary, since some people fill out the diaries inaccurately to reflect idealized listening in order to keep their favorite programs on the air or to make themselves seem more responsible by listing high-brow programming such as public broadcasting. Other methodologies used by smaller ratings services and stations themselves include telephone and face-to-face surveys. Whatever the method, it is usually good enough for most advertisers.

Once the information is acquired by the ratings services, daily, weekly, and monthly reports called books are circulated. These books report listener behavior broken into time slots called **dayparts.** The ratings figures provide the following information:

A **rating** is simply a percentage of the total households out of all possible radio owners listening to a particular radio station. A share represents a station's portion of listeners who are actually *using* radio. This measurement is used as a basis of comparison. A share tells the station how it is doing in relation to its competition. Finally, a PUR, or **People Using Radio,** provides a ratio of how many people are tuned to radio in general.

But what if you have a 15 share at 9:00 A.M. and then another 15 share at 9:15 A.M.? Have the **same** people been listening, or are they new listeners? The **cume,** or cumulative statistic, represents the number of different people who tune into a station over a period of time.

Selling the Product

Basically, a radio station's sales department is responsible for selling listeners to clients through advertising. Salespeople, called account executives, sell air time for these advertisements by calling on local, regional, and national area advertisers. Account executives must rely on their own initiative since they are paid a commission of usually 10 percent to 15 percent. They spend long hours generating new accounts, servicing their existing accounts, and researching new angles and advertising packages for clients. Radio station advertising is handled by local and national representatives and agencies.

Local sales refers to advertising sold to local businesses in the station's service area. Some businesses do not have the knowledge or the time to create an advertising campaign and put together a coherent advertising schedule, so they hire someone else to do it for them. Sometimes a local advertiser is handled by an account executive at the station, and sometimes that executive will work with an agency who then works with a client. Advertising agencies create and place advertising purchases for a client. Agencies typically work on a commission based on how much advertising the client purchases. Salespeople can have mixed feelings about working with agencies. On the one hand, large agencies tend to be good clients for stations since they buy a lot of advertising for a number of different clients. On the other hand, agencies can drive a hard bargain due to their knowledge of the ratings process and their desire to get the most out of their client's advertising dollars.

National advertising is characterized by big companies purchasing media from markets all across the United States. It would be difficult for a single salesperson to deal directly with a large national client, not to mention the headache the client or its ad agency would have in attempting to buy from thousands of stations individually. This complex process has been simplified by firms that represent many radio stations nationwide. A national client simply buys advertising from one of these station representative firms, called *media reps,* which distribute the advertising spots to the appropriate programs of individual stations based on the desired target audience ratings. Many national advertisers become involved in the advertising process on the local level by offering shared cost incentives to its retailers. For example, if a local department store sells Blue Moon blue jeans and buys $500 worth of advertising with a station, on a 50/50 co-op agreement, the manufacturer would pay half of the advertising bill, or $250. Co-op incentives can also include providing slick radio spots to local businesses that can be personalized. For example, a radio spot might end with: "Blue Moon blue jeans are available at . . . ," at which time the local retailer can add its own name and address.

An anchorwoman reads the news on the air at KCBS San Francisco.

Serving the Community

Radio has the great potential of serving the community because broadcasting has the power to call the attention of so many people to an injustice or problem, which may help facilitate action. It is said that the media do not tell people what to think. They simply tell people what to think about. Radio serves the community with daily news coverage of local events, and by producing brief public service announcements for local nonprofit organizations or full-length documentaries on community issues.

News Production

Radio news is the most expensive type of programming for stations. It costs a great deal in terms of personnel, work time, and equipment with very little advertising revenue return. Consequently, unless a station adopts news as its basic format, you'll not hear a lot of radio news on music format stations.

Still, radio is the most instantaneous, flexible, portable, and adaptable of all news media. For example, when the 1989 Loma Prieta earthquake occurred in California, it was radio that provided the most immediate coverage, especially to those in the area who had lost all power. Even people who still had access to television were limited by the television crews' ability to get themselves and their equipment to the affected areas, while radio was able to take phone calls from people everywhere. And battery-operated audio tape recorders are light and can be taken anywhere and used by one person. Radio does not need an entire crew of people to acquire, edit, and assemble news. Finally, the medium of radio itself is incredibly flexible, which provides for easy insertion of news stories between programs or postponing or canceling radio programs altogether.

Public Affairs Production

Most radio public affairs programs are local productions about community problems. **Public affairs** programming usually consists of interview and discussion programs. Broadcasters have mixed feelings about these programs. First, they feel that very few people listen to public affairs programs, which ultimately costs the station money. In addition, if a program presents information on a controversial topic, the station must give the opposing side an equal opportunity to respond, again adding cost. On the other hand, it is good for the public's perception of a station to see it actively involved in the community, which might lead to more support, higher ratings, and better revenues.

In addition to full-length programs, public service announcements also fall under the category of public affairs programming. Typically, these are short spots that provide information about events or services of nonprofit organizations.

THE PEOPLE BEHIND THE SOUND

Radio stations, even public stations, are businesses. Typically, personnel in radio stations have widely diverse backgrounds and skills. Although audio production can be handled by one person, it takes the combined efforts of many people to accomplish successful radio production. In fact, most production decisions are based on programming decisions. A radio station must create and maintain a unique and identifiable station sound or it will be unable to acquire a listenership and compete in the marketplace. Just about anyone can learn how the equipment works and what buttons to push. A successful producer must also be able to create interesting and effective messages in a variety of ways that fit within the programming specifications.

Ironically, just about everyone in a radio station can be involved in the production process: sales managers might record and assemble commercials; the news director produces the news; DJs put together their own live delivery mixed with prerecorded components to form their shows or air-shifts; and public affairs directors produce their own programs as well.

Program Director

It all begins with programming. The **program director,** or **PD,** is ultimately responsible for how a station sounds. Without consistency in programming, a station cannot acquire and keep a constant listenership and, therefore, will not be able to compete in the marketplace. The PD's most important job is to monitor the station's sound and evaluate its competitive and earning potential.

Imagine if there were no program schedules or station formats. The situation would be chaotic. One minute you'd be listening to Garth Brooks, the next minute Aerosmith, then Nat King Cole, then the Mod Squad, then the Glen Miller Orchestra. If you enjoyed listening to a particular kind of music, what station could you count on if every station just played whatever music it had laying around? And how could a station sell to advertisers when the audience is changing from one song to the next? PDs concentrate on format consistency by overseeing the station's music selection, format creation, music library maintenance, commercial production, and scheduling of the programs for play. PDs are typically in charge of the announcing staff, which means hiring and firing DJs as well as scheduling DJ air shifts.

The program director also provides information to assist the radio production person in creating the most effective message possible. Some of the important programming input includes:

1. Scheduling information that provides insight into what type of audience may be available to listen, what programs will precede and follow the new program, and what type of program will be consistent with the station's overall sound during a specific time period.
2. Programming feedback about how other station programs are doing in terms of audience popularity and how the competition fares in comparison.
3. Source availability information so the producer can take advantage of the wide variety of resources.

Promotions Director

The promotions department is in charge of organizing the promotion and positioning of the station. The goal is to get as large an audience as possible. Again, the promotions planned must work within the boundaries set by the programming department. The station image must always be consistent with its sound. The **promotions director** is the station's marketer and must develop over-the-air promotions, solicit or secure the merchandise for contests and giveaways, and handle all of the station's advertising placed on other media.

Production Director

Production directors oversee all of the production facilities, equipment, scheduling, and individual projects. Since good radio production is the result of a station's programming, audio producers must tailor their work to reinforce the station's sound. The production department in a large station will typically employ people who produce the written scripts for radio **copywriters,** who assist in assembling effective communication messages or programs. In smaller stations, the account executives write their own copy. A production director must ensure that every element of production fits with the overall sound of the station. This includes the pace of programs, the music used for beds of commercials or promotional spots, and the styles of the announcers.

Sales Manager

The **sales manager** controls the assignment of accounts, sets quotas, and keeps the sales staff motivated to ensure that those quotas are achieved. In the old days, the sales staff often dictated the type of programming, the type of music to be played, and even the selection of announcers. This was before formats and before the scientific sampling of the audience. Now the sales manager must work closely with all other departments. For example, the programming of a station, its format, and thus its audience determine what types of products can be advertised and what programs will be scheduled to reach potential audiences; production creates the actual spots based on the requirements of clients; and traffic provides time availability information. Simply put, the sales department is how the station makes money, including the revenues that pay all station employee salaries.

News and Public Affairs Director

The **news and public affairs director** oversees all public affairs programming, including news production. Specific duties might include scheduling program guests, reserving studio time for production, and becoming involved with the community in order to ascertain needs and issues that should be covered by public affairs programs. Specific forms of news and public affairs and their production will be detailed in the chapter on news production.

Traffic Director

Most people think that the function of the traffic department is to inform commuters about accidents or traffic jams on their routes to work. In fact, the **traffic** department works as the communication center of the station's programming. This department prepares the station log, or the written schedule, of what programs and commercials will be aired. Commercial scheduling is a highly complex endeavor. For example, if an account executive sells one hundred commercials, the traffic department must schedule all of those commercials in the log during the appropriate daypart while making sure that no other similar advertisements air before or after them. In addition, traffic must keep all account executives apprised of time availability, called **avails,** so time will not be oversold or, more importantly, undersold. Traffic also routes written commercial copy or taped commercials to the control room in time for airplay. As the account executives sell, the avails and the commercials change. It is a great task to keep straight all of the information. If a mistake does occur, the station will offer to run additional commercials for a client free of charge. These free spots are called **make goods.** The traffic director oversees all of the information that flows to and from the department.

Business Manager

The **business manager** handles the financial matters of the station. Once commercials are played on the air, the business department bills clients and monitors their payments. Other duties of the business department include budgeting, accounting, personnel records, payroll, and office supplies.

Chief Engineer

The **chief engineer's** main function is to keep the station on the air. Once the station is up, the engineer must ensure the signal conforms to the technical requirements mandated by the FCC. The engineering department is responsible for equipment inside the station as well as the maintenance of the transmitter, wherever it is located. When you hear an announcement that a station is "experiencing technical difficulties," you can bet that an engineer is frantically working to solve the problem. The truly big stations still have an engineering staff. However, because of recent cost-cutting in broadcasting and the reliability of the new solid-state equipment, many stations only contract out for engineering.

General Manager

A **general manager,** or **GM,** may be an executive from the parent corporations that own stations or they may be owners themselves. The GM's primary mission is to maintain station operations in terms of generating a profit. They are the chief fiscal officers of the company. Even in noncommercial stations, GMs are actively involved in fund-raising. All other managers and departments answer to the GM, who handles any major disputes and sets company policy. GMs are also responsible for hiring or firing all of the other departmental managers. It is the GM who keeps the entire station and its discrete departments functioning as a profit-making business.

SUMMARY

Radio stations are licensed by the FCC and must agree to adhere to the rules and regulations set by this federal government agency. Since stations are licensed to serve in the public's interest, community involvement is crucial to ascertain the needs and issues that should be addressed. Public service is typically manifested in news and public affairs programming. But radio stations are also businesses very concerned with generating a profit. Stations sell listeners to advertisers. These buyers can be found locally or nationally and are sometimes represented by advertising agencies.

Stations are all structured differently. Depending on the type of station and the size of its market, the specifics of jobs and the number of responsibilities assigned to each person vary. Nevertheless, certain basic functions need to be served regardless of station size: administration, programming, sales, and engineering. These functions are achieved through the hard work and dedication of many individual station employees.

Most important, radio stations use audio production to help the audience create the mental experience of a communication message. All production is created in accordance with an overall consistent station sound. In fact, most production decisions are very much influenced by programming decisions. A radio station must create and maintain a unique and identifiable station sound or it will be unable to acquire listeners and compete in the marketplace. In order for a station to achieve an audience in the first place, promotions are used to gain public attention. Radio stations also use positioning statements to establish an image that distinguishes themselves from other radio stations or mass media outlets.

ACTIVITIES

1. Pick up a copy of *Broadcasting Magazine* or *Electronic Media* and read about the contemporary issues facing the industry today. Then go to your library and find an issue of ten years or more ago and note how radio broadcasting has changed. How have these industry changes affected the production aspect of radio stations?

2. Monitor an hour of radio programming by writing down the number of segments of music, commercials, promos, DJ talk, and so on. Tune in a station that has a different format and compare the two programming strategies.

3. Find a public or noncommercial radio station, listen to it for a couple of days, and then answer these questions: What kind of programs did the station air? How do underwriting spots compare to commercials? What was the overall station sound?

CHAPTER
11   *Formats*

▼

When television was introduced to the public in the late 1940s, people in radio got nervous. Television was appropriately nicknamed *radio with pictures.* By the beginning of the 1950s, television had mimicked radio's programming strategies. Television hired radio talent and technical people. When television took over as the most popular entertainment medium, radio was devastated. Radio could not compete with the new and exciting phenomenon of television. When given the option of listening to a radio drama or watching drama on TV, the public chose TV. Radio had to change.

THE NEW RADIO AUDIENCES

As advertising revenues declined and radio talent left to join the ranks of the new television studios, radio was abandoned and left for dead. Sure, the invention of the transistor changed radio receivers from huge and heavy pieces of furniture into portable, mobile units that could be taken just about anywhere. And more people were commuting longer distances in their cars, where they could be served best by radio, not TV. All this helped radio a great deal, but if radio was to survive, there would have to be a big change in its programming.

Niche Programming

Obviously radio could not compete with television using the same programming scheme consisting mostly of dramatic and comedy shows. Instead of trying to win back the mass audience and be everything to everybody like television was doing, radio stations were forced to serve very specific segments of the overall audience in order to attract advertisers who wanted to reach those specific people. This programming strategy is called specialization, or *niche,* programming. From just a handful in the 1950s to many dozen today, there is a format for every audience niche.

Demographics

The key to programming is knowing the demographics of the listener. In order to serve an audience, you must ascertain what your audience is. Who is listening out there? Are they men? Women? How old are they? What are their interests? What are their incomes and education levels? What kind of programming do they want? The answers to these questions make up the crucial audience information called demographics introduced in the previous chapter. Since advertising is the way in which revenue is gained, radio stations must clearly define their programming, called a **format,** to reach a specific demographic in order to provide those specific listening ears to the advertisers. Since the target audience affects programming, production also will be affected. All aspects of your production projects, like message, music, and announcer style, must be created to reach the selected group of people. If a specific audience is already being served by another station, you would be competing with that station for exactly the same people. Your programming approach would have to be just different enough to lure away enough listeners to obtain economically viable ratings. Counterprogramming is strategy used to avoid this difficult head-to-head competition. Counterprogramming involves ascertaining the demographics of an audience that is not being served well by the other stations in your market, then programming your station to serve those "missed" people.

TABLE 11.1	*Demographics Broken into Categories and Dayparts*

Audience Demographics

Persons	12+
Persons	12–24
Persons	18+
Persons	18–34
Persons	18–49
Persons	25–49
Persons	25–54
Persons	35+
Persons	35–64
Women	12–24
Women	18+
Women	18–24
Women	18–34
Women	18–49
Women	25–34
Women	25–49
Women	25–54
Women	35+
Women	35–44
Women	35–64
Women	45–54
Women	55–64

TABLE 11.1	*continued*	
Men	12–24	
Men	18+	
Men	18–24	
Men	18–34	
Men	18–49	
Men	25–34	
Men	25–49	
Men	25–54	
Men	35+	
Men	35–44	
Men	35–64	
Men	45–54	
Men	55–64	
Teens	12–17	

Ratings Dayparts

Monday–Friday	6 AM–10 AM
Monday–Friday	10 AM–3 PM
Monday–Friday	3 PM–7 PM
Monday–Friday	7 PM–Midnight
Monday–Friday	10 AM–7 PM
Monday–Friday	6 AM–7 PM
Monday–Friday Combined Drive	
Monday–Sunday	6 AM–Midnight
Saturday	6 AM–10 AM
Saturday	10 AM–3 PM
Saturday	3 PM–7 PM
Saturday	7 PM–Midnight
Weekend	6 AM–Midnight
Sunday	10 AM–3 PM
Sunday	3 PM–7 PM
Saturday	7 PM–Midnight
Weekend	6 AM–Midnight

How Formats are Constructed

While demographics are the most important factor when choosing a station's format, they aren't the only concern. Promotions, public relations, technical sound, and equipment availability all affect the overall station image. Finally, two stations might adopt exactly the same format but present it in completely different ways. Besides the music, personalities, pace, scheduling, and style of presentation also distinguish one station from another. And style very often makes the difference between success and failure.

Initially, you might be concerned that programming or format boundaries could possibly limit options or stifle creativity. A more positive way to think about it is to stretch your own creativity once these necessary boundaries have been set. It may take a little more effort, but the results are worth it.

Again, the purpose of a format as a programming strategy is to reach a specific audience. Therefore, productions should be tailored to speak to that certain group of people. For example, a script will be most effective if references are used that are relevant to the target audience's life experiences. Consequently, the better you know your audience, the better you will be able to communicate with it. The following information highlights several radio formats that are currently used in the industry. Keep in mind that this list is constantly changing as audience preferences change or as listeners grow tired of a particular music type or presentation style. Nevertheless, it is necessary to become familiar with these formats in order to create productions that will support them.

MUSIC FORMATS FOR LOCAL RADIO

Music is very important to society because it both reflects culture and creates it. Music formats change constantly because audiences are always changing. New music fads emerge, peak in popularity, then often fade from public interest while other music formats are revitalized and perpetuated to serve original audiences of the past or newly enthused audiences of the future.

Vintage Rock and Roll

Oldies rock and roll logically attracts the oldest listeners of rock music, the over-35 age group. Oldies rock typically consists of music from the 1950s and 1960s highlighting the so-called golden age of rock and roll. The idea behind this format is to take you back in time. To accomplish this, some stations adopt the same presentational styles that were used back when the music was first released; other stations maintain the music sweep format. Nostalgia and trivia dominate contests and promotions.

Another variant of the vintage rock format is called classic rock. It highlights the more recent old music of the 1970s and 1980s and consequently is popular with younger listeners ages 25 to 39.

Middle of the Road

Of all of the radio formats, there is one that does seem to try and be everything to everybody. It is called **middle of the road,** or **MOR.** Because of its lack of consistency or loyalty to any one type of music or format, some believe that it can't be or shouldn't be classified at all. The idea behind MOR is to concentrate on good music in general, no matter what kind it is, where it comes from, or who it is meant for. MOR also presents a great deal of news and information talk programs that concentrate on general topics of interest. There are very few stations left using this format, although in the 1980s, there was a version of it called "music of your life," a format featuring the popular hits from the 1930s, 1940s, and 1950s that was pitched to dying AM stations because of their older demographics. Rather than MOR, it was known by some as **nostalgia.**

Adult Contemporary

Adult contemporary, AC, is a common music format on AM. It targets a very broad audience of 24 to 39-year-olds. You might be surprised to know that this type of format boasts the largest adult audience of all formats. It is a spin-off of **middle of the road, MOR,** beautiful music, and mellow rock. Some AC stations play "lite" music, which tends to be softer, while other stations mix in newer and more upbeat music. Since the audience is more mature, the copy used in AC production tends to be a bit more sophisticated than that of pop-rock stations. Cliches, slang, and colloquialisms are typically avoided. The tone tends to be relaxed rather than high-energy or upbeat.

Album-Oriented Rock

Album-oriented rock, AOR, is second only to CHR in drawing rock listeners. Some AOR formats concentrate on older rock songs like classic rock; some formats boast broadcasting the newest rock releases like cutting edge rock, and finally, other AORs do a combination of both old and new. But no matter what era of rock is being highlighted, the presentation approach is similar to all AOR formats: lower repetition and **music sweeps,** or long uninterrupted blocks of music. These long blocks of time allow this format to present special features, such as live concerts or benefit concerts. Unlike the constantly changing CHR format, AOR doesn't drop a song when it falls from the charts. Continuity is the mainstay of the AOR game plan. Programmers concentrate on meshing hits within music sweeps to keep a consistency of sound. AOR also engages in promotions and contests that complement the overall sound. For example, AOR stations will only give away tickets to bands whose music is featured in their format. AOR is particularly popular with the male 18 to 24-year-old group.

Contemporary Hit Radio

In 1990 nearly 20 percent of the radio audience, or nearly half of rock music listeners, turned to **contemporary hit radio, CHR.** This format, formerly known as top 40, airs the fastest-selling pop music, which means the programming is changing all the time to adjust to music sales. Consequently, CHR maintains a very busy and high-energy programming style using many contests and promotions to keep the twelve-listener excited and engaged. CHR also has very broad age demographics, 12 to 34-year-olds, so the presentation and the advertising messages are kept simple in order to reach this broad spectrum of listeners. In order to keep their listeners from switching stations during commercial breaks, programmers typically schedule high-energy spots at the beginning of a break followed by more low-key spots at the end of the break. Because of the aging of the population, however, the CHR format is losing popularity and stations.

Urban Contemporary and African American

This format is currently one of the most fast-changing specializations. At one time these stations were called Ethnic, Soul, Rhythm and Blues, and/or Black. The concentration was on awareness of black culture, issues music, and social and political material. As some stations started to become more integrated and highlighted specific music, such as disco in the late 1970s, a handful of stations evolved into the **urban contemporary** format, which attracted 8 percent of the total radio listening audience.

Most recently the African-American format has seen yet another major trend with the emergence of hip-hop and rap music. Since rap, by definition, requires poetic monologue or dialogue, there has been a resurgence of cultural, racial, and political issues in the music. Some interesting examples include issues such as drugs, violence, AIDS, discrimination, prejudice, sex, feminism, homosexuality, and the homeless. The sound of rap is constantly changing. For example, some of rap's sound may result from sampling (i.e., incorporating bits of previously recorded music by other artists to create/recreate a new result). A current trend is the sampling of old disco music or jazz. In addition, a *rougher* version of rap called *underground rap* exists and is typically featured during late night or over night shifts because of its extreme profanity, violence, and/or sexually explicit content.

Interestingly, the urban contemporary format demographic is the most ethnically diverse of all radio formats with 16 to 28-year-old African-Americans, Hispanics, Asians, and whites. In fact, these diverse groups have incorporated this originally "black" format to advance their cultural concerns by infusing specific music, languages, and political issues to create their own rap.

Some stations try and expand their audience by combining the contemporary hits format with the urban contemporary format. This marriage is often referred to as "Churban" radio. All of these formats concentrate on the latest and greatest hits yet lean toward music with a dance beat and a message. Again, since the urban contemporary format is quite trendy, relying on the latest dance crazes and current events, the sound is constantly changing. In order to maintain the hippest sound and keep the dance rhythm going, programmers must closely monitor all of the station's music, commercials, and promos.

Jazz

The Jazz musical format was developed in the United States based upon African and European music. It is characterized by its melodic and harmonic sophistication, its rhythmic syncopation, and its fundamental dependence on improvisation. Subformats (or styles) such as Be-Bop, Swing, Fusion, Big Band, Latin Jazz, Hard Bop, Free Jazz, etc. have evolved during different stages in the history of jazz, although they all exist contemporarily on stations that adopt the jazz format. Finally, Jazz has also been associated with other formats. For example Urban Contemporary and Jazz formats seem to meet in a quieter, softer, more mainstream version of music called "Light Jazz" or "Light Urban Contemporary".

Hispanic

Hispanics make up the second largest racial minority in the United States, which has resulted in the establishment of more Hispanic-format and Spanish-language stations. It typically has a very broad approach in order to be a full-service format for this specialized audience. Though this diverse programming tends to be lumped together under the somewhat generic term, "Hispanic," in reality the music formats might incorporate popular music from other formats and then add music from Latin American, Mexican, Puerto Rican and other Spanish-speaking country artists. Other segments might include Hispanic awareness public affairs programs, Hispanic news reports, interviews, telephone call-in talk shows, community hot lines, and panel discussions. Scripts for this format tend to be bilingual and closely tied to specific cultural needs.

Asian

Like the Hispanic programming, these formats also tend to be non-specifically categorized under one simplistic and sometimes inaccurate format label: Asian. Chinese, Japanese, Vietnamese, Tiawanese, Korean, etc., all provide programming in their own languages featuring music, news, and public affairs content that focus on the interests and needs of their specific audiences.

Easy Listening

Consisting mostly of quiet instrumentals with a few soft, slow songs, you might have heard this type of format described as *elevator music*. Now *new age* is often considered a subformat in the easy-listening category. It might surprise you to know, however, that **easy listening** is number one in the ratings in many cities across the country. This means it beats rock and country and contemporary formats. Formerly known as *beautiful music, semiclassical,* or *dinner,* this format sweeps music with very little interruption by the DJ.

The goal of an easy-listening format is to provide a haven of calming, free-flowing music for those who are tired of the hard-hitting, high-energy contemporary stations. It concentrates on creating a mood to fit the different moods of various times of the day. Subtlety is a must. So when there are contests or promotions, they tend to be very low-key. Commercials adopt a soft-sell attitude, and scripts tend to be straightforward without glitz or sugar coating. Obviously, any music beds must be consistent with the music played within the format or the audience will be blown out of their seats at each commercial break. Over the past ten years, the easy-listening format has changed from all-instrumental versions of popular songs into a format featuring the softest of the soft rock artists including many vocals. Today, so-called beautiful music is more like adult contemporary than its original incarnation, once called elevator music.

Classical

Classical programming using live orchestras was radio's first format. The use of recorded classical music began on some smaller stations in the 1930s. And though this format is not large—only 2 percent of stations and listeners are listed in this category—its audience is extremely loyal. Advertisers are especially interested in this audience because, of all radio users, classical boasts the most educated and professional demographic, usually between the ages of 30 and 55. Obviously, classical concentrates on large sweeps of music, particularly since many music selections are quite long or are made up of several movements that can't be interrupted with commercial breaks or personality talk. Since credibility is most important to classical stations, announcements are carefully constructed to be grammatically correct yet not overly complicated. Announcements are kept short, simple, and to the point. The idea is to stay away from stereotyping the audience as cultural snobs.

Country

Country music, also called country and western or C & W, has been on the scene almost since radio began, although until the 1960s it was considered mostly a southern United States interest. Today, more stations are using the country music format than any other single form of music programming. This is partly because many country artists and songs have crossed over onto the pop charts. The country format has adopted styles that span the music spectrum, such as "lite" country, which has a softer sound; traditional country, which brings back those golden country oldies; hit country, which features the latest songs to hit the charts; and rebel country, which is a harder country and rock combination. Contrary to the stereotype, script dialogue used in country production does not have to be twangy or reflect slang and bad grammar. You don't have to say "Y'all come on down, ya hear?" in order to remain consistent with the format. On the contrary, country targets quite a sophisticated adult audience. In fact, the country format enjoys the widest range of age demographics of all formats.

Religious

Religious stations are typically found on the AM and noncommercial FM bands. This format has a very specific goal: to spread religious ideas and information to as many people as possible with the aid of the mass media. Many people refer to religious stations as Christian stations. This label is only partially correct since many religious stations are concerned with sects such as Hebrew or Moslem.

Some religious stations are referred to as religious talk because they devote little time to music. Often these stations feature only the voice and viewpoints of the founder, or they sell blocks of time to any practicing preacher. Others program long music sweeps featuring inspirational songs with positive, life-affirming messages. This music can originate from many different formats, such as rock, country, or contemporary. Personalities presenting this music are expected to become personally involved by offering comments and observations about the songs or the religious messages. For the most part, copy is written conservatively, keeping a close eye on what words are chosen to describe products or services. Using God to sell your product or exaggerated claims are typically frowned upon. Simple honest and straightforward messages are the rule.

Talk

The **talk**-based format dominates AM programming and draws nearly 7 percent of the overall radio audience. The all-talk format is substantially less expensive to produce than all-news. The goal of talk radio is to let the audience do most of the talking. The basic component of the talk format is the telephone conversation, which only requires one on-air personality and a small support staff to produce. Talk radio is the most interactive format because it allows the audience to become directly involved with radio and be heard on-air as part of the public forum process. Though found predominantly on AM stations, talk radio is slowly spreading to smaller FM markets.

Commercial and promotional breaks during the news and talk formats are especially challenging because they consist mostly of words with very little or very subtle musical beds. Nevertheless, the commercial script must be unique from the news and talk copy so that audiences can distinguish between them. Humor and drama are fine as long as it meshes well with the usually serious or conservative overtone of the formats. There are several different talk formats used on talk radio or on talk segments of music radio. A few of the most common are interviews, phone-in shows, and discussion programs.

News

The **all news** format emerged in the 1960s and is now programmed by a relative handful of major- and large-market AM stations. There are two reasons why there are so few all-news stations on-air today, and both have to do with cost. All-news stations are very expensive to maintain because of the number of people it takes to produce the programming. It is the most staff-intensive format, typically requiring more than one on-air newscaster at a time, many field reporters and writers, and multiple support people. The second overriding cost is equipment. Portable equipment must be provided to all reporters, and monitor equipment purchased to receive special reports such as weather, stock market, and international news. Because of the high cost of this format, networking and ownership groups tend to create the larger and more successful operations. The news is programmed much like music in that news stories are placed according to their rank and scheduled in long news sweeps with clustered commercial and promotional breaks. Though all-news does reach people as young as in their twenties, the target audience for this format is men from 39 to 54 years old.

NONCOMMERCIAL FORMATS

You are probably quite familiar with the various music and talk formats that have been presented in this chapter so far. But what happens when a program is produced that does not "fit" into these popular formats? What if a program is directed at a very narrowly defined or localized audience, which makes it economically nonviable on commercial stations? Since the program won't be played on these stations, does that mean that it simply will never be aired? In fact, there is a place on the radio for specialized programming: noncommercial radio.

Since commercial radio dominates the airwaves of today, it is ironic that radio began as a noncommercial enterprise. Originally, stations were supported by community entities such as schools, universities, churches, newspapers, and local businesses. It wasn't until August 1922, when WEAF in New York tried an idea to sell radio time, then called toll broadcasting, that advertising became the mainstay of radio. This new revenue system spelled doom for those stations that produced programming that didn't play to a large audience. How could these noncommercial stations, running on very limited funds, compete with the larger financially successful stations? They couldn't. The number of noncommercial stations dwindled to just a few in the late 1930s. With the reallocation of FM to 88–108 mHz, the FCC in 1948 set aside the lower twenty channels (88–92 mHz) exclusively for noncommercial stations. The 1967 *Public Broadcasting Act* brought further support for public radio with the creation of the **Corporation for Public Broadcasting, CPB.** This government-supported organization was created to promote the development of public broadcasting. It helped establish and fund the **National Public Radio, NPR,** network. NPR produces and distributes public programming and represents the interests of public stations across the country. However, of the more than thirteen hundred noncommercial stations in existence, only three hundred are affiliated with NPR.

Noncommercial stations are divided into three types: public radio, college radio, and community radio.

Public Radio

Since public radio stations are noncommercial and cannot compete in the market-place with their economically more viable commercial counterparts, they are funded partly by the government, by underwriting grants from private corporations, and by listener support. It also helps to be affiliated with NPR because expensive, high-quality programming is provided by the network, relieving much of the programming cost responsibilities. The main goal of public stations is to involve the community as much as possible in local, regional, and national issues. They don't just want to be background noise. They want to be a tool for public use. The most common formats of public stations are news, information programs, jazz, and classical music. If a public station does adopt a specific format, it follows the format consistency rule in terms of musical beds, scripts, and style, just as a commercial station does. The main difference is that revenue received by public stations is put back into programming and operations because public radio is nonprofit.

College Radio

College radio stations dominate the noncommercial channels with more than eight hundred educational institutions holding licenses. These stations typically present *alternative* programming, that is, programs you probably wouldn't hear on other commercial stations. College radio is notorious for its eclectic, hectic programming schedules that are not easily categorized. They pride themselves on the idea that you are never quite sure what you will hear next. College radio does not program around one consistent format or audience. Instead, it uses all types of formats at different times of the day or week. Nearly 90 percent of college stations are oriented toward music. Some examples of specialized music that have been featured by college radio stations are world beat, reggae, rap, new wave, new age, jazz, folk, funk, disco, new music, classical, eclectic, choir, religious, heavy metal, all-Elvis, feminist, comedy, Dr. Demento, Native American tribal chants, and music from other countries and cultures around the world (usually presented in the native language). The possibilities are limitless in college radio. Most college radio stations are programmed by students either as learning laboratories or school activities.

Though music dominates college radio's focus, public affairs programming is also presented. The topics covered by these programs are as wide-ranging as the music programming and usually concentrate on those groups and opinions traditionally ignored by commercial stations—topics such as the environment, gay and lesbian rights, parenthood, children, politics, poetry, writing, language, literacy, cooking, sports, health, racial and sexual discrimination, law, animal rights, science, and specialized cultural programs in the native languages. The important contribution of this programming is that it allows groups that are typically politically disenfranchised by the commercial mass media to have a voice through the medium of radio.

In addition to providing unique music and public affairs programming, college radio stations have another primary purpose: to teach students about radio. Most college radio stations are run by students. Consequently, students are able to learn about all aspects of the business of radio, including management, promotions, public relations, announcing, production, personnel, accounting, business organization, programming, music, news, underwriting or sales, and engineering. Since college radio allows volunteers to work with any and all departments, students are able to gain first-hand experience in a variety of areas, which provides them with a good "big picture" of the business of radio.

Community Radio

Community radio represents the smallest number of stations in the country, and it usually operates at a lower power level. Stations are economically supported by community groups, local business underwriting, and listener donations. Like college stations, community radio provides alternative programming through a variety of different formats. Some of the characteristics or stated goals of these stations include:

1. They are nonprofit organizations.
2. They are run by groups representing the overall community and work to serve everyone instead of special-interest groups.
3. They allow general public access to their airwaves and work to present a wide range of cultures, especially those that are typically ignored or overlooked by commercial media.

Because of their montage of formats, college and community radio typically schedule programming in large blocks, called **block programming.** This allows programs to be scheduled at the same time each day or each week, which provides scheduling consistency while still maintaining several quite diverse formats.

These dozen or so major formats are only the most visible. There are many more that are tried, tested, and discarded daily. All play-by-play, all-shopping, all-Elvis, all-Beatles, all-comedy albums, and on and on. If it makes money, it makes it as a format.

It is important to re-emphasize that all production is based on programming decisions that evolve from the station's format. Format is much more than music. It also includes production, programming, style, and personality. Any type of production you create, whether it is a commercial, public service announcement, talk show, or music or public affairs program, will be directly influenced by the format in which the production will be played. Maintaining consistent quality within the parameters of the format is the ultimate goal. For example, to fit in with the various format requirements across the country, a national company that wants to reach a very wide demographic will produce several different versions of its commercials, such as a rock version, a country and western version, an easy-listening version, and a noncommercial underwriting version. However, consistent quality often requires inconsistency of program content. Formats that rely on the latest music trends must constantly change to stay abreast of what is "happening now," even if it is new music that has little relationship to previous trends.

SUMMARY

The key to programming is demographics. Once you have ascertained what your target audience is, you have to program to reach it. Typically, you can compete with other stations with the same format or you can counterprogram to reach audiences that are currently missed by the other stations in your market. Although demographics are the most important consideration when establishing a format, other factors—such as public relations, promotions, presentational pace and style, personalities, scheduling, and the overall style of the station—greatly affect the success of the basic format.

While some formats are perpetuated or are constantly being rejuvenated, most radio formats are constantly changing as the times and the audience change. Some commercial formats that are currently in use are rock, easy listening, urban contemporary, classical, Hispanic, adult contemporary, country, middle of the road, oldies, religious, news, and talk. Noncommercial stations include public, college, and community radio, which tend to adopt various formats as a rule. They are structured as nonprofit organizations with the basic goal of providing access and service to the public, especially those groups that are typically overlooked by commercial media.

It is important to re-emphasize that all production is based on programming decisions that are typically manifested as the station's format. Format is much more than music. It also includes production, programming, style, and personality.

ACTIVITIES

1. Listen to two different local stations and try to write down a typical hour's clock or format. Start with a blank clock face.
2. Write for a program guide from a local college, public, or community station. Note how every hour features a different program type.
3. Invite a program director to your class to tell about how his or her format works and why it is successful.

Producing Short Announcements

Most of the production heard on a radio station is determined by its programming. The format of the station, the music it airs, and the audience it seeks all have a great influence on the type of production a station employs. Whether a commercial station is operating as a profit-making business, a listener-sponsored community station using volunteers, or a college station designed to train students, a radio station's programming directly affects its production. Every radio station consciously picks an identifiable production sound and style to sell products for its advertisers, serve its community through public service announcements, and, in general, promote the format, the talent, and the special events of the station.

Most of what is defined as production on a radio station is in the form of short announcements, sixty seconds or less. Sure, many stations have a weekly public affairs program or two lasting an hour or thirty minutes, but most of the continuous, repetitive production that defines a station and reinforces its format is presented in increments of sixty-, thirty-, twenty-, and ten-second recorded announcements. These announcements are spots or PSAs designed to promote a commercial product or nonprofit organization, underwriting messages allowed by educational stations, and promos used to build good will and thus a larger audience for a station. Behind each minute or thirty-second announcement, there is an entire production process, from idea to script to production to air.

INTRODUCING THE SHORT ANNOUNCEMENT

Have you ever stopped to wonder how many short announcements a typical radio station airs in an hour? A day? A week? A year? During the busiest time of the day—morning and afternoon drive times—a commercial station may air up from twelve to fifteen minutes of produced commercial announcements per hour. A few of these may be a minute each, but most will be thirty seconds or less, adding up to a possible total of thirty or more commercials hourly. Add to that PSAs and promos, and in one busy drive time hour it's possible for a commercial station to broadcast up to fifty short, produced announcements of from ten to sixty seconds. Even a noncommercial station that airs only four PSAs per hour will have aired thirty-five thousand in a single year. The short announcement. It's the production heard most on radio today.

PSAs and other short announcements appear on the program log.

KSJS 90.7								
PROGRAM LOG			M	T	W	Th	F	PAGE 4 OF 12
AM TIME • CLASS A •CHANNEL 214 • WEEKDAY				DATE				PDT

SCHEDULED TIME BEGIN END	ACTUAL TIME ( ) AIR	PROGRAMS and/or ANNOUNCEMENTS TITLE/GRANT	Source/Grant	GRANT NUMBER	PROGRAM MATTER OR ANNOUNCEMENT Length	Type	NOTES
6:00	6:00	LEGAL ID	L		:05	ID	
6:25	6:25	SAFER RESTORATION	LOC		:30	PSA	
	6:26	PREVENTING STROKE	L		:30	PSA	
6:40	6:41	HIGHER BLOOD PRESSURE	L		:30	PSA	
	6:42	EXCHANGE STUDENTS	LOC		:39	PSA	
6:52	6:52	PEEL OUT IN THE STATES	LOC		:58	PR	
	6:53	WX	L		:18	I	
7:00	7:01	LEGAL ID	L		:05	ID	
7:25	7:25	SUMO ST. FAIR	loc	ars	:30	PSA	
7:25	7:26	SMOKE DETECTORS	L		:30	PSA	
7:30	7:31	Rhythm Wave Concert Calendar	loc			I	
7:40	7:41	FIRE SAFETY	L		:30	PSA	
7:40	7:42	SF 200	loc	ars	:30	PSA	
7:52	7:51	THIRD WORLD AIRWAVES	LOC		:53	PR	
	7:52	WX	L		:18	I	

ON	OPERATOR or ANNOUNCER	OFF	ON	OPERATOR or ANNOUNCER	OFF
6:00	Sharon Jennings	cont	cont	Sharon Jennings	cont

There are at least three categories of produced short announcements broadcast by a radio station: the commercial or underwritten message, called the **spot;** the public service announcement, or **PSA;** and the station promotional announcement, the **promo.** Related to the promo are the very brief station positioners or identifiers sometimes referred to as **shotguns** and **liners** because their length is usually limited to a couple of words or a single sentence. A few of these in each category may be read *live* by the DJ or announcer on the air, but most are individually produced or prerecorded with music, sound effects, and voices. The differences among the spot, PSA, and promo are mostly in who pays for them and for what reason. The similarities are that the production of each is a predictable process involving a sponsor, a production person, and a plan.

If you ask a disc jockey on a commercial station what the most important thing he or she does during a typical hour is, chances are the answer will be, "play music." Ask the same question of the station manager and that individual will always say, "play commercials." Commercial radio is big business, and the sale of advertising time is the only way that a commercially licensed station is able to generate income. The money collected from airing hundreds of commercials daily pays the rent, utilities, and equipment costs of offices, studios, and transmitters, and it pays the salaries of all the administrative, support, and programming people. Everything that a commercial station is able to do as a broadcaster is directly dependent on successfully persuading businesses to spend money on commercials.

To a lesser extent, public radio, college-run, or community-owned nonprofit stations depend on money from the same businesses as commercial stations. Because these stations are licensed by the FCC to operate as educational, the commercials they air are limited in their content and are called **underwriting,** a term for a commercial-like announcement on a noncommercial station. Even when a public or community station gets most of its money from its listeners in the form of regular on-air telethons, it still may depend on donations of money, or underwriting, in return for a mention of that sponsor's product to pay some of its bills.

Like the commercial station, a potential donor or advertiser will have to be contacted, and an announcement written, produced, and aired. Unlike the commercial station, most of the educationally licensed station's employees are volunteers, and its facility will certainly be less costly to operate than that of the commercial station. Nevertheless, paid underwriting by the same businesses that advertise on commercial stations is becoming increasingly important to the nonprofit radio station.

Public service announcements are aired by all radio stations. Whether a one-sentence announcement read live between commercials or a complete thirty-second produced production, the PSA is designed to promote the business of a nonprofit organization. Similar in purpose to commercials, PSAs differ only in the definition of the organization they represent. To legally qualify as a PSA, the sponsoring group must be chartered not-for-profit, like a community foundation, a charity, a church, a city, or a school. Like a commercial for a profit-making business, a PSA can actually try to sell or convince the listener to give money, attend an event, or even buy a product, as long as it is offered by a recognized nonprofit organization. Public, community, and college stations see the airing of PSAs as their main mission; commercial stations may view them as a necessary public relations cost of doing business in a community.

The sponsor of a station promo is the station itself. The goal of the promo is to sell or attract attention to the on-air programming of the station or to an outside event sponsored by the station. A promo can serve several possible purposes. On the commercial station, a series of ten-second produced promos might be used to announce that the station "plays more music," a ploy the management hopes will attract more listeners. Any increase in the audience size means higher ratings, and that can translate into more money for commercials. An educational station might use a produced announcement to promote a weekly music or public affairs program. At either type of station, the goal is always to attract favorable attention to a station's programming and projects, and thus increase the number of listeners.

Commercial stations and noncommercial educational stations all use the short announcement for profit, for public service, and for promotion. Whether profit-making as a result of selling time to advertisers or whether operated as community, public, or college, all stations have the same goal: to get an audience for their programming. It may be entertainment programming for a narrowly defined audience and done for obvious commercial reasons, or it may be public affairs and minority programming for the greater good of a community. Whatever the station and whatever the intended audience, all stations will air thousands of brief messages yearly that are designed to sell, to persuade, and to promote. The creation of these short announcements is the main activity of radio production.

PRODUCING THE COMMERCIAL

Most American broadcasting is advertiser-supported. Beginning as far back as 1922, when New York station WEAF ran that first radio commercial for a housing development, it is the money of business and industry that has defined the nature of radio, both its programming and its audiences. And the way advertisers use radio has changed, just as the programming has changed. In the early days when radio was presented as fifteen-minute, half-hour, and hour programs, a sponsor or its agency paid for the entire program. At first, the system seemed to be a real convenience to station owners. But imagine one sponsor being responsible for an entire hour. Imagine the power. Eventually, owners of broadcast facilities and the creative people involved in radio began to see the problems caused by this total advertiser control. Instead of a programmer making a creative decision on what was radio in the public interest, it was the sponsor who picked the talent and the music, and approved the script. Whether good radio or not, if the sponsor didn't like it, it didn't air. From the mid-1920s until the early 1950s, the sponsor and its advertising agency were the program producers for much of radio.

Because the commercial radio station of today is based on a format rather than longer programs, its income depends on a steady stream of short sponsored messages or spots. Now, instead of a single advertiser buying an entire block of time and controlling the content of the program, many individual sponsors will participate in the programming of the station by purchasing short announcements of a minute or less. Instead of an advertising agency making the creative choices for a station, the station itself decides on a programming format and attempts to get a specific audience. Once the audience is identified through ratings, the station's salespeople or their representatives are able to go to the sponsors and advertising agencies and sell **availabilities,** or individual openings, for spot announcements in various hours of the day. The time of day determines the cost to the sponsor; the largest radio audiences are in the morning and afternoon commuting hours, called **drive times,** and are most expensive. It is less expensive to advertise in the middle of the night because fewer people are listening.

Advertisers also look at audience research data to help them decide the content of a commercial and the specific audience to which it will be targeted. **Demographics,** a measure of the composition of the audience, are used by advertisers to decide which station to give their money to and during which time of day. Demographic data show exactly how many men, women, and teens are listening, as well as their ages, education, and income levels. A sponsor knows where to advertise with certainty. The maker of a high-priced European luxury auto, for example, is now able to place spot announcements on the radio station that has the listeners able to afford the product. Before demographics, the choice of station was based largely on intuition. Now every decision on what to sell to what audience is based on science.

As a professional producer of short announcements for radio, much of what you do will be in the service of advertising. Soon you'll realize that, more than anything else, advertisers want results; they want to sell their ideas, products, or services. Sophisticated advertisers with agency representation and a large local or regional

---

TABLE 12.1   *How a Local Commercial/Spot Gets on the Air*

1. A business has a product or service to sell to the public and money to spend on advertising. The money can be part of a regular budget for advertising, which includes newspapers, radio, television, direct mail, and billboards. The money can come from sales revenues or cooperative cash agreements with manufacturers of the product sold by the business.

2. The business contacts an advertising agency representative or an **account executive,** the salesperson, of a radio station directly. Eventually, the advertising agency will have to go to the radio station sales department. Agencies are found in medium, large, and major markets. If they exist in small markets, they are usually print-oriented.

3. The agency or radio station salesperson gives the business ratings and marketing information about the station's audience and the cost per spot during different times of the day. A list of the advertising costs of a station is called a **rate card.**

4. If the business or agency has already produced the spot, the only task of the radio station production person is to put it on cart for air. Contracts have been signed, and the radio station traffic department has scheduled it on the program log.

5. If the business is a small one or a first-time advertiser, the radio station salesperson may actually bring the sponsor into the production facility for a conference. This meeting may include only the production person, the sponsor, and the salesperson, or it may include all three and a writer. The sponsor will explain what product, service, or idea he or she wants to sell and give the creative people important details about the business.

6. The production person may be asked to come up with an idea or an actual script, even produce a **spec** spot for the advertiser to approve. After approval, the advertiser will ask that it be run on the air. It is a simple process. Using the information about a station's audience, the sponsor works with advertising and salespeople, writers, talent, and other creative people to get just the right message to precisely the right audience.

---

budget will know exactly what they want to say and for what audience. For them, every word in every spot must be there for a reason. Most businesses, however, will depend on you to suggest the best approach for reaching your station's specific audience. In a small market, there are no large advertising agencies, so the business owner who wants to buy time for spots must go directly to the radio station. As a production person, you will be involved. There is a process that can be followed to get an idea onto the air for an advertiser, shown in Table 12.1.

Working with Sponsors

It's not enough to just be a creative production person in commercial radio. When dealing with the people who control the money, the sponsors, you must also be part businessperson and part psychologist. Sure, you're the one with the creative ideas and the technical tools who knows how to make the announcement for an ordinary product stand out from the other twenty or so commercials heard every hour. The problem is, you have to present these ideas to someone who may only understand that there is a product that must be sold using your station. You may have great ideas on how to use humor to attract audience attention to a product; the advertiser may be a humorless individual who wants the name of the product shouted many times throughout a serious spot. When creative people work directly with advertisers, compromise and understanding are important. In small-market local radio, a production person may have plenty of direct contact with the business owner.

In larger markets, advertising agencies are the buffer between the sponsor and the radio station. An agency makes it simple for a medium- to large-size business of regional or national influence to present a unified image and develop an overall commercial strategy that includes all media. For a percentage of the budget, the agency person does all the research and all the liaison work between the business owner, the creative people, and the radio station. Unlike the small-business owner who must call or visit each newspaper and radio station separately every time he or she wants to advertise, the large business simply gives all the advertising budget to an agency professional. The agency representative will have the choice of sending you a prewritten script with instructions on how to produce it or a complete produced spot.

So whether you have direct contact with the sponsor or the sponsor's agency representative, there is a good chance that you'll be involved creatively with many local commercials. In fact, in small- and medium-size radio markets, much of the production directed by agencies may be done in the production facility of a radio station. When the budget is large enough, the radio station production people and the agency people often decide to go into a recording studio for those productions too advanced for the station to handle. If you are a skilled radio production person, there will be many times when you will be paid extra to write the script and produce the spot, either at your station or at a more advanced facility.

Writing the Script

Part of the creative process of radio production is writing the script for a commercial. Even though there are people whose main creative task is script writing, much of what goes on the air locally will be written at the agency or station level. The very large stations may have the services of a part-time or full-time writer; at smaller stations, writing is often done by salespeople, secretaries, and announcers. Writing an effective commercial is the first step in radio production. Often, an advertiser will come to you with only a fact sheet. You must decide how to craft an effective message from those facts before presenting it to your audience.

First, you will want to know the objectives of the advertiser before you can choose the correct words for a commercial. Is the main goal of a spot to sell a specific product? As the writer, you'll have to present enough information to the listeners so that they will know enough about the product to decide in your favor. The outstanding attributes of a product like quality, style, and price are always written into the spot along with a comparison with competing brands or why the advertised product is better. Every product spot should tell where to purchase it, even the hours of the store. What about a service? Similar to selling an actual thing, a product, the idea is to motivate listeners to go somewhere and spend money on an activity or service. And some advertisers will want their commercials to be used to sell an idea or build good will for their name. The main goal of this "institutional" advertising is to affect public perception of the advertiser, as opposed to selling a specific product or service.

TABLE 12.2   *Writing the Spot, Questions to Ask*

1. Who is the intended audience for the spot? While many people may want a sporty car, most of the listeners will not be able to afford this one. Here, the price of the product alone will help to determine the intended audience for the commercial and thus the station on which it will be advertised. The audience will probably not be a CHR or AOR audience; rather, it will be a station listened to by those with high incomes, perhaps all-news, jazz, or classical. Because it is a sporty car, it will be pitched to moderately high-income persons in the 30 to 50-year-old range, and those with a higher than average education level.

2. What is the one main idea to be contained in the spot? Sure, you can say a lot in thirty seconds or a minute, but because the listener can only retain a fraction of what is contained in the commercial, it must be made simple. You'll have to decide on whether the car will be advertised to appeal to the consumer who is interested mainly in price, style, or quality. The cost is high and the quality is assumed because of the well-known manufacturer, so it is decided that the main idea will be its attractive, sporty appearance, so a major appeal will be that of popularity. Drive this beautiful car and get noticed.

3. What are the secondary ideas that must be included? The driver of this car must be made to feel that he or she made the right decision, from a safety and value point of view. The spot will infer that the person who buys this car will not only have an attractive, sporty car, but a safe one as well. The educated consumer for which this car is intended wants to be known as a savvy buyer.

4. What important details must be in the spot? Because market research shows a high consumer interest in sporty import cars of quality, the feeling of what it means to drive the car will be stressed. The appeal to youth, the feeling of wind in your hair, the excitement of driving a car that will make people notice you, will comprise the content of the spot. Details on those safety accessories found only in expensive cars may also be included.

5. What details should not be in the spot? Price, for one. Since you are selling a sporty driving experience, it's probably not a good idea to remind listeners that after taxes and financing, their payments may be $600 a month. It's also not a good idea to remind them about how driving on most roads with the top down is a crowded, noisy, smog-filled experience. Information about dependability will not have to be in the spot either. Since it is a well-known import, the listener already has decided that it is a product of quality. Years of advertising have already done that job.

Once the objectives of the advertiser are clear, the next step is to determine the best way to reach the audience. Here, the writer needs to be aware of the psychology of the consumers and those values that are important. Once these values are known, a commercial can be written that matches the product, service, or idea to the listeners.

As the writer of the commercial you are about to produce, you have many facts about the product. You also know the objectives of the sponsor and a bit about the audience. Now it's time to put all this information into words. Table 12.2 shows a checklist of questions to ask before a commercial can be written. It is going to be a local dealer spot for a sporty convertible, an import, $25,000 to $30,000, made by a well-known manufacturer.

This thirty-second commercial will be written to convince an upper-income, educated professional who wants the feeling of driving a sports car, and wants to be perceived as an individual who buys only the best. It will have to be straightforward and believable. The spot will have to be written in the present tense, and it will have

TABLE 12.3	*A Sample Script for this Product*

SFX: Pleasant outdoor, birds, breeze, gentle engine and under

ANNCR: You're listening to a remarkable driving experience. . . . (pause) Imagine yourself behind the wheel of a machine that responds to your slightest touch, a car so advanced that it has antilock brakes and dual air bags as standard equipment. . . .

CROSSFADE TO SFX: ocean waves, happy crowds and under

MALE VOICE 1: (walking through the parking lot at the beach) (low key, monotone) I'd love to get a new car, but they all look alike . . . (excited) whoa, look at that!

MALE VOICE 2: It's the new xx. (sighs) Linda, at the office, has one. It's really a beautiful car . . . She's offered to let me take it for a spin someday. . . . (excited) I can't wait. . . .

ANNCR: The new xx, a real experience you'll be proud to drive.

---

to be written using words that connect with an educated person, like the example in Table 12.3. Once written, the spot, like all short announcements for radio, must be easily read aloud. Always read all copy out loud before finalizing.

One good thing about this entire process is that you have just written a script that communicates what the spot will sound like without ever having stepped into the production facility. Now, you can present the copy to the sponsor or agency representative and get approval before you complete the production. Once you have this approval, the rest of the process will be your creative choice. You can select the sound effects and music, and you can pick and prepare the talent for the day of production.

Doing the Production

For this simple commercial, you'll need an announcer, two male voices, and several sound effects. You may even decide to mix in some light jazz music with the sound effects, but only under the announcer's voice. If you're working at a small station where the cost of production is free to a local advertiser, then you'll be the announcer and two men from the station will be the two male voices. The sound effects will come from your library, and the entire production will be done in your facility. If the advertiser has allocated money for this production, you may be able to hire a couple of professional voice actors for the male parts and a well-known voice for the announcer. Your role would be that of producer and director.

Before you actually go into the production facility, plan on some advance preparation. Whether you are using professional talent or people who work at the radio station, give everyone a copy of the script to read over. Even if the voices you are using lack experience, your written instructions on the copy and a brief rehearsal should yield a decent performance. Audition the sound effects ahead of time and note their position on the disk. Gather all music, effects, and open-reel tape, and begin production. There are several ways to approach the production of this simple example.

TABLE 12.4   *Producing the Simple Commercial*

METHOD 1 (Combo, Real-Time)

Here is the fastest, easiest way: Do the entire spot in real-time, right to reel-to-reel tape. Put the two SFX cuts on separate tape carts or cue them up on separate CD players. If music is to be used along with the SFX, premix it along with the sound effects and put them onto two carts. Put the prepared carts in separate playback machines and set a level for each. Have one microphone for the two male actors and the combo microphone for you as the announcer. Start the tape, start the first cart, open the combo microphone, fade the cart under, read the first ANNCR part. While reading the first part, start the second SFX cart and crossfade to it, open the second microphone, fade the cart under and cue the male voices. Read your final ANNCR part, fade out the SFX and stop the tape. If there is to be a music ending, edit it on later. Dub to cart for air.

METHOD 2 (Combo, Multitrack)

Carefully time the voices and the pauses in the dialogue. Record them in real-time onto track one of a four-track recorder. Assign that track to audition, an isolated monitor, or headphones so it plays back in sync with the next real-time recording. Add the SFX's directly from CD players to track two at the proper time during the dialogue. Place this track into playback/sync/monitor, along with the dialogue track. Add the stereo music to the third and fourth tracks. Now put all four tracks into normal playback and assign them to their own playback modules. Set levels, adjust the pan, equalize, and add processing as needed. Mix to a two-track stereo master for distribution and to a cart for air.

METHOD 3 (Studio and Control Room, Digital Workstation)

Using a digital workstation, record each individual voice and every sound effect onto a separate "track" or location on the hard disk storage medium. The advantage of this method is that the starting and ending cues for every voice and SFX can be moved until the very precise timing is realized. Once it sounds right, play all the sounds back for the correct mix. Once you become proficient at assembling a multiple voice, multiple effect commercial using a computer, you'll never touch reel-to-reel tape again.

PRODUCING AN UNDERWRITTEN MESSAGE FOR NONCOMMERCIAL RADIO

An underwritten spot announcement is the noncommercial station's version of a commercial. Even though there are FCC content restrictions on what an advertiser can say in an underwritten message, in many cases it will sound just like a commercial to the listener. How did underwriting become such a necessary part of noncommercial broadcasting? It started long ago. In the 1950s, those few educational radio stations on the air had programming that mostly consisted of aiming a microphone at a teacher lecturing in the classroom. It was boring stuff, but it cost very little to produce; the university or city only had to pay the electric bill of operating the station. Later, as competition from other stations became more intense and as audiences became more sophisticated, government was pressured to monetarily support noncommercial radio. High-quality programming, it was argued, cost just as much as if it were made for a profit-making station.

Noncommercial radio did not want to continue as a second-class service. For a while, there was even some financial support by the federal government. Eventually though, stations and their institutional licensees ran out of money. It looked like many stations would have to cease operation. Where would the money come from for noncommercial broadcasting? The era of on-air begging began, which meant that four times yearly the noncommercial stations went directly to their listeners to sell memberships in the stations. But because income from listeners wasn't enough, there was pressure on the FCC to allow commercial-like spot announcements from profit-making businesses, called underwriting. Allowed since the 1960s, underwriting has evolved from the simple corporate mention to the use of the audio logo and slogan of a business. Today, there remain few restrictions on underwriting. It is one of the few ways that a noncommercial station can raise the revenue needed to support its broadcasting activities.

The process of getting underwriting for a station is also different from that of getting advertisers for commercial radio. Usually, underwriters are local community businesses that are interested in getting their names associated with the public service work of an educational, noncommercial station. Instead of highly paid sales forces and advertising agencies, it is often the volunteer programmers of the station who directly contact merchants for their donations. In return for a tax-deductible donation, the underwriter can have his or her business and products announced and feel good about supporting a struggling local radio station. Often, the station gets needed furniture, supplies, and equipment in return for a mention on the air. Compared to commercial radio, underwriting for the noncommercial station is a low-key affair.

Writing and Production Strategies

Once a profit-making business is contacted about supporting a nonprofit station, what must the business be told about what the message can say? First of all, forget the common commercial appeal to consumer values. Underwriting by law has to be *value neutral*. You are allowed to mention the product, but you can't compare it to a competing product. You can't say it's the best car on the road, you can only say it is a car and it is, in fact, on the road. You cannot use any quantitative or qualitative descriptions, either. You can't say that there are twenty in the package or that the package is the largest available. You can't say that the car is the most beautiful red car on the road, but you can say it is a red car. You cannot use directives like "come on down and buy one today." You cannot mention price, discount, or sale. Writing an underwriting message is a real creative challenge.

TABLE 12.5	***Two Scripts for Same Business***

Compare the two scripts below, one a commercial, one an underwritten message. Obviously, the commercial can say more than the underwritten spot. Note the underlined and numbered parts of the spot; they draw attention to: (1) qualitative, (2) quantitative, (3) directive, and (4) price language not allowed in underwriting for a noncommercial station. The question is, do they both sell?

EXAMPLE A: Commercial

Come down now (3) to the Spartan Bookstore on the San Jose State campus. Spartan has the largest (2) selection of high-quality (1) SJSU T-shirts and sweatshirts. Buy one at the regular price, get one free. (2 and 4) And see the exciting (1) MacIntosh Classic. You'll go right to the head of the class, your grades will improve greatly (1), when you use this powerful (1) computer. Prices start at $900. (4) And while you're at Spartan shops, tell 'em you heard about it (3) on this station and receive a 20 percent discount (4) on everything you buy. Spartan Bookstore . . . on the San Jose State campus.

EXAMPLE B: Same Sponsor, Noncommercial Station

Spartan Bookstore is located on the San Jose State campus. It has SJSU T-shirts and sweatshirts, and, of course, textbooks for your classes during the coming semester. It also has the Macintosh Classic computer in stock. Spartan Bookstore on the San Jose State campus, another supporter of University radio, KSJS, 90.7 FM.

And if this isn't confusing enough, these rules only apply to profit making organizations. Nonprofit groups who pay for underwriting on your station can sell their nonprofit activities just like a commercial. And the range of what noncommercial stations will allow as underwriting varies greatly. The larger stations often limit their underwriting to brief announcements at the beginning, middle, and end of the program or hour, "this program (hour) is brought to you through the courtesy of Spartan Bookstore." Other stations limit their underwritten messages to public service with wording like:

"Spartan Bookstore, located on the San Jose State campus, would like to remind you that drinking while driving is the leading cause of fatal accidents among college students. Choose a designated driver before you party. This reminder was brought to you in the public interest by Spartan Bookstore."

In the underwritten PSA, directive language is permitted in the PSA content, but not the underwriter's part.

There are no real restrictions on the techniques of production used for the underwritten announcement. Music, drama, comedy, many voices, music, and sound effects all can be used as long as the message remains value-neutral. This usually means that as long as the copy doesn't violate the FCC-imposed criteria, the underwritten message can sound almost like a commercial. Often those stations that serve a small community or those who must aggressively raise money will have to make their underwritten messages into highly produced, slick spots that sound almost like the real thing. Most listeners cannot tell the difference anyway.

PRODUCING THE PUBLIC SERVICE ANNOUNCEMENT

The PSA is a common short announcement that you will produce for radio. In a public service announcement, you often use the language and techniques of a commercial to "sell" an idea or product or to publicize an event to benefit a not-for-profit community organization or charity. Nonprofit groups and their events include most government-, church-, and school-sponsored events, public libraries and municipal recreation programs, United Way agencies, and the charity activities of service clubs like Rotary, Kiwanis, and Lions. In short, all the volunteer activities of your community in which money or goods are solicited to be used for the work of a nonprofit organization qualify as content for PSAs. Even when written and produced for a noncommercial station, a PSA for a nonprofit group can sell a product or an idea using directives, qualitative and quantitative language, and even price descriptions.

Why Public Service?

The Communication Act of 1934 requires all radio stations to operate in the "public interest, convenience, and necessity." Practically put, a station must augment its commercial entertainment programming with noncommercial programming in the public interest. In the days when radio consisted of completely sponsored programs of a half hour or hour in length, stations were required to air a reasonable number of programs that were nonsponsored, or **sustaining.** Sustaining programs, mostly educational, community service, and news, were public service programs. As the disc jockey program began to appear in the middle 1940s, stations began to air individual selections of music and spot announcements as programming. But because they still had a mandate to serve their community of license, stations began to air their public service in the form and length of a spot announcement. The thirty-second PSA replaced the one-hour sustaining program.

The production of PSAs gets the radio station involved with public service groups in its community. Before deregulation of broadcasting in the 1980s, stations regularly had to *ascertain community needs and interests* in order to look good at license renewal time. Every few years, representatives from a station would go into the community and survey the public service needs of the people. Local civic and religious leaders would be asked to respond to questions like "What are the major issues confronting our community?" and "How can this station solve the problems that you identify as community needs?" Community needs and interests would then be used in the FCC license renewal application and would determine the PSA campaigns that the station would produce and air. Some stations took this task very seriously; many more believed it was a nuisance activity that took time away from the real business of radio, that of making money.

Whenever public service is taken seriously by a station, both the station and the community benefit. The station benefits at license renewal time because there is no doubt as to its public service commitment. Potential local advertisers may also be impressed. If a station, for example, spends some original effort on a PSA for a volunteer organization's charity event, the effort might be noticed by an owner of a business who is also a volunteer. Impressed by the station's public service efforts, he or she may be more likely to buy advertising time. Public service benefits the community by letting listeners know about charity events and campaigns they might not otherwise know about. Through its public service efforts, a radio station can define itself and become an important institution in the life of a community. Public service awareness can help all feel more positive about where they live.

Script and Production Strategies

PSAs often arrive at the station from a nonprofit group in a prescripted form, even preproduced, ready to read or to cart for air. Other groups will send a general press release to all radio, television, and print outlets. As a production person, you'll have to take the main points contained in a page-length news story and turn it into a short announcement. Often, it will be written in the newspaper style of the **inverted pyramid,** with the who, what, when, why, and how of the content all in a very long and complex opening paragraph. In a press release, like a news story, the first, or **lead,** paragraph will usually have all the information about the event and its sponsoring nonprofit agency. The main points will have to be identified and written into a shorter message.

Often, you'll have to write a PSA from a list of facts. Some PSAs arrive only in the form of an idea or request by a community organization, and you must determine the content of the announcement. Rather than a script, you may get a question, "Can your station tell your listeners about our annual pancake breakfast that benefits the school library fund?" As a producer, you have to ask some questions in order to write an effective PSA. First, you'll have to know the basic details about the event: where is it located, the date, and the time. Next, you'll have to know what the main objective of the event is to be. Why is money needed? How will the money be used? With enough facts, you easily can write a brief PSA.

Many production options exist for producing a public service announcement. Consider drama. What if you are trying to publicize the opening of a new city-sponsored day-care center for low-income working mothers? Using actors, you might write a brief conversation between two working mothers describing how they don't make enough money to afford adequate child care. The announcer then gives the solution that is provided by the city. Or what about using **actualities,** the real voices of mothers who are satisfied with the service. Simply take a portable tape recorder to the day-care center and ask the same question of a number of mothers, such as "Why do you need day care?" Edit the best responses into a PSA. Like the commercial, the production of a PSA can include all the language, music, and effects needed to persuade listeners to support, to believe, to buy, or to act.

TABLE 12.6   *Sample PSA Written from Fact Sheet*

Facts:

Pancake breakfast, Saturday, July 24, 6:00 A.M. to noon, Vine Hill School parking lot, an annual
    affair, money used to buy books for the library since funds were cut five years ago.

PSA:

(cowboy voice and western music) Howdy pardner. Do you like pancakes? Bacon? Sausage? If so,
    you've got a great chance to fill your tummy and the bookshelves of your children's school library
    at the same time. It's the annual school district "eat to read" pancake breakfast. It's this Saturday
    from 6:00 A.M. to noon at the Vine Hill School parking lot. See you there.

You have just taken a list of unrelated facts and turned it into a script for a public service
    announcement. Now try to read it aloud. Like the commercial or the underwritten announcement,
    a PSA must be able to be easily read by an announcer. When writing for radio, sentences always
    must be shorter, ideas simpler.

Finally, consider the role of a radio station in developing a complete public service campaign for a group traditionally underserved by the media. Well-organized groups affiliated with schools, churches, and the business community often have access to media professionals who can write and even produce the PSAs for their events. Large nationally based organizations even hire advertising agencies to develop their campaigns, and some even use celebrity voices for their preproduced PSAs. All these groups can really inundate you with ready-to-use material. Small charities and minority groups, on the other hand, have little access to media and no media savvy. This is where the local radio station can help. You can be a resource to these groups by actively contacting them and then inviting them into the station to help plan public service announcements. Your station will have performed real community service, and you'll have some original produced PSAs on your air.

PRODUCING A STATION PROMO

A **promo,** or promotional announcement, is basically a commercial that the station produces to sell itself; after the commercial, it is probably the most important task that a station does. So what is so important about a promo? First, a promo helps to define the station sound and the structure of its format for the listener. All a listener has to do is push the button to hear a certain kind of music. A promo can be used to reinforce or to solidify this choice in the mind of the listener. Short, produced announcements telling about new music the station is playing or how much music the station is playing may help build the audience numbers, which allows the salespeople to charge more for advertising.

Second, a promo can act as an informational vehicle for the station. If a personality is appearing live in the community, a promotional announcement can inform listeners. If a station is **block-programmed,** that is, it has individual programs instead of a single format, promos are important because they tell interested listeners where to find, for example, classical music, jazz, news, interviews, and other specialty programming. A promo can also inform listeners that a contest is going on, even tell them when to listen for the best chance to win.

Third, and most important, a promo can simply be a repetitive reminder that they are listening to "90.7 FM, KSJS." It can be recorded in any number of ways, combined with so-called positioning statements, those liners or shotguns that in a few words describe the station. If you ask a modern programmer what the three most important things are that must be heard between every record, the answer will be, "call letters, call letters, and call letters." As a production person, much of your creative production efforts will be devoted to promoting the station.

Promotional Strategies

Like the commercial or PSA, the production of a station promo involves a process and, initially, a group of people. When planning for a PSA, community leaders often will work directly with the production person. For commercial production, a salesperson, an agency representative, or even the sponsor might work with you on a project. The people involved in the production of a station promo may not include any of these individuals because programming is directly involved. The promotions director, program director, a marketing person, and even the entire production staff will probably be asked to give input on the design and execution of a station promotional campaign. Here is what they must consider:

The need must be determined. A station's need to have its call letters continuously before the public is ongoing. Special occasions arise, however, when just the mention of the call letters is not enough. An example of this is when a station must react to what the competition is successfully doing. If another station is playing more music or giving away more prizes, a new campaign is needed. Short promotional announcements must be made to assure listeners that if they leave the dial right where it is, they won't miss anything. Ratings are also an important clue as to the type of promotional campaign needed. If the ratings show, for example, that not enough women are listening, a campaign might be launched that gives away a shopping spree at a local department store or supermarket. And special shows, contests, and one-of-a-kind events always present the need for a special promotion.

The central theme must be decided on. What will you call the promotional campaign? Will you use that name on the air? The campaign idea that "May is more music month" or "win with 103.7" is a theme for a campaign that can also be used on the air, both spoken live by the announcer and included in produced promos. If the promo is for a specific event or program heard on the station, deciding on the promo's central theme will be just like that for a commercial. Whatever the promo, what is the main point that you want the audience to get? Is the goal of the campaign simply to get the listener to believe that your station plays the most music and gives away the best prizes? Or, will the promotion only be used to draw audience attention to a special Saturday night presentation of oldies?

The plan for producing and airing the campaign, the number of different produced promos involved, and the frequency of airing must be decided on. This is the easiest part of the campaign. First, consider the audience for the event or idea promoted. If it is a general awareness campaign, like frequent mention of call letters, and if there are many different versions, several times per hour makes sense. Conversely, if it is a concert of interest mainly to your night-time audience, play it mostly at night. Contests tend to run during the daytime hours, but promos for them can run anytime. Promos can be added to the log by the traffic department.

Writing and Producing the Promo

A promotion is one of those cases when a programming need immediately translates directly into a writing and production need. First, the writing. Make it simple and direct. Tell the listener, in as few words as possible, exactly what you want him or her to know, believe, or do. And, since promos are just another intrusion into the airing of a listener's favorite music, they need to be shorter than commercials and PSAs. If most commercials are thirty seconds long and PSAs ten to twenty, most promos should be five or ten seconds at a maximum. Exceptions must be made for those promos explaining a contest or telling about a live concert featuring a number of performers.

A lot of the promos you'll write will be the very brief station identification promos variously called **spot breakers, shotguns,** or **liners.** These mostly take the form of produced positioning statements that reinforce the way a station wants to be perceived in the mind of the listener. "The Bay Area's best new music" is one example. To a listener, it means that the station plays new popular music, not oldies, not jazz, not news. Or, the famous news station liner that appeared in many produced incarnations, "You give us twenty-two minutes and we'll give you the world." This is another example of a station promo designed to tell the listener what the station is all about.

In the final analysis, production is production is production. A promo, like every other short announcement produced for radio, will need to start with an idea and lead to a treatment of that idea, including the best way to write it and the best way to produce it. If drama works, use it. If comedy is effective, use it. If a straight sell is the best way to communicate to an audience, do it.

SUMMARY

The short produced announcement is the basis of modern format radio. Whether a spot announcement for a commercial station, an underwritten message for a noncommercial station, or a public service or promotional announcement, it seems like a radio station is always trying to sell you on an idea or a product or service. It's true. Modern radio, and its daily presentation of several hundred produced short announcements, is a fact of life we are all used to; it's the price we expect to pay for the privilege of hearing our favorite disc jockey play our favorite music, or our favorite talk show host interview famous people. And it's not just commercial radio. Even public, community, and college stations are constantly asking you to become a member, attend an event, or support a charity.

Fortunately, this proliferation of short produced announcements presents a real creative opportunity to a radio production person. By now, you know how to use the tools of production, and you have some idea of the tremendous variety of options available when presenting a short message on the radio. You know why a station needs a commercial, PSA, or promo, and you understand more about how to write the script. The short announcement is the most common form of radio production. As a production person, the commercial, PSA, underwriting announcement, and promo will be your greatest opportunities to creatively contribute to broadcasting.

ACTIVITIES

1. Listen to a sample hour of your favorite station. Write down every short, produced announcement heard during this hour. Try to identify whether they are commercials, PSAs, or promos.
2. Tape several commercials currently aired on a local station. Examine them to determine the main points, the values they are aimed at, and the audience they are trying to reach.
3. Complete the PSA/promo assignment in appendix B.
4. Spend some time discussing and writing down all those organizations in your community that need community awareness.
5. Design a promotional campaign for a new program on your college's radio station.

Producing News and Information

Radio programming described as *informational*—news, public affairs interview, news magazine, or audio documentary—will require some time in the production facility. From recording voices to adding theme music to final editing into a complete package or show, the production of information programming benefits from processes similar to those used for the commercial, promo, or PSA. News and information must sound like they fit in with the rest of the station's programming, so the techniques employed in their production are motivated by the same goals as music programming. Like all other production, those factors that determine the way that a station's audience will be served by its music will influence its news and informational programming and its production.

The two most common forms of informational programming are the straight newscast and the longer produced public affairs, news magazine, or documentary program. Both require a production facility for completion. For the straight newscast, the voices of newsmakers and reporters on the scene of a story often will have to be edited into a short package and transferred to a cart for use during a live broadcast. Production for a half-hour or hour public affairs documentary may require you to follow a process similar to that used for an informational video. After deciding on an idea, research, script writing, audio recording, and editing are done. Then music, sound effects, and credits, may be needed to finalize the show for air. For either form of informational programming, the production skills you've learned so far will be enough. Along with the content decisions you make, an informational radio production can be a very creative experience.

A CHANGING ROLE FOR RADIO NEWS AND INFORMATION

In the beginning, a handful of pre-World War I wireless experimenters read from the newspaper the events of the day. An early documented use of the broadcast of straight news to an audience of more than one was the KDKA offering of the Harding-Cox election returns in 1920. Because of the primitive equipment used, no production was possible; it was just an announcer reading into a converted telephone. By the mid-1930s, radio had developed a love–hate relationship with the news. On one hand, some of the most powerful radio stations were owned by newspapers. Broadcasting seemed a natural addition to the business of print journalism—gathering and interpreting world, national, and local events for a mass audience and selling the package to advertisers. So major newspapers went on the air to read short pieces of news for the purpose of promoting what was to be found in their soon-to-be-released papers. Eventually, all radio stations began to read from the papers, and later directly from the Associated Press wire service. This created a minor news war with the papers crying foul, and, for a while, radio was restricted as to what it could use from the wire service; stations even had to wait until the papers were on the street before they could read stories from them.

Several events in the middle to late 1930s came together to secure the position and importance of news and information programming on radio. To a lesser extent, it was prodding by the Federal Communications Commission, increasingly upset at radio stations for too many commercials and too little public service. Required to operate in the "public interest, convenience, and necessity," radio stations were made to believe that the airing of nonentertainment, nonsponsored news, and community affairs was a quid pro quo for license renewal. Local stations and networks began to develop their own news operations, staffs increased, and radio relied less on newspapers to inform audiences. Most important, the late 1930s saw the rise of Hitler and Mussolini and an increasing awareness that war in Europe was imminent. Was America going to war, too? Everybody was listening to the radio for information that seemed to change hourly.

Radio's place as an important source of news and information was solidified during World War II and continued throughout the late 1940s and 1950s. By the late 1960s, America was at war once again, but this time it was television, with its visual impact, that stole the show and the news audience from radio. But radio had also changed. While it began as a full-service medium for the entire family with shows for kids, soap operas for mom, and news and information for dad, radio had gradually evolved into a series of formats, each one for a specific, narrowly defined audience. Stations whose audiences were mostly young people eager to hear the hits of the day relegated their news to a few minutes each hour and their longer informational community service programs to early Sunday morning. With the deregulation of the 1980s, stations were no longer required to do news, and those that didn't need it for competitive purposes dropped it. Now, this type of programming is found on public and community stations, news and talk stations, and so-called "full-service" stations.

THE FIVE "W'S" AND AN "H" OF INFORMATIONAL RADIO

The journalist's familiar "who, what, when, where, why, and how" is one way to understand the purpose and scope of informational programming and the techniques used for its production. But first, look at the similarities and differences between the two most common forms of informational programming: the *straight newscast* and the *documentary*. Both present information, as opposed to entertainment, and both use the facts and opinions surrounding an event in an attempt to synthesize them into a story the listener can comprehend. The straight newscast is usually just the facts of an event with the opinions of those involved. The purpose of this form of journalism is to get both sides of the issue and present it without comment. The type of production for this form of informational programming is mostly confined to recording and editing voices.

Documentary programming on radio is often opinion, commentary, a roundup of news in magazine form, even the re-creation of the events of the day. Differing from the straight newscast, its goal may be to call for action on a community issue or to present a historical perspective on a local event. Unlike the straight news story, a documentary may be the obvious editorial position of the station, and it may use in its production music and sound effects, even actors, to present and reinforce that opinion. The public affairs documentary may not even be the content responsibility of the station, but rather air time given to a responsible community group for the presentation of its ideas. The public affairs documentary can run the gamut from a simple assembly of the pro and con voices of the experts on an issue to the complete investigative report by itself or as part of a longer magazine, an audio version of "60 Minutes."

For all types of informational programming, look at who produces it, what they produce, when they air it, where they produce it, and why and how they produce it.

Who

Who are the people responsible for the news and informational programming of a radio station? Depending on the size and format of the station, some informational programming may originate locally and some may be delivered by satellite from a national news network. At the network and major station level, an entire staff could be devoted just to informational programming. There are the management and organizational personnel whose role is to determine which stories get covered, which reporters cover it, and where in the newscast it appears. Networks and the large all-news stations have a news director who is primarily responsible for the journalistic content and integrity of both the straight newscast and the documentary programming. Under the news director, there may be an assignment editor who decides what stories will be covered by what news reporters, and there may be a managing editor or producer who puts each hour together.

In the actual production of the informational programming of a network or all-news station, there are producers whose only job might be producing long-form documentaries on government or community issues. A station may even have a community affairs director, an individual responsible for deciding what the community needs in the way of information and who the spokesperson should be to present this

An editor works on assignments at KCBS San Francisco.

News is written at KGO San Francisco.

information. For the production of the straight newscast, there will be writers, reporters, and readers, known as anchorpeople. Also involved may be the analyst or commentator, usually a respected member of the journalism profession with enough earned credibility to present personal opinion. In the largest operations, there will be separate engineers who operate all the equipment, either because management realizes that a reporter or anchor needs to better concentrate on the content and presentation of the news or because a technical union requires it in its contract.

The newsroom is a busy place at KCBS San Francisco.

Locally, a station may have a news director who doubles as a reporter and a news reader. In the major- or large-market station whose primary format is popular music, it may be a single individual who does news during morning and afternoon drive times. This person may be called the news director but in reality is the entire news department. He or she may call a few local sources for news, read the papers and wire services for stories, and then do all the writing, production, and delivery on the air. Once a week, this person may produce a one-hour public affairs interview show. In the medium- and small-market station, the generic announcer may be required to read the news from a wire service printer in the morning and come back later in the day as a DJ and production person. In the very smallest station, one person may do every task known in radio production from DJ to news writer/ reporter/reader to sales to engineer to janitor.

What

What is the typical form of the news and information aired by a station? Again, this always depends on the size of the station, its market, and its commitment to informational programming. The continuum of options for a station whose format is primarily music includes brief headlines, a five- or ten-minute hourly newscast, a half-hour news roundup, and a complete public affairs program. The all-news station will air informational programming that consists of elements of all these forms. Such a station will begin with headlines, then read the stories behind the headlines, and then present some of the stories in great detail as a feature or commentary. Most of these stations have some network services, including hourly newscasts, health and sports features, and continuous coverage of major news events. Whether music or all-news, much of a station's informational programming content will contain produced elements or be totally prepackaged.

At all-news KCBS San Francisco, one member of the anchor team runs the board and both read.

At music station KHQT San Jose, a single newsperson reads headlines on the morning show.

On some of the large-market music format stations, only the **headlines,** or the highlights, of the news are used, perhaps a sentence about each of four or five stories. During this service, the minute or less of news is augmented by traffic, sports scores, and weather, just enough information for the busy commuter who, after all, has selected a music station. Stations with a greater commitment to news may have a traditional time when a listener can expect to hear an actual newscast. Five minutes every hour, on the hour, is typical. Small-market stations, especially those that are the only one in a community, may try to present all the news in a half hour form, sometimes called a *roundup.* The small station may have several public affairs programs that are done by local civic and political leaders and produced by an announcer at the local station production facility. Most small stations will not have the resources to produce a full-length documentary.

When

When is the produced output of news and informational programming aired? As one popular all-news station declares "all news, all day, all night." To this station, news is a format, just like the station that plays the same forty records over and over. When selecting a format station, the listener does not tune in to hear a specific program but tunes in to hear an identifiable sound, whether news or music. Music-formatted stations schedule news when they believe their audiences want to hear it, and they schedule longer public affairs shows when they believe their music audiences are the smallest. It's all done with ratings in mind. To music stations, the continuous airing of music with the least interruption is the most important thing they do.

The frequency of news on a music-formatted station depends on market size. In the large and major markets, there are usually plenty of radio stations where the news can be found, all the time and in depth. Music stations usually only air brief news headlines during the morning and afternoon drive times. Here, audiences are largest, people are commuting, and even though news in detail can be found elsewhere, their surveys show that their listeners want to know at least the important stories between 6:00 and 9:00 A.M. and 3:00 and 6:00 P.M. If details are necessary, the commuter will catch the television news at home. Public affairs programming and documentaries on a large-market music station are usually buried, relegated to a time when few people are listening, often very early or very late on Sundays.

In the medium or small market, where there are fewer sources of news available, even a music formatted station may have a five-minute newscast every hour. Unlike the major market, a listener cannot push the button and get news all the time, and it is for competitive reasons that a music station may need a continuous local news presence. The audience has fewer choices. In the one-station market, there may be a half-hour news roundup at noon or 6:00 P.M. In the tiniest of markets with a single station and no daily newspaper, it is often the radio station that people turn to first for any news of local significance. Many of these smaller stations broadcast an hourly satellite-delivered national news service and augment it with local news.

Besides the all-news station, there is another category of station that may have a great commitment to airing both the straight newscast and public affairs/documentary programming. The so-called educational, noncommercial, public, college, or community station with no commercial restrictions can broadcast as many hours of informational fare as it can afford. When are they usually scheduled? Anytime. Because these stations are often **free-form,** or without a format, the longer news features, public affairs shows, and documentaries can be presented at a time convenient for the intended audience. National Public Radio offers its member stations a three-hour news block for airing during morning and afternoon drive times. In a small market without an all-news outlet, this is an important service for the commuter. The typical community station may have access to NPR news and documentaries, and it may have a large group of community volunteers that produces local public affairs programs.

A news production studio.

Where

Where does production take place? At the network level, there are dedicated studios where news personnel and production people can put together news stories and longer programs. At some of the large all-music stations, a news reader may actually come into the on-air room and banter with the DJ team as part of the popular morning zoo format. At big all-news stations, some production is actually done in the newsroom. When a reporter gets audio for a story from the telephone, it's recorded right where the writing, gathering, and preparing of the news is taking place. Sometimes, the live newscast originates from the newsroom because the sounds of telephones, typewriters, and wire service printers add an immediate kind of audio ambience. Most larger news operations also have several minimal production rooms where a package for a straight newscast can be assembled. All the familiar production elements are present: a way to tape from the telephone, a small console to allow mixing of live microphone and taped sources, and a cart machine used to dub the complete package for air.

Conversely, the production of longer programs must take place in a quiet studio and production facility. If people from the community are to be interviewed, and if they must speak into several microphones, the newsroom ambience would be too distracting, too noisy. For the production of a documentary, people are sometimes interviewed in segments in a studio. Later, parts of these interviews are edited together, using an announcer for transitions and music or sound effects to make an interesting, even compelling, audio presentation. Unlike most production for the straight newscast, the longer documentary always can be planned, researched, scripted, and produced into a creative radio program.

Why

Why does a station include informational programming in its schedule? An all-news station does it to get an audience for its format, news. A public radio station does it because it believes it is the best way to be an alternative community broadcasting service.

A music station does it for more complex reasons. One reason might be that the owner of the station has decided that something is owed to the community in the form of informational programming. Even though the music format is relatively inexpensive and any money spent on news is without immediate profit, the way the citizens and the advertisers in a community view a station can have a long-term value. Another reason that a music station will have an informational presence is for competitive reasons. The question is always asked, "If the other stations are doing it, can my station afford not to?" Finally, and of practical importance in this era of ownership by large, impersonal media conglomerates, stations feel they have to present some informational programming just to keep other companies from challenging their licenses to operate. A decision to air informational programming is a business one.

How

How is production for informational programming organized and completed? Now that you understand the who, what, when, where, and why of informational programming, knowing how will become more obvious. Now it's your turn. Below are all the steps to producing two of the most common informational audio programs. One is the basic produced news package used in the straight newscast; the other is the long-form public affairs-type documentary.

RADIO NEWS PRODUCTION

Listen to a typical five-minute news broadcast. Notice that some of its content appears to be read by different voices and contains voices of actual newsmakers, called **actualities.** An actuality is usually part of a **package,** a produced news story from thirty seconds to several minutes that contains an introduction read by a reporter, several actualities, transition narration, and a conclusion by the reporter. The voice of the reporter before and after the actualities is called a **wrap-around.** This entire package with its actualities and wrap-arounds must be planned, written, and produced using familiar audio production equipment. Look at a summary in Table 13.1 of the entire process from assignment of the story to its final production. You'll see that decisions on the content of the story begin in the newsroom; its production happens partly in the newsroom and partly in a production facility.

TABLE 13.1   ***Order of Tasks to Complete a News Package***

What	Where	By Who
Story is assigned	Newsroom	News director or you
Content resources and interview subjects are found	Beat sheet, newspaper, other reporter, news conference, or other radio station	You, news director, or editor
Interviews made of subjects and recorded	By phone or at the scene	You or assigned reporter
Actualities selected and edited	Production facility	You, engineer, or producer
Wrap-around written	Newsroom	You or writer
Wrap-around recorded	Newsroom or production facility	You
Package assembled	Production facility	You or engineer
Package dubbed to cart for air	Production facility	You or engineer

The Newsroom

It starts in the newsroom. Look closely at the organization, the staff, and the facilities of a typical large-market radio station whose primary format is music, a station in a market not served by an all-news operation. This station believes that news is important to its image and ratings, so there is a sizable staff and enough resources to support a credible news operation. The major news effort is the presentation of a three- to five-minute newscast every hour from 5:00 A.M. to midnight. In addition, the news staff produces two weekly half-hour public affairs documentaries; one is a straight interview program, and the other is a compilation of the week's local news highlights. Obviously, much of the content for the latter will be material originally used in produced package form on an hourly news broadcast.

Our example station is well-equipped. Its state-of-the-art newsroom has all major national, state, and local **wire services** offering prewritten news stories sent by telephone line to a computer-like printer. Most stations will have at least an **Associated Press,** or **AP,** service and a state or local service, depending on the size of the market. Some stations will have audio services featuring the voices of national newsmakers, delivered by phone line or satellite dish. There are facilities for recording from the telephone, plus portable cassette recorders and microphones that can be taken into the field by a newsperson.

Adjacent to the newsroom itself are several small production rooms for putting together packages using material gathered from the field and the phone. When the newsperson goes on the air live, it is all done from a small console in the newsroom. For the production of the two weekly shows, the radio station's main production facility is scheduled.

KGO San Francisco subscribes to all major wire services.

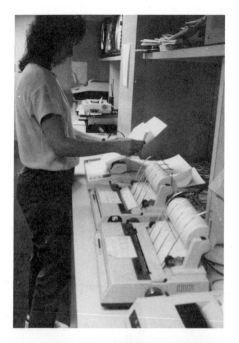

At KCBS San Francisco, there is a separate studio for traffic reports.

Personnel at the station consist of a news director and a staff of five, all of whom write, gather, and report news at the station and in the field. On a normal day, the news director will be on duty in the newsroom from five A.M. to noon to help coordinate the day's activities, going into the field occasionally for a breaking story or an important local press conference. The news director will help with writing and gathering during the busy morning drive time hours. The five news people will each spend three to five hours of their day writing, preparing, and reading on air, and two to three hours reporting from the field and producing packages in the newsroom. Table 13.2 shows the daily schedule for this staff.

TABLE 13.2   *News Operation Schedule*

Person	On-Air	Reporting and Production
News director	Fill in and vacations, special stories during A.M.	Coordinates staff of 5 for daily news operation, does weekly news roundup show production, works on morning news
Person A	Five A.M. to nine A.M. writes and anchors	Ten A.M. to one P.M. either on phone to prepare packages or at scene of news event with recorder
Person B	Nine A.M. to one P.M. as above	Two P.M. to five P.M. as above and helps afternoon drive (person C) with activity in newsroom
Person C	One P.M. to four P.M. as above	Either A.M. or P.M. produces the weekly interview show, plus reporting and production of packages
Person D	Four P.M. to seven P.M. as above	One P.M. to three P.M. reporting and preparation of packages
Person E	Seven P.M. to twelve A.M. as above	No reporting but prepares packages for next morning's news during quiet times

This is a realistic schedule, because most news events requiring on-the-scene or over-the-phone reporting occur during the business part of the day. Newsmakers and politicians schedule press conferences during the morning, and most of the service activities for the commuter are broadcast during the morning and afternoon drive times, 5 A.M.–9 A.M. and 3 P.M.–7 P.M. Unless there is a breaking story, the nighttime newsperson reads wire copy for current news stories and airs previously produced packages during the 3–5-minute newscast.

a   *b*

(a) At KCBS San Francisco, newswriters prepare electronic copy, which is read on air by anchorpeople. (b) KCBS electronic copy on screen.

Now that you understand a bit about the setup of the newsroom and its staff, look at how content decisions are made and how those decisions translate into production decisions. Which stories will be read directly or rewritten from wire copy? Which will be local productions? Like elsewhere in radio, a programming decision must be made before the production can take place. This time, the decision is based on a journalistic judgment of what is important enough to cover in detail and what the defined audience of the station will be interested in hearing. The decision is also influenced to a lesser extent by the amount of time and resources available, which is largely dependent on the format and the relative importance of news to a station. So the question is, "Given the amount of time and resources available, what stories should be made into a produced package?"

This decision may depend on the availability of local content people. If, as a reporter, you have been summoned to a city hall press conference where the mayor has announced that funds have been secured for a new freeway that will surround the city, a major story is feasible. How will you treat this very important local story as a package? First, the news director has determined from reading the local newspaper and the city wire service that a press conference will be held to announce the long-expected freeway. Tape recorder in hand, you attend the conference and record the remarks of the mayor. Meanwhile, it is decided that some phone contacts will have to be made for reactions for and against the proposed freeway. The voices of well-known civic spokespeople and the voice of the "person-in-the-street" will be used to put together a strong local package. From the newsroom contact sheet, the news director or another reporter calls the chamber of commerce president and the council member who represents the district affected by the freeway. On the way back from the press conference, you stop at a shopping mall near the location of the proposed freeway and record the opinions of people there. You return to the station.

Producing the Package

Before production of the package can begin, look at some of the elements you have already gathered and what you still need to complete the package on the new freeway announcement.

Table 13.3 shows the elements that you will shape into a two- to three-minute package for air. Because this is an important local story, you may want to do several things with the information, some immediate and some later. On the next hourly newscast, the news reader on duty will at the very least need to read a modified version of the wire service report. If time, you may be able to put on a cart a few seconds of actuality from the mayor's statement. And it should be mentioned that, "We'll have local reaction later." This will give you, as an experienced reporter, an hour or two to prepare and produce the package. What is the best way to proceed?

Review all the material and select those segments that best tell the story. Listen to the tapes to find what the television news people call the *sound bite*. In your case, the sound bite is an audio actuality, the voice of the newsmakers, content people, and others recorded for this story. An ideal sound bite has all the important elements of the speaker's opinion or *slant/spin* of the story in ten or twenty seconds. Skilled

TABLE 13.3   *Elements of the Package*

1. The mayor's three-minute announcement, on cassette.
2. Comments of five people at the shopping mall, also on cassette, who were asked: "What will this new freeway mean to you?"
3. A one-minute statement from the president of the chamber of commerce, recorded from the phone, on open-reel tape.
4. A rambling, five-minute phone interview with the city council representative of the affected area, also on open-reel tape.
5. A printed summary of the mayor's announcement and local reaction from the city news service wire.

politicians and professional spokespeople always include a sound bite in public appearances; this makes it easy for busy newspeople to excerpt exactly what the speaker wants the public to hear, see, and understand. A disorganized speaker who requires too much editing may not be used by a fast-paced news operation.

Once they have been determined, put the audio segments into a production format for rapid access. Many newspeople will put the selected segments, in order, on a single cart. That way, all you have to do is read opens, closes, and transitions, the wrap-arounds, and press the button on the cart player each time an actuality is introduced. For this story, there will be two exceptions to this simple method. The mayor and the chamber of commerce president were prepared with their statements, which included the usual sound bites. These have been identified and will be transferred to cart. The city council person, however, was not prepared, so his long, rambling statements will have to be edited down to a short actuality before its transfer to cart. The answers of the "people-in-the-street" also will have to be condensed and edited. Editing will take place using either reel-to-reel or the cassette audio will be transferred to a digital sampler and edited quickly using a mouse. All audio can now be put on cart in the proper order, with timings and *outcues,* or the last words of the segment, included.

This cart has all actualities recorded in the correct order for production.

TABLE 13.4   ***Order of the Actuality Cart***

CUT 1: Mayor speaks, 27 sec., "many years"
CUT 2: C of C pres for, 32 sec., "important"
CUT 3: Council against, 48 sec., "in this"
CUT 4: 3 people at mall, 18 sec., "and dust"

TABLE 13.5   ***Script for the Package***

ADAMS: Today in San Jose, Mayor Janet White announced the funding for the long-awaited outerbelt freeway. . . .
CUT 1: (mayor) "Finally, after . . . many years"
ADAMS: We asked Harry Angstrom of the Chamber of Commerce what this new freeway will mean to the business community. . . .
CUT 2: (Angstrom) "We have waiting . . . important"
ADAMS: Not all are pleased with the project. City Council Representative Stanley Baran believes that a major project like this will disrupt one of the city's oldest neighborhoods. . . .
CUT 3: (Baran) "The people in my district . . . not part of the decision-making in this"
ADAMS: But what do the people of the Willow Glen area think about a major freeway bisecting their neighborhood? We went to the Valley Plaza shopping center and asked. . . .
CUT 4: (misc people) 3 voices, woman last ". . . not so sure I'll like all the noise and dust"
ADAMS: But this issue is far from being resolved. An environmental impact study and several promised court challenges may mean a decade before that first piece of dirt is ever moved. For KSJS news, I'm Mike Adams.

After listening several times to the four segments on the cart, some writing will have to be done. The wrap-arounds, which include an open, introductions and transitions between taped actualities, and a close, will be written in the newsroom. Once the script is written, you find that your facility offers two choices for putting together the final package. One option is to go into the production facility and, using a live microphone and a cart playback, record the entire package onto open-reel. If any further editing is required, it can be done before the transfer to cart for broadcast. The other option is to go directly to cart for air. Because of time constraints, you have chosen the second option. Table 13.5 shows what the finished script might look like.

Production of the package is very straightforward. Set levels on the playback cart, set your own announcer level, erase and place into the cart recorder a tape of sufficient length, record the package, and play it back. Now that you have completed it, there is one final task to consider. If you have actualities on cart, will they be needed for the weekly half-hour local news roundup? Probably, as this is a story with much local significance. Put the cart with the actualities, along with your script, into the "in" basket for the half-hour show. Now, when the news director is ready to write the weekly show, all that has to be done is to assign the stories an order or a priority. And if, as is done in the modern newsroom, every script is on computer, all the news director has to do is assemble the half hour from the daily menu.

And that's how to approach, plan, and produce a package that can be used in a straight newscast and a weekly news roundup show. Production of the news package is the most common type of informational production done in a radio station. If the disc jockey spends most of his or her time in the production of brief announcements like commercials, PSAs, and promos, the newsperson will spend most off-air time preparing and producing the package. The major differences between the two will be in the content and the amount of production equipment required for each.

PRODUCING A RADIO DOCUMENTARY

The term documentary, as applied to media, may have begun with Robert Flaherty's early 1920s silent film, *Nanook of the North.* Later, radio adapted the basic film documentary style to its own technology. In the documentary, the meaning added by the producing organization varied from the impartial "both sides of the issue" treatment by the major news organizations to a sponsored program designed to present that sponsor's opinion. Compare a network documentary on an oil spill to one made by an oil company. Same facts. Different point of view.

Most long-form informational shows that you will produce for radio will not be in the tradition of the complete documentary. It's more likely that you'll do interview shows with community newsmakers or magazine-like news shows, a roundup of the week's news with added commentary for perspective. The interview show is the most basic long-form informational format. You'll contact one or more content people, perhaps for and against a local issue, bring them into a studio, set up microphones, and roll tape. As the newsperson, you'll ask the guests questions and organize the discussion as the moderator. For the magazine-like news roundup, you'll simply take a week's worth of stories and actualities and rewrite it into a half-hour show. For the news roundup, you may want to bring in an expert to interpret the significance of those stories. Those are the basic public affairs shows done by most broadcasters.

Production of a documentary is more involved. To a radio station, the true documentary is a thoughtful and well-researched presentation of an issue of community importance. The station is allowed to take sides, but it must identify its position if it is not obvious. Unlike the public affairs interview or the news roundup compilation, the documentary requires a lot more production time and resources. A newsperson will interview and record on audio the people involved in an event of importance to its listeners, edit it, and add narration to clarify or influence the meaning. A documentary begins with many hours of taped material that must be edited down to a final program of thirty minutes. The person who selects what to include and what to leave out is really the editor, and his or her editorial judgment affects the meaning of the topic explored in the documentary. The radio documentary can be a very creative experience.

TABLE 13.6	*Order of Tasks to Complete a 30-Minute Documentary*

1. Select an idea. It can, for example, be based on personal observation, ideas based on recent news stories, or tips from listeners.
2. Decide on a treatment of the idea. Will you use voices of experts or the actual people affected by the issue, or a combination of both? Will it be narrated, or will the actual people tell the story in their own voices? Will there be music and sound effects? And re-creation by actors?
3. Do research. You may read all that has been written about your selected topic and you may ask experts on the subject matter. Know as much as possible about your subject and where to find the people to interview who will tell your story.
4. Write a script. This could be in the form of a complete script when you have all the information and you know basically what your interview subjects might say. It could also be an outline. Often, it is only after listening to the interviews that you can write the complete narration.
5. Do the interviews. Tape recorder in hand, go to those locations and people who have agreed to have their voices recorded for your production.
6. Listen to the interviews and select the segments you need to complete your show. If you have done the interviews on cassette and transferred the selected parts to open-reel, put each edited segment on a separate small reel. You could also transfer each edited actuality segment onto its own separate cart, timed and labeled. If you are operating in the digital domain, each segment is given a location on the hard disk.
7. Time the segments. You'll want a time for each segment and a total running time.
8. Write, time, and record final narration. Like the package, your narration will be written just like a giant wrap-around.
9. Select music and sound effects, if needed. Often these elements are used to add meaning to a documentary.
10. Put together the final show, either in real-time from carts or in segments to be edited later.

The Process

Like the production of a news package, the documentary requires a logical process to get you from an idea to a final product for air. Unlike the package, you may have to convince the public affairs director, news director, program director, or station manager of the importance of the topic that you wish to spend your time and station resources completing. Since documentaries are primarily aired on noncommercial stations, getting air time will not be a major problem. While commercial stations have weekly public affairs time slots, they are usually at a time when no one is listening; besides, it's a station where most listeners do not expect to hear anything outside of the format.

Once you have convinced station higher-ups that your idea is worth exploring, you'll need to organize for production. Table 13.6 shows the steps and activities to consider.

Now look at each step in detail. The idea and its treatment are the most important decisions you'll make in the production of a documentary. Think about it . . . you have been noticing that public opinion about the homeless in your downtown area has gradually changed from pity to tolerance to anger. At first, you and your friends wanted to help. You gave money every time homeless people asked, you wrote many news stories about their plight, and you even tried to influence the construction of a temporary shelter. That was five years ago. Today, when the seemingly same faces again ask you for change, you brush them off. And, whatever happened to the shelter? Can nothing be done to solve this ever-present problem? Why do you have less compassion today than two years ago? . . . Now you have an idea. Your documentary is going to be called "The Homeless of Downtown, Revisited." Using radio, you are going to explore why attitudes appear to have changed.

You have decided that the best way to treat the subject is to interview a sample of city officials, people who work downtown, social workers, and leaders of the homeless themselves. There are at least a dozen of each of these. You'll interview city officials to get facts on the increase or decrease in the numbers of the homeless, programs available, funding and job issues, and changes in the past five years. You'll ask residents who work downtown to describe how and why their attitudes have changed. You'll ask social workers and other welfare agency people for their opinions, and you'll interview homeless people and their spokespeople to find out what has changed. It is planned that some music will be used for transition and under some of the narration you will write. The music will be selected to reflect the narration's conclusion that little has changed and the situation is getting worse.

Research and interviews can be done concurrently. For this production, your experience in the newsroom has prepared you with a list of civic and welfare spokespeople, even leaders of the homeless community, to contact. You already know some of these individuals, and you make appointments for a tape-recorded interview. For the less structured interviews, you take to the streets of downtown with a tape recorder and interview workers and homeless people. Now you have the story. It's a complex one, too. By carefully drawing out people through an informal interview style, you have drawn these conclusions:

1. The homeless are increasing in number.
2. The homeless population is changing from just the wino stereotype to include middle-class families, women, and children.
3. The homeless population is becoming the victim of more crime and violence downtown.
4. Federal money is decreasing.
5. There is no training or work for these people.
6. Welfare agencies are decreasing their staffs because of budget cuts, so they have many more people to deal with.
7. Downtown real estate is too expensive to permit a shelter to be established, and the suburbs promptly hassle and jail the homeless. So they have no choice but to live on the downtown streets.
8. There is an attitude that homelessness is a problem that can't be solved, a result of our economy.

You have discovered that this is a very complex issue, one that definitely requires a half hour to thoroughly explain. You may begin to write some narration to amplify and clarify the information you gained from doing the interviews. Most of this narration will have to be finalized after the interviews have been listened to and parts selected. At this point in the documentary process, you have one foot in the door of the production facility as you listen to the interview tapes and the other foot beneath the word processor as you work on the narration. Before you put both feet inside the studio, consider how you will treat the narration.

Narration is designed to contribute to the understanding of the content of a production. How will you approach its writing? It should be active and descriptive without being redundant; it shouldn't repeat exactly what the interview subject has just said or is going to say. Write most narration in the present or future tense. The past tense cannot be used in most cases because, for example, interviews, while certainly occurring in your past, will be very much in the present to the listener. Most narration is written in the second person as it is a good compromise between the very personal and the very detached and will sound like, "You can learn much from a visit to our downtown . . ." An exception to this is the narration you might write if you are personally involved in the content of a show. Here, it might be appropriate to use first person like, "I certainly learned much from my day on the streets. . . ." The third person gives a rather stuffy, pedantic, impersonal feeling to a narration like, "One can certainly learn much from a visit to. . . ." Radio is a personal medium and the third person is rarely used.

Write narration to be read aloud. Use short, declarative sentences, and always practice any narration by actually reading it out loud. Compound, complex sentences that read well on paper may be impossible to speak. Many narrator scripts are written in thought groups or fragments of complete sentences, marked for easy reading by an announcer. Punctuation need only occur in the mind of the listener. Again, the narration that you finally write will change as you listen to the tapes and select and time the best parts.

There is one more task before you finally go into the production facility. Look again at your list of conclusions. Have you started to identify several short segments out of each interview that reinforce and amplify those conclusions? You'll also have to decide on an order that best presents them. Ask yourself: "What do the city officials think is the main reason why less money is available for more people?" "Is it an economic recession or the attitude of elected officials?" You listen to the social workers as you wonder, "What do they think has changed within the homeless population? More families? What do your fellow workers in the downtown area believe? Are they more cynical about the ability of government or society to really solve this problem?" What about your own feelings? As the producer, your attitudes and values will determine what segments you pick and the relative weight you assign to each opinion. Everybody has a different answer. Which one will you believe the most? Now you're ready for production.

The Production

The first step, then, in the actual production is to listen to and select those segments that best tell the story. They will have to be edited, timed, ordered, and transferred onto the production format of choice. You have several options. Consider the tape format that you have recorded the original interviews on, and the formats available to you in the production facility. You probably recorded all the interviews on a high-quality cassette. The problem with the cassette format is that no matter how good the quality, it is not a production format; you can't edit on it, you can't cue it up. The cassette always has to be transferred to another format, either open-reel or digital workstation. Once this is done, you can select segments and edit them for clarity and time, all before you use them in the final production. Like the news package, each edited segment can be put on its own cart or separate reel of tape or digital workstation location, all with its timing on a label or the screen.

The next step is to finally write, record, and time the narration. How much you need will depend on what you have to say and on the time remaining after all the segment times are added together. Subtract time for opening and closing music and sound effects; what you have left is the amount of time left for narration. Should the narration be recorded? Again, it depends on the equipment in the production facility and your skills as a production person. As with the interview actualities, you may decide to put each narration segment on a separate cart or location in the digital sampler. Another choice is to record it in real-time, as you play the segments from cart.

Adding meaning to your topic are music and sound effects, which you select for some of the same reasons that you used when picking music for a commercial or PSA. On one level, music in your production could be a simple opening and closing theme to establish your show. At a higher level, music can be used to accent an important thought in the show, to be heard under narration, or to establish a transition from one idea or interview subject to the next. Library music may suffice, but if you are a more ambitious producer, you might even consider an original soundtrack for the production. Sound effects may not be needed for this production since most of the on-location interviews already have the city street noise background. That may be sound effect enough.

All these elements can now be combined, mixed, and edited into a final show. How this is done will depend on the facilities at your disposal. The simplest, quickest way is to do it in real-time, just like being on the air during a DJ show or a newscast. Think about what you do during a five-minute newscast; you read copy and push buttons containing taped actualities. Doing a documentary in this way is no different. With the addition of a CD player for the theme music, you simply load up all the cart playback machines with your edited segments, start an open-reel recorder, start the clock, and do the show in real-time or several longer segments. After it is done, edit out the pauses and mistakes. It's the fastest way.

Another way is to have everything on cart and just push buttons while following the script. Start cart one, the music, fade it down, and start cart two, the one with all the narration cuts in order. At the cue, start cart three for the first actuality. Back to cart two for the narration, back to cart one for the next actuality. If this is how you work best, do it. You could also have each segment on a separate small reel of tape and splice them all together, edit it some more, dub the finished tape to one track of a reel-to-reel master, and add the music to a separate track. There is one caution. If you began with a cassette interview of much of the show, dubbed it to reel, edited it and dubbed it to cart, transferred it back to reel, added music and dubbed, for a fifth generation away from the cassette original, you could encounter technical problems. Like the copy you make of a home videotape, a consumer analog format like the cassette loses quality and gains noise with every copy. Of course, if you are working entirely in the digital domain, no problem.

You have followed the traditional documentary process. You had an idea, researched it, and drew conclusions from the research. Now you are able to inform and even influence your audience into believing that in spite of all the talk about the homeless, no one has really solved the problem. It's only getting worse. Now that's something for your listeners to think about. It's what documentaries are all about.

SUMMARY

Objective news reporting and documentaries are different, of course, but both are expected of a radio station. There are times when a listener just wants to know about the events of the day, and there are times when a detailed treatment, complete with the editorial opinion of the broadcaster, is valued. With any informational format, just like any commercial, PSA, or promo, the most creative use of content for radio requires some production. Whether a package of a single story, a news magazine, or a complete documentary with music and sound effects, it is the production you do that makes the programming work. For you, it will be the production that turns the programming into a creative experience.

ACTIVITIES

1. Listen to an all-news station for a sample hour. Try to figure out its format. Is there a predictable time during the hour when sports, traffic, and weather are presented?
2. Listen to a typical five-minute newscast on a local station. What percentage of the total time devoted to news is "produced packages"?
3. Organize the class into groups and complete an informational magazine half-hour show.
4. Listen to your favorite music-formatted station. When does it air news, if any? When does it schedule longer public affairs shows and documentaries?
5. Ask your local public broadcasting station when it airs traditional radio documentaries.

Producing Drama and Comedy

Comedy and drama on radio peaked, died, made a comeback, and died again. It's back again, but instead of the half-hour comedy specials featuring the great comedians of the past, comedy is typically found in commercials and on specially produced bits for a morning DJ show. And, as with cable television, there are some full-time comedy formats delivered by satellite. These feature both contemporary and classic comics recorded in concert. Drama today is used like comedy, in commercials and features on music shows. If a full-length dramatic presentation makes it to the air today, it will be either in the form of an old show from radio's golden age or an experimental production done by a college or public radio station. Full-time comedy and drama are not money-making formats, but they are exciting to both produce and hear.

THE WAY WE WERE

Radio drama peaked as the driving force of radio in the decade of 1935–1945. After television took over drama entertainment, radio drama was virtually extinct by 1953. But it has slowly made a comeback. For example, in the 1970s, the original radio programs of the 1930s and 1940s, such as "The Shadow," "Fibber McGee and Molly," and "The Lone Ranger," were syndicated to radio stations across the country. Sears began sponsoring nightly dramas, comedies, and mysteries in 1979. In the 1980s, National Public Radio created a popular series called "The Spider's Web." NPR eventually collaborated with the **British Broadcasting Company, BBC,** to create programs such as "Masterpiece Radio Theatre," taken from the television series. Even thirteen episodes of "Star Wars" and "The Empire Strikes Back" were produced by this collaboration.

Radio comedies and dramas have their advantages, even if they can't compete on the same scale as television. Television's pictures are limited by the size of the screen, whereas radio's "pictures" can be any size at all. Virtually any situation can be created with good writing, good sound effects, and the right background music.

Your grandparents listened to old-time drama on a radio like this.

Consider these examples: people talking while underwater or inside a washing machine or even inside a dog's mouth; a live newscast from the planet Pluto; a piece of paper telling you how much it tickles when you write on its tummy. On television, these situations would cost a great deal of money and time to create. Radio's possibilities are limitless because it relies on the imagination of the listener, unlike television, which provides audio and visual information that guide the audience toward very specific meanings. Radio requires more work from its audience because it is the audience that ultimately interprets information and makes meaning of it. For example, radio needs its audience to fill in the missing visual information or perceptions of time and place. Consequently, the radio writer must choose words that create appropriate pictures in the listener's mind.

Radio dramas and comedies can be entertaining, but they can also influence and motivate the listening audience. The most notable example of a radio drama's power to influence people's imaginations was during the 1938 presentation of Orson Welles's "Mercury Theatre on the Air" broadcast of "Invasion from Mars," also known as "The War of the Worlds." The program depicted the Martian invasion in an emergency news format, which fooled listeners into believing the invasion was happening, causing a nationwide panic.

COMEDY AND DRAMA TODAY

Since radio drama will probably never be able to attract enough loyal listeners away from TV to make it economically feasible, it is most prominently found in radio commercials, because any commercial that tells a story is a mini radio drama. These little dramas have characters and a plot, typically a problem that can be solved by using a specific product.

BOX 14.1

Contemporary Radio Drama

One example of a new radio drama tradition can be found in "Grand Boulevard," a radio soap opera featuring the usual "soap" topics of love, marriage, philandering, murder, lying, cheating, medical exploits, and morals. But what makes "Grand Boulevard" different is that it features an all-black cast. It is based on the real-life Grand Boulevard neighborhood of Chicago, an historical place where blacks gathered at a time when they were restricted from other parts of the city.

Its producer, Tony Green, is a former aide to Jesse Jackson. Green describes his characters as "people who are driven by a purpose" and who come from all vocations in life, including doctors, lawyers, teachers, social workers, preachers, and judges. He feels this is especially important in these times where there are so few role models in the mass media available to blacks in this country. Green spent a great deal of time and energy promoting the program, and his persistence has paid off: "Grand Boulevard" is now syndicated five days a week to several major cities, such as Chicago, Los Angeles, Washington D.C., New York, and Cincinnati.

But despite its popularity and loyal following, Green is still having trouble finding advertising support for "Grand Boulevard." It seems advertisers are not easily convinced of the potential buying power of blacks. However, as more and more programs such as "Grand Boulevard" emerge and succeed, perhaps advertisers will recognize the economic potential of this demographic group.

PRODUCING AND DIRECTING A RADIO DRAMA

As a class project, the production of a drama for radio can be a creative challenge. The advantage of such a production is that you can take as much time as needed, an entire semester, to write or find a script, select and rehearse actors, and mount the actual production. If your school has a college radio station or if your community has a willing nonprofit station, you can get a drama on the air. Now consider format, script, talent, and production.

Format

There are several different formats that a radio drama can adopt, for example, mystery, adventure, soap opera, or science fiction. However, no matter what format is used, the target audience of the drama must be consistent with that of the station's. A comedy or drama featuring mature people over the age of sixty may not do very well on a heavy metal station. In fact, a radio drama would most likely not be considered for a music format because it would cause severe programming inconsistency. Consequently, what few radio dramas are presented can be found on talk-format stations or public radio stations. So the format you select for a college station can be practically anything.

The Script

The first step in producing a radio play is getting a good script, and there are only two ways to do this: use an existing script or write a script of your own. Existing scripts can come from a variety of sources. Libraries typically maintain collections of radio plays that have been produced over the years. Audio tapes are available that feature broadcasts of some classic radio shows like *The Lone Ranger* and *The Shadow*. Also, keep in mind that regular stage plays also can be adapted for radio. If you are planning to use an existing script, you must recognize that this material is copyrighted, which means you are not allowed to broadcast it without permission. If you plan to produce a play for profit, you must receive permission to use the script, which usually means paying a copyright fee. Costs vary from play to play. Even the use of a script on college radio requires permission and the payment of a reduced fee.

If you are going to write your own play, remember that the script is meant to be heard and not seen. Write for the ear, not the eye. You can take an original story or use an existing plot, poem, song, play, photograph, or painting and adapt it for radio. When writing the script, you must be familiar with standard script format for efficient production and so that others will be able to produce your script, as well.

Once you have decided on a script, become very familiar with it. The best way to do this is by reading the script out loud. You can read it alone or alternate characters with an assistant to get a feeling for how the script will be actually broadcast and to help alert you to the specifics of dramatic moments or good places for sound effects, music, and so on. This exercise also provides an estimate of the overall length of the production.

Timing the first reading of a script will give you a rough estimate and indicate whether major cuts must be made if it runs too long. Using a stopwatch is the best method for timing because you can stop the time if you are interrupted during the reading. Once you have established the pace of the production and ascertained the mood that you want to communicate, it is time to cast the characters.

Talent

When producing a radio comedy or drama program, the requirements of your cast members are quite different from those of a straight announcer. Voice affectation and quality are most important. Audition as many people as possible for your production in order to take full advantage of the available talent. Remember you can recruit just about anywhere. Place an ad in the school newspaper, post flier announcements, or even produce an announcement for auditions and play it on your college radio station.

Keep written records on those who apply. Make notations about an applicant's name, address, phone number, voice quality, experience, audition performance, and availability for work. These records will also allow you to recall people for future productions. Since you will most likely be involved with students, it is important to remember that students move around a lot. Include a line for a permanent address and phone number so you can contact these people from semester to semester. Box 14.2 gives an example of an audition card.

▼

BOX 14.2   *Example of an Audition Card*

Personal Information

1. Name:
2. Address:
3. Phone: (   )
4. Permanent Address:
5. Permanent Phone: (   )
6. Date of graduation:
7. Please consider your school schedule and other obligations and indicate what times you are available to work on this project.
8. Age:
9. Gender:

Experience and Training

1. What experience have you had in speech, drama, radio, or television? Please indicate dates, names of productions, positions held, and parts played.
2. Do you speak any foreign languages? How well?
3. What dialects or accents can you do?
4. What impersonations can you do?
5. Can you produce any sound effects with your voice? (For example, a siren, a dog barking, a motorcycle accelerating, etc.)
6. Do you sing?
7. What type of music?
8. Do you play any musical instruments?
9. Any other qualifications you want to tell us about?

Audition Results

1. When speaking naturally, what kind of voice does this person have? Child? Boy or girl? Juvenile? Mature? Aged? Other?
   For the following sections rate the voice using the shorthand:
   G = Good
   F = Fair
   P = Poor
2. Are there any defects or noticeable voice qualities?
   Pronunciation?
   Pace?
   Energy?
   Accent?
   Colloquialism?
   Artificiality?
   Other?

▼

BOX 14.2   *continued*

   3. How was this actor/actress able to affect the following characters?

      Child?

      Boy or girl?

      Juvenile?

      Mature?

      Aged?

      Foreign (what nationality, type, and age)?

      Caricature (animals, lisps, snobby nasal talk, etc.)?

      Other?

   4. Acting abilities:

      Dramatic quality

      Articulation

      Volume

   5. What was your overall impression of this voice?

   6. Additional comments and notes.

Once you have auditioned all applicants, weigh your choices according to these considerations: individual voice qualities, the combination of different voices (think contrast!), acting abilities, and any special qualifications for specific parts. Making casting decisions is not always an easy process. Again, you must be flexible and make the best of the available talent. As soon as you have reached your final decision, post a casting sheet, along with the schedule of rehearsal times. Do this in a timely fashion; don't keep candidates waiting. Of course, as a practical matter, you'll probably be assigned an entire class with which you are expected to work.

Sound Effects

Once you have cast your play, you should then begin to collect your sound effects, **SFX.** One of the best ways to determine what sound effects you will need is to have your cast read through the entire script very slowly and note every place a nonvocal sound can be used. Keep this list for a reference. Remember, you don't have to limit yourself to what sounds are available in your SFX library because you can go out and record—actually create your own sounds as is necessary. Since SFX bring life to your production by providing information for the listener's imagination, it is very important to take your time and choose them carefully. Once you have acquired all the SFX on your list, collect them onto a single reel of tape. You don't have to record them in the order they will appear, but it does make your production run much more smoothly if the SFX are ordered. Either way, make sure you keep a log of exactly what is on the reel.

Music

Once you have collected all of your SFX, you can turn your attention to music. Music can be used to communicate a variety of feelings or emotions. In addition, music can set a mood, establish a time or place, signal a change of time and place, and build tension toward a climax. It isn't necessary to have music playing continuously throughout the play. Shorter music cues can have a better effect. Background music is designed for the background. Don't let music overpower a character's dialogue. Choose music that blends in well and isn't distracting. Don't forget that music is also copyrighted, so you must get permission to use it or utilize a music library where the rights have been purchased already.

Keep all your music cuts on the same reel, just as you did with your voice tracks and sound effects. Be sure to allow yourself more music than you think you will need because you can always fade out if the music runs too long. If you run out of music, you'll be stuck and will most likely have to do it again.

DRAMA PRODUCTION

The actual production includes a few initial rehearsals, then a final dress or studio rehearsal, complete with equipment and engineers. A director will be needed, and sound effects and music will have to be ready. Finally, it will all be put onto tape for later broadcast.

Before the Taping

The cast must be able to rehearse the script many times before actual program presentation or production. The first reading of the script gives the cast a feeling for the movement of the story from beginning to end. At this time, you will have an opportunity to correct mistakes. Cast members might mispronounce a word or misunderstand a line or a point in the plot. You need to correct these mistakes right away before the cast gets used to the wrong way and it becomes too difficult to change later. Don't over-rehearse the cast or it might lose its excitement for the program. Instead of going over the entire production every time, initiate a cue rehearsal. This rehearsal covers only the difficult or rough spots of the script and skips those scenes that have been well-rehearsed and have no problems.

The initial rehearsals do not necessarily need to be conducted in the sound studio. However, you must conduct at least one dress rehearsal before the production. This rehearsal is conducted in the studio and requires every person involved with the show to be present. This is the closest rehearsal to the actual presentation and, consequently, contains all aspects of the program, including special effects and music.

This rehearsal is not interrupted. It is conducted as if it were the real thing. After the studio rehearsal, you will present your impressions of the actor's performances and make any changes before the final presentation.

In the Studio

The director is an important person. Directing is an exercise in the creation of art. Good directors realize that each sound, whether it is speech, a sound effect, or music, has aesthetic value and causes the listener to think and to feel. When directing, you arrange many of these important and powerful sounds in a meaningful way. As with all production, radio drama and comedy can be performed live or can be prerecorded. Again, the advantage to live production is spontaneity and possible audience reaction input. However, prerecorded programs allow you retakes and editing options. Your first production using drama and actors will be a taped one.

Recording the voice tracks is the first step in prerecorded production. Ideally, it is best to record your talent at the same time in the studio. Allowing cast members to be in the presence of each other can often add to better rapport and interaction. If you must record the voices separately, edit them down to one voice track to be mixed with the other aspects of your production later. Remember that voices are unique in pitch and volume. Therefore, if you have two or more people sharing a microphone, a strong voice could distort while a softer voice could be lost. It is best to mic talent separately, as it makes mixing so much easier. When using separate mics, leave enough room between them to avoid one voice being picked up by another person's microphone and wave cancellation, an out-of-phase effect. Also, make sure to position your microphones where the talent can see you at all times. Cast members cannot respond to your direction if they cannot see you.

When possible, route individual microphones to different channels on the audio board so you can easily adjust levels. If you have too many cast members, take their voice levels carefully. Those voices that produce similar levels should share the same microphone so your engineer will not have to constantly adjust. Distance to the mic also plays a major role in creating the illusion of place, movement, and background noise. You won't create a believable illusion of a person calling someone from across a field if you place the mic two inches from his or her mouth. Since every studio is uniquely configured, experiment with various sounds to achieve the desired effect. Do remember that the actual slamming of a door may not be "heard" by the microphone the same way your ear hears it. Play it safe and dub in sound effects when possible.

Keep in close contact with your engineer throughout the production. The engineer is a technical expert and can often make very useful suggestions about how a specific desired sound effect or music bed can be accomplished. In addition, the engineer will be able to predict possible audio and technical problems in advance of the actual production, which can save you a great deal of time and trouble.

COMEDY ON RADIO

Comedy uses the same production procedures as drama. You still work with a script, organize the production, audition and select talent, choose appropriate music, and utilize sound effects. You still must create while adhering to the boundaries set by programming and more specifically, format. Full-length comedy programs are as few and far between as radio dramas; however, using mini-comedies in the form of commercials, station promotions, contests, and DJ programs is a widely popular programming approach. Most comedy today found on the radio is in the form of small, produced segments heard on the morning zoo DJ formats and on commercials.

Comedy is more of a style than a format. The basic goal of comedy is to amuse the audience. The idea is, if listeners are enjoying themselves, they might tune in more often to have fun. Typically, humor is used to grab the listener's attention. However, humor should be used to enhance the message, not overpower it.

Developing comedy is not as easy as it sounds. Very few people are actually good at this, and there is nothing worse than an unfunny person trying to be funny. If you are writing humorous scripts, remember that what may be hilarious on the page may sound quite ordinary when read out loud. The best way to determine how comedy works, and thus be able to recognize or even create funny material, is to study those who are successful in the field. Listen to comedy DJ teams, watch stand-up comics on TV, and consume funny material wherever you can find it. Once you have created humor of your own, be sure to "test it" by letting others listen to your ideas. Try to find people who will be honest and not simply tell you what you would like to hear.

KHQT's morning team works in separate studios but they see each other via small TV cameras and monitors.

Mini-radio dramas and comedies are frequently used in commercials, contests, DJ programs, and promotions. But what if you decide to test your skills and produce a full-length drama or comedy program? Where will you go with the finished product? Who will play it? As discussed earlier, public radio stations, and especially community and college radio, aren't as concerned about a program's economic viability as they are concerned about serving the public with novel and original programming, especially that created locally. And since these stations typically adopt a wide array of formats, it is much more plausible that they could and would fit a radio drama or comedy into their programming schedules.

SUMMARY

In early radio, especially 1935–1945, drama and comedy were the mainstays of the medium. But with the advent of television, these formats were abandoned because they could not compete with the new visual medium. Nevertheless, mini versions of these styles can still be found in commercials, promotions, DJ programs, and contests. Production concerns for radio drama and comedy include:

1. Working within the programming format.
2. Writing or securing the rights to a script.
3. Auditioning, selecting, and rehearsing talent.
4. Choosing music.
5. Acquiring the appropriate sound effects.
6. Technical considerations.
7. Working with the engineer.
8. Establishing distribution outlets.

Radio dramas and comedies, unlike television pictures, are not visually limited. By effectively using sound effects, music, and dialogue, you can create virtually any situation with the help of your listeners' imaginations.

ACTIVITIES

1. Go to your favorite music store and buy some old radio programs, usually found on cassette tape. Take your time listening to how pictures are created in your mind by the sounds put together in the programs. Note how many different sound effects were used in one program alone.
2. Check your local public radio station for more contemporary radio drama programming. Tune in to hear how these shows are being produced.
3. Create a ten- to fifteen-minute radio drama or comedy of your own.

15

The Disc Jockey

▼

What is the first thing you think about when you turn on the radio? Commercials? Probably not. News? Perhaps. The truth is, if you're like most listeners, the first image received when the radio is switched on is that of the disc jockey. The disc jockey, or **DJ,** is a concept that has been evolving for more than eighty years. Today, the disc jockey is simply the person who pushes the buttons that start the music that a station plays, tells the listener about that music, and, in between, reads live or plays prerecorded commercials, PSAs and promos, tells the time and the weather, and even tries to be funny. Above all, the DJ is a performer, an unseen entertainer who comes out of your radio. The disc jockey has always brought an element of "show business" to the business of radio.

And the major activity of the disc jockey? You guessed it: nonstop production and lots of it, all in the presentation of a particular station's format. In fact, if your experience in production for radio until now has been that of the individual, planned-in-advance project, the experience of being a disc jockey will be a brand-new and different creative challenge. As a DJ, you are really performing continuous production. Instead of starting the music, fading it under, and talking in the production of a single, well-rehearsed commercial, PSA, or promo, you'll repeat these tasks and more dozens of times during a three- to six-hour air shift. Make a mistake? When you are the DJ, there is no going back. Whatever production you do, it's live and in real-time. The disc jockey is the person at the music-formatted station responsible for the on-air programming of the radio station by performing continuous production.

THE VERY SLOW RISE OF THE DJ

Disc jockeys have been both some of the most obscure and the most visible people in broadcasting. It all started at the turn of the century, when the term *radio* had not yet come into popular use. Then, it was **wireless,** so-named for a telegraph without connecting wires, and so it was only the dots and dashes of Morse code used for two-way communication. Some wanted to go further; seeing the advantages of a wireless telephone, a handful of experimenters were learning how to make the new device talk, even play music. In 1906, Canadian inventor Reginald Fessenden developed

The Herrold College, shown around the time of World War I. (Courtesy of the Perham Foundation Electronics Museum, San Jose, CA)

one of the first methods for broadcasting the human voice using wireless telegraph technology. He talked, and he played phonograph records. His audience was only a handful of listeners.

But there was one individual who first really performed many of the activities of the contemporary DJ: announcing records on a weekly program, playing listener requests, and even getting record service from the local music store. Her name was Sybil Herrold. The story of the world's first disc jockey begins in 1909 in the Garden City Bank building in downtown San Jose, California. It was at a school that trained men for new jobs in the shipping industry that required knowledge of radio apparatus and some skill in sending and receiving messages between ship and shore stations. The job title was wireless operator, and the school was Charles D. "Doc" Herrold's College of Wireless Engineering.

To broadcast, Herrold tapped into the electrical supply used for the streetcars and ran it through a water-cooled telephone microphone. This was connected to a transformer designed to increase the voltage and generate an arc to which an antenna was connected. Normally, an arc like this would have been turned on and off using a telegraph key to send code. Herrold substituted the telephone for the telegraph key, and when it was spoken into, the resulting variable voltage modulated, or affected, the arc and audio was heard. Voices and music on radio.

Herrold began a weekly broadcast schedule, and, while no formal audience surveys were done in those days, letters from listeners proved that people did tune in on a regular basis to hear the broadcasts of talk, music, and news. Herrold and his wife asked the local record store if some sort of arrangement might be worked out whereby the station could play the latest records in exchange for telling its growing audience where the records could be purchased. Sybil Herrold was the one who sat in front of the microphone and played the records on a wind-up gramophone, the horn of which was aimed at the telephone microphone. She announced the titles of the records, which she said could be purchased at the local store. Apparently, her program sold records. She even held weekly contests and awarded a small prize to the listener who called in with the correct answer. Sound like radio today? This early attempt was perhaps the first "sponsored" DJ broadcast.

The Charles Herrold radio station, circa 1912. (Courtesy of the Perham Foundation Electronics Museum, San Jose, CA)

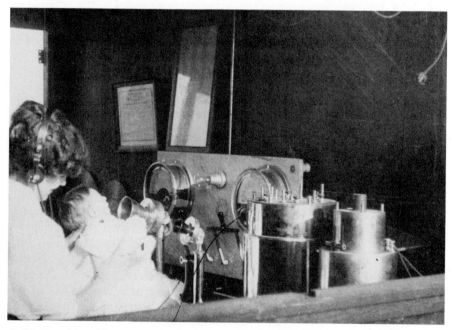

Sybil Herrold and her son, Robert, are "on the air." (Courtesy of the Perham Foundation Electronics Museum, San Jose, CA)

Herrold was broadcasting long before the federal government even thought of issuing licenses for stations. Organized commercial broadcasting would have to wait until the conclusion of World War I. A number of stations went on the air in 1920, KDKA in Pittsburgh, WWJ in Detroit, and WHA in Madison among them. Throughout the 1920s, the broadcasting era came to full fruition as the public made, and later was able to purchase, commercially built radios. By the end of the decade, the Federal Radio Commission had been established to license and regulate the hundreds of signals.

If smaller stations were still playing phonograph records, most were experimenting with other forms of entertainment. Taking their cues from the public entertainment of the times—live theater, music, and vaudeville—programming on the new medium of radio was provided by all kinds of performers, actors, comedians, and musicians. With the exception of the rare sustaining interview or news show, broadcasting was mostly sponsored, entertainment-based programming. Throughout the 1930s, national networks and their high-priced shows dominated, and radio became the most popular medium ever. It was the era of the highly paid personality and the strong entertainment industry labor union.

One of the most influential and powerful unions was the American Federation of Musicians. As an organization representing anyone who recorded or played live music on radio, the AF of M was able to effectively influence, even control, the format of musical presentation on radio. To this group, it could only be done live. The nationally popular shows had to be done live twice, once for the East Coast and again for the western time zone. Acetate disk recordings of entire shows, called **transcriptions,** crude as they were, were not allowed by the union. The union even forbade major networks and large- and medium-market stations from playing their members' records on the air. If any broadcaster other than those in the smallest markets tried to put a disc jockey-like program of recorded music on the air during the 1930s, the union could prevent its member musicians from ever appearing live on that station or network again. Since major programs depended on live musicians, it was too great a risk.

Historians point to an accidental event in the late 1930s as the official start of the modern disc jockey era. New York announcer Martin Block felt he had no choice but to play phonograph records when the scheduled orchestra failed to appear for a program. The resulting disc jockey program, later known as the "Make Believe Ballroom," was a large success. It finally demonstrated that the audience liked hearing the hit music of the day on the radio, and it proved to musicians that broadcast exposure could also sell their records. Musicians, who formerly believed that **canned,** or recorded, presentations of their work would prevent them from getting paid live jobs, thus reducing their incomes, now saw great wealth coming from records. The unions, already under considerable governmental and business pressure to curb their monopolistic practices, had no choice but to go along with the membership. The door was open for the DJ.

The disc jockey remains the major staple of radio. Sure, the job has changed a lot since big-city personalities received cash, known as **payola,** from record companies for playing a new record. Just as the demise of AM led to the rise of FM, digital systems and direct broadcast satellites will challenge FM as the main delivery format. Whatever that outcome, radio will still be a distributor of specific formats of recorded music, designed for a very narrowly defined audience. And the more things appear to change, the more they remain the same.

Take the morning show, for example. In the early days of radio, the morning drive-time program was usually a glib personality, often a comic, sometimes a musician, but almost always a magazine show of entertainment and information. Today, the morning zoo format is little more than an updated version of the "Don McNeil Breakfast Club" of a half century ago. Still entertaining, still zany. Only the names of the personalities and the music have changed.

THE ACTIVITIES OF THE DJ

What about the on-air life of a modern disc jockey? It's all about music sweeps, stop sets, and following the clock. These three commonly used terms are all a part of the lexicon of radio, in which each hour of programming is broken down into the specifics of the format for the disc jockey to follow while on the air. The **clock,** sometimes known as the format wheel, simply shows when the DJ must play music and from which category, and when the DJ must talk and play commercials or other prerecorded material. The typical hour may begin with a twenty-minute block of music as specified by the rotation sequence of the format, uninterrupted by commercials, but with quick five-second recorded promos or call letters interspersed between the songs. This is known as a **music sweep.** The music ends and the DJ may **back announce** the titles of the records in the music sweep and then play several commercials, PSAs, or promos. This is called a *stop set.* A typical hour clock on a music-formatted station may require the DJ to play three music sweeps and three stop sets.

What a DJ Does

Look at a day in the life of a disc jockey:

The clock radio next to your bed has suddenly come alive with a song in your rotation. Through the mist that is waking up, you imagine that you must be on the air. The record suddenly ends, you grope for your headphones, frantic because you have to talk and you can't find the microphone switch on the console. You can't even find the console! Then a familiar voice jolts you into reality. It's the voice of the overnight DJ, and you realize that you have to get up fast and prepare for your air shift. It's 5:00 A.M. and you have to be on the air in one hour. Another day of morning radio awaits your experienced touch. The audience will be waiting for you. A quick shower, a jolt of coffee, and you're on the freeway for your premorning drive-time commute.

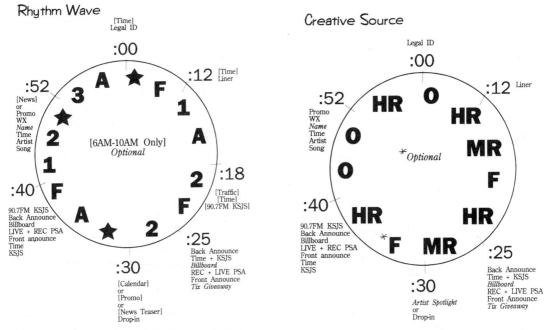

Shown are two variations of the format clock.

Thinking back, it seems like only yesterday you were in college. Ah, college radio: Those were the days. You were quite a star on the station there; you held the student positions of chief announcer, production director, and program director. You did a somewhat humorous morning show; you always liked to get up early, liked to be a major part of people's day. In fact, you were so confident of your skills that it was a bit of a letdown when a small local station hired you to do overnight, two A.M. to six A.M. The graveyard shift. Well, at least it was a job in radio, even though it wasn't the big time. Then it happened. The morning DJ got a better offer, and your persistence with the program director, those daily visits with the tapes of your overnights, paid off. You were given a chance to do the all-important morning shift. Of course, this is a small station and the morning shift is no zoo; it's just you as DJ and a news reader who comes in for a few minutes each hour. Uh, here's the parking lot.

It's still dark as you press the night bell, smile at the TV camera above the door, and wait to be buzzed in by the DJ on duty. Now the human population of the station has doubled, and the all-night DJ has a live person with whom to interact. You banter for a few minutes as you look at the program log to determine what the spot load is going to be like. It's a Monday, so there aren't very many commercials during most hours. Friday is real hectic; that's the day when everyone wants to advertise. But today you can play more promos, and you can use more of your prerecorded comedy bits and production goodies, those creative bits of production that are uniquely you. Anyway, you grab the music log that has been prepared for your shift and quickly glance at it. One great thing about a tight music format is that you don't have to spend time searching for music and planning what you are going to play. It's all done by the music director, a person you believe is really a computer. You can spend all your creative time on what you are going to do and say for your listeners. Ten minutes till air time.

You have a couple of tasks to complete before the change of the shift from overnight to morning drive. You go to the news wire and quickly scan it for features like "today in history," "famous people's birthdays," and all the lighter side stuff that DJs have been using for decades. You have to be more careful this morning; the newsperson was a bit upset on Friday because when you cleared the wire, you left all that you didn't use in a giant heap. After a few minutes with the wire, you sit at a desk and rewrite the local weather forecast from the morning paper, and call the weather station for the temperature and call the highway patrol for the traffic updates. Next hour, all this will be done for you by the newsperson, but now it's all part of your preparation routine. Five minutes till air.

You unlock a cabinet and get out your personal headset and a stack of carts. You scrounge around the office for a decent pen and head into the on-air control room. The overnight DJ is nowhere to be found. Knowing you are here, he simply put on his final song, grabbed his pen and headset, signed off the log, and split. You are in charge, and the song is ending, the request line is flashing, the transmitter warning light is blinking, and the studio is littered with paper, soda cans, and candy wrappers. Now to an outsider, it might seem like a time for panic. To you, it is the start of a very typical day. Quick as a flash, just like shifting gears on a car, you plug in your headset and adjust the volume, set the console for your voice level, adjust the microphone to your height, pop a CD into the empty player, select the cut specified on your music rotation log, all in about five seconds. The phone and transmitter lights can wait.

You give a **legal ID,** an FCC requirement for call letters and location at the top of the hour; "KSJS, San Jose." You say something very funny (to you, at least), start the CD, and your show is under way. First things first. You grab all the CDs for the first music sweep, you look at the log and pull all the scheduled tapes for the first stop set, even load the first three into the cart machines. Now you can relax a bit and finish setting up the room. You sign on the transmitter log and press the "power lower" button so that the pesky warning light will go away. You sign on the program log, and then you place all logs, weather copy, and carts in an easy-to-grab place. You even spend a second or two cleaning up from the last shift. You can even think about what you are going to say while you segue through a few songs.

Now the typical hour is under way, an hour filled with continuous, nonstop production. It's another hour where, at any given moment, the DJ is a few minutes or a few seconds away from that unacceptable silence, the dreaded **dead air.** Table 15.1 shows some of the activities you will be expected to perform in your role as a never-stopping radio production person, a disc jockey.

TABLE 15.1   *The On-Air Activities of a DJ*

What	When	Why
Keep program log, write down everything aired	All throughout the air shift	Record-keeping for FCC and advertisers
Keep engineering or operating log	Start and end of shift	FCC requires it several times daily, some stations hourly
Follow music log	Every time a song is played	Rotation of music format, what to play and when
Follow clock	Always	Station format
Play prerecorded commercials, PSAs, and promos	When scheduled on clock or log	Contract with advertisers or station format
Play music	Scheduled on music sheet or log	Station format
Announce, talk, read	On clock, format	Station format
Talk on phone	Scheduled contests, when listener feedback is wanted, requests	Station format
Operate equipment	Continuously	

What a DJ Says

Sure, most stations have a format that is tight, or specific enough that a DJ knows exactly when to play a certain song and when to play commercials, PSAs, and promos. But what about the rest of what the DJ says? This is often part of the format, just like the music. Some stations hire generic announcers and tell them exactly what to say and when to say it; some stations hire personalities and give them some guidelines; and other stations don't care what their DJs say as long as they say it quickly and get back to the music. What a disc jockey must say and is allowed to say is, of course, up to management and the particular programming philosophy of the station. And like all of radio, what the DJ actually says has changed much since Martin Block began to very formally announce the hits of the day.

In those early days, everything was scripted, written out ahead of time. But starting in the 1950s, most of what the DJ would say began to be more **ad-lib,** an abbreviation for add liberally. In the beginning, the disc jockey felt like he needed to speak the language of the teenager of the time. Whether the jive talk of New York DJ "Murray the K" Kaufman on WINS or the soulful communicating of LA's "Wolfman Jack" on a powerful Mexican border station, the early DJ had no real rules; just get a big audience, and the sales department will try to do the rest. If talking the language of the kids worked, great. Later, as more stations realized that what the audience really wanted was much more music, the personality of the disc jockey began to be severely reined in. Signs on the control room walls of 1960s rock stations stated simple programming philosophies like "be bright, be brief" or "time and temperature only."

As radio stations became more competitive, and as more stations in a single market began playing similar music, the personality was all but replaced by a human machine. The rules were simple: when the record ends, announce its title, give the station call letters, say the correct time. No more, no less. Push the button and start the next song or commercial. It was a successful formula that seemed to work for the typical AM powerhouse in the 1960s, one that played the same forty songs over and over. But another revolution was simmering. With the popularity of the Beatles and the release of albums containing songs lasting five or more minutes, an *underground* music audience was growing, one that was getting tired of the formula radio of time and temperature, bright and brief. Formerly money-losing FM stations began to find an audience, so-called *progressive rock* radio happened fast, and once again, the DJ had no rules. Again, the disc jockey was free to talk about the music, to speak the language of the audience.

Today, most music-formatted stations still require their DJs to say specific things at certain times during the hour. Call letters and place on the dial, such as "90.7 FM, KSJS," are usually heard after every song. Positioning statements like "the Bay Area's best new music" are said often. Liners announcing contests and other features like "instant request radio," add to what the on-air DJ must continuously say in the service of a consistent station sound. Even when the morning DJ or team of DJs, known as the morning zoo, can seemingly say whatever comes to their minds and develop outrageous comedy bits, a closer listen will reveal that the important elements of the modern format are still there; the call letters are still heard after every song or comedy bit, the positioning liners are still present. There is still a planned, overall station identity.

The disc jockey has served radio well. He or she has slavishly followed rules that seem to change every time the ratings fall or the next big innovation is embraced by management. But the basic activities of the DJ, what the DJ says and

Positioning information in control room of KHQT, Hot 97.7, San Jose.

does, have not changed all that much since Martin Block was forced to fill in with records and talk because of a missing orchestra. Following and keeping the program schedule or log up to date, announcing song titles, turning on and off a microphone, and starting the music and other recorded production all have been lifelong duties of the disc jockey. Music changed from big band to rock, AM was replaced by FM, and records gave way to CDs, but the DJ remains at the heart of the radio station.

When the Music's Over

Most air shifts are short enough that the on-air disc jockey is expected to perform other duties as a full-time station employee. The most common of these duties is production. At many stations, there is a production director who looks at all the requests by sales and programming for produced commercials, PSAs, and promos, and then assigns the concept or script to a DJ. On the production request form, information about the production is listed, like the type of music or treatment wanted, the air dates, the log number that is to be put on the label of the cart, and the **kill date,** or last day of broadcast. At large- and major-market stations, an **AFTRA,** or **American Federation of Television and Radio Artists,** union contract may even specify exactly how much production a DJ is expected to perform and at what compensation level.

Sometimes, the DJ is expected to attend store openings, visit sponsors, and even make personal appearances at schools, parades, and community and civic events. At other stations, the DJ wears a sales or management hat either before or after the air shift. In the very small markets with very few employees, the morning DJ often will make some sales calls after the shift has ended. In small towns, this is often an advantage because an announcer can make personal contact with the advertiser and make some extra money in sales commissions. At the medium-market station, when there is no union restriction, management and administrative types like program director, production director, promotions director, and music director will be expected to fill an air shift. Instead of doing production after the air shift, these individuals may attend meetings or, in general, plan the activities required to support the format. At smaller stations, even the DJ/program director will have to do some share of the production.

NONFORMAT DJ PROGRAMMING

While most commercial station disc jockey programming is highly formatted, there are some exceptions. Specialty music shows on format stations and college and community radio stations with their blocks of programming often provide opportunities for a DJ to do something original, out of the format. What is nonformat DJ programming? It is simply a program where the normal scientific rotation is suspended for a good reason. A station whose format is popular music may decide that it can

*A student does production
for a college radio station.*

benefit from a Saturday night program of all listener-requested oldies. In this case, the listeners, rather than a computer, program the station. Or a jazz station may decide that it will air a two-hour blues music program on the weekend. Although the stations are not seriously altering the music their audience expects to hear, these examples are deviations from the normal format. Such a show often can find a sponsor on a commercial station, perhaps during a nondrive time when most advertisers would not be interested in spending their money.

Community and college stations are often *block programmed.* This simply means that every hour or two-hour segment of time could conceivably have a totally different kind of programming, all in blocks, each one done by a different DJ. Such a station might have post-modern rock from 6 A.M.–10 A.M., jazz from 10 A.M.–2 P.M., rock again from 2 P.M.–6 P.M., news from 6 P.M.–8 P.M., and classical music from 8 P.M. to midnight. This nonformat programming is mostly done by individual DJs, as opposed to a program director and music director, and the listeners always need a program schedule to find out when the type of music they are interested in will be aired. Many of these stations have members or paid subscribers who receive a monthly program guide showing the schedule of the programs offered.

What are the qualifications for being a nonformat, specialty music DJ? Years of experience in radio? A college degree? Not at all. The only radio experience required is some knowledge of equipment operation and an FCC operator's license. What is really required is that you be an expert in your chosen area of music and, in the case of some nonprofit stations, have a collection of music for your program.

A college radio station uses a flier to recruit students.

The most interesting nonformat specialty music shows are done by volunteers who are themselves musicians or music historians, people who have spent a lifetime pursuing the hobby of collecting a type of music while learning enough to talk about on the air. If the station already has determined that it will play, for example, jazz during a certain block of time, all you have to do is go to the station and show that you are knowledgeable about jazz music. You'll be put into the station's training program, you'll send for a license, and soon you'll be on the air. In the past, DJs actually had to take an FCC exam; today, a simple postcard with your name and address is all that is required.

Other community and public stations may have an open format; they may have lots of air time and have to fill it with anyone who wants to be on the air. Stations that air any innovative type of music programming usually want a brief written proposal and a sample tape. If they like the idea and if it fits within the mission and the political bent of the stations, they may train you right away so that you can eventually do everything involved in the show's production on your own. Many volunteers will actually produce the program at their homes or an outside studio, and they simply show up each week with the tape. This is one way the smaller college and community stations are able to stay on the air. There are usually plenty of opportunities to produce and package a program of your favorite nonformat music at small community stations. You won't get paid, but you'll get experience.

KSJS
TRANSMITTER LOG
90.7 MHz

	E.B.S.
KSJS	
KSJX	

DAY _SATURDAY_

DATE _MAY 29 93_

CARRIER ON _CONT_

CARRIER OFF _____

PROGRAM ON _CONT_

PROGRAM OFF _____

CARRIER ON _____

CARRIER OFF _____

PROGRAM ON _____

PROGRAM OFF _____

OPERATORS	
ON 12m	OFF 2m
ON 2:00	OFF 6:00
ON 6:00	OFF 10:00
ON	OFF
ON	OFF
ON	OFF
ON	OFF
ON	OFF
ON	OFF
ON	OFF
ON	OFF

TIME	PLATE VOLTS(2)	PLATE AMPS(4)	RF OUTPUT(3)	REMARKS
12:00 AM	3068	.305	100%	
1:00 AM	3075	.307	100%	
2:00 AM	3070	.309	100%	
3:00 AM	3054	.303	100%	
4:00 AM	3061	.304	100%	
5:00 AM	3103	.305	101%	
6:00 AM	3067	.303	100%	
7:00 AM	3068	.308	100%	
8:00 AM	3063	.307	100%	
9:00 AM	3061	.304	100%	
10:00 AM	3065	.305	100%	
11:00 AM				
12:00 PM				
1:00 PM				
2:00 PM				
3:00 PM				
4:00 PM				
5:00 PM				
6:00 PM				
7:00 PM				
8:00 PM				
9:00 PM				
10:00 PM				
11:00 PM				

REMARKS:

A log must be kept of transmitter operations.

TABLE 15.2	*Structure and Elements of the Audition Tape*

(a) Song one fades out, 5 seconds.

(b) You back-announce song, give call letters of station, 5 seconds.

(c) You read a PSA, 20 seconds.

(d) Song two begins, you announce over instrumental open, music establishes, edit to ending, 15 seconds total.

(e) You give call letters, and read weather and temperature, 10 seconds.

(f) You start three 30-second productions showcasing the variety of your production (one straight, one comedy, one with technical originality if possible, all stuff you have written and voiced).

(g) Add a minute of news or a segment of produced informational if you have it (optional).

Total = 3 to 5 minutes

PRODUCING AN AUDITION PACKAGE

If you are serious about a paying radio career, you'll always need three things: a brief audio sample of your latest and best work, an up-to-date resume, and a cover or transmittal letter to each individual employer. All three are important, all three are part of the *audition package:*

1. An audition tape, usually three minutes or less, that highlights your best work will be requested by every employer when applying for an on-air position. If you have been an on-air DJ at the college station, you already have samples of your on-air performance. "Telescope," or condense, the best parts of the tape and leave only the opening few seconds of the music after you have finished announcing music or reading a PSA. Put on a few of your best-produced PSAs and promos, and even a bit of a newscast, if you have one. The tape should be recorded using the best possible equipment, mastered, and edited on high-quality reel-to-reel, then dubbed to cassette for mailing.

2. A resume should give any vital information that can be of value to an employer seeking to hire someone in any area of radio, on-air or off. After your name, address, and phone number, list your education, what schools and when attended, and when you graduated. You should list high school, community college, trade and specialty schools, and four-year university and graduate programs, but don't bother with grade school and junior high. This listing should be simple. Add dates of attendance and degrees completed, if any. After education, list relevant work and professional experience, paid and unpaid. It's probably not important that you delivered newspapers in the sixth grade, but the internship at the local television station, your college

radio career, or your DJ job at the club will interest the employer. The most important thing about the resume is that it must be honest. A long resume that is padded with useless and dubious information will be very obvious to any employer.

3. A cover letter is simply a letter of interest and intent, designed to be the first thing that the employer reads. A phone call to the station to find out the name, exact title, and correct spelling of the program director or manager will give you information that will allow you to speak directly to that person by letter: "Dear Mr. Crane . . . I have just graduated from San Jose State with a degree in radio and television. I have been on the college station, KSJS-FM, for the past two years and was the program director during my senior year. As you know, we were named 'Best Station of 1991' by the National Association of College Broadcasters. I have learned much from college radio and now that graduation is near, I want to work in commercial broadcasting. Please listen to the enclosed tape and I'll contact you by phone in a week. Thanks, etc. and etc." To the point and sincere, the cover letter sets the tone for the attached tape and resume.

Both the production quality of the tape and the appearance of the written communication will speak volumes about you as a radio person. If your tape is not tight or does not represent your best work, never send it out. A company is not likely to hire you for radio production if your tape is sloppy. And, if you appear to misrepresent your background, past jobs held, and other experience, you'll not be trusted, not hired. The physical look of your printed materials is just as important as the sound of your tape, because, in a way, you have produced the resume and cover letter using some of the same organizational skills that went into the tape. You decided what was important and its order; you edited. Always have someone check your written materials for spelling and grammar. Even for an audio production or disc jockey job, it's more important than you think.

Either mail or deliver your package in person to the person in charge, usually the program director, personnel manager, or general manager, depending on the size of the station and the job you are seeking. Always follow your package with a phone call: "Did you get my package?" "When can I come in for a personal interview?" "I realize there are no jobs now, but I just graduated and I am very interested in working for your station in the future." "Can I talk to you about my tape?" If it is a station where you really want to work, ask if there are any non-DJ jobs that you might be able to perform. If not, ask what kind of experience will best prepare you for a job at that station. All this is great experience. Rejections, the usual advice to go to a small town in Iowa for that first job—this is the stuff of radio careers.

SUMMARY

Disc jockey-based programming is the economic basis of modern radio. Under direction, it is the disc jockey who is responsible for presenting directly to the listener all of the programming heard on a radio station. The typical day for a disc jockey might consist of an air shift of from three to six hours, four being the average. The DJ may also be responsible for a one- or two-hour production shift where he or she can expect to apply creative ideas in the service of a sponsor, a nonprofit organization, or in the promotion of the station itself. At medium- and small-market stations, the program director and other administrative programming personnel will all have a DJ shift.

So while you may spend considerable time as a production person in the studio designing a single thirty-second PSA, chances are you will spend most of your radio career on the air as a DJ. And while someday you may produce a documentary, a comedy series, or a radio play, you will first be a disc jockey because that is the main business of radio. Once you have established and proved yourself, you may have a chance to do different types of production. Once you have decided that you have been a DJ for too long but that you still want to remain in radio broadcasting, you may finally be able to leave the air and go into sales, management, or programming consulting.

ACTIVITIES

1. Do the basic disc jockey assignment in appendix C.
2. Listen to the radio station of your choice for several sample hours. Try to figure out the format. When are the promos aired? When are the music sweeps and stop sets? Can you draw a sample of how that station's clock might appear?
3. Attend the meeting of your campus radio station. Find out what is required to get on the air as a disc jockey. Many college radio stations are on the air continuously, even when school is not in session, and they always need new people.
4. Produce the audition package.
5. Send your resume and audition tape to a local station. Try to arrange an interview with the program director to get an analysis of your tape and your chances in radio.

Radio in Transition

Radio has always been in transition. Some would say that is why it has survived changes in audiences, competition from other media, and constant technical changes for close to a century. Whether the transitions have been accidental, forced, or voluntary, on balance the people behind the radio business, and those behind its programming and production, have apparently managed the fortunes and fates well. As the twentieth century winds down, there are more stations, more listeners, and more interesting programming and production on radio than at any time in the past. Of course, that doesn't mean that the familiar radio of today won't sound different in ten or twenty years. As a final perspective, we'll look at where radio has been, where it is now, and where it is going.

WHITHER RADIO?

Rumors of radio's demise have always been greatly exaggerated. Take the early 1950s, for example. Television was the new kid on the block, and the doomsayers were predicting that it would certainly make radio obsolete in a few years. Of course, they were also saying the same about the movies, and theater owners waged many campaigns against such heinous conspiracies as pay TV.

But radio did have a real reason to be worried—its programming. When television began to repackage the same big radio stars and all the radio drama, comedy, and variety shows with pictures, there was no way that the American listener-cum-viewer would ever come back to a box that didn't show you anything. The great illusion that had been radio was no more. Most believed that radio, absent its programming, would just go away in a few years. Americans wanted pictures in their homes.

So during the 1950s, radio reluctantly parted with the likes of the Lone Ranger and Jack Benny, giving them and others up to television. In their place, demoralized stations turned to playing the hit music of the day from phonograph records, and local announcers suddenly became disc jockeys. It was a time of true transition for radio, its most serious challenge. What about the hit music that stations were playing during much of the 1950s? Whose music was it, anyway? It was *Your Hit Parade,* the music of the generation that had gone to war in the 1940s, music that mom and dad danced to in their youth. What about their kids? Most radio programmers didn't know it, but the salvation of radio was at hand, and it would be driven by high school kids. Transition time.

It happened because when men returned from World War II in 1945, they married and started families in record numbers. Their children, called the baby boom generation, were born in those few post-war years, and they represented a formidable challenge when they came of age in the late 1950s. More affluent than their parents and with more leisure time, they wanted their own identities in clothing, speech, and music. They were consumers, there were lots of them, and they saved radio, literally took it back from their parents. It was the music. Elvis Presley and others mostly copied obscure African-American music and made it acceptable to white teenage audiences, if not to their parents. It was different, it was loud, and radio was fun again.

The new sound was further refined by a new breed of radio programmers, and the concept of "top-40" radio took off, making radio very popular for several decades. It was a new type of programming, fast-paced with a format of forty songs repeated over and over, and it was supported by production that was characterized by loud and fast music, plenty of echo, and lots of hard sell. Along with this change in the sound of radio, another event that helped save radio was the application of science to the art of programming. Demographic research enabled stations and potential advertisers to know exactly what age group was listening to what type of programming, and music formats were designed to reach the newly empowered teen consumers. Newly revitalized radio was very successful. The youth of the day bought it for a while.

By the mid-1960s, when programmers had grown very wealthy and too complacent, another transition was in the making. And again it was in the music. The Beatles and others began to turn from the predictable two-and-a-half-minute song favored by the top-40 format and to experiment with new recording technology and longer and more complex forms of music. Along with the music came the dress, the drugs, and a new social consciousness. Soon there was a growing audience that began to rebel against the hard-sell top-40 sound, the bland two-minute love song, and the Vietnam War. The social, political, and cultural climate of the late 1960s was about to affect radio again. Radio would have to change to survive. Long songs? No problem, just put 'em on FM, no one's using FM for anything anyway. AM was still very profitable. What happened, of course, was that this music by new, socially aware artists was recorded using modern recording technology, and it sounded very good on FM. It spoke to a new generation. Again, radio was in transition.

THE TRUTH ABOUT RADIO

Although national radio networks and big stars dominated programming during its first two decades, radio is at its best when it's a highly personal local medium. No matter how many new formats, no matter how much the audience may change, no matter how many new networks are introduced, radio is still very tied in with the social, cultural, and political fabric of its community of license. Radio is local. Radio is always there. Think about how you rely on radio. Most people listen in their cars, for entertainment and information on the way to work and play. Television viewing has never caught on in the car. Radio is an obvious medium to turn to for continuous news when a local disaster hits and the power goes off. Most people don't have porta-ble, battery-operated televisions for use in emergencies. And, unlike television, the economics of radio make it possible for every town, no matter how small, to be served by local radio. The truth about radio is that it is still a local, cost-effective method of mass communication unlike any other.

Consider the business, the programming, and the technology of what is now called radio. Where has it been and why? Where is it going? What part will you play in its future? What are the truths about radio?

Business

There are too many radio stations in some markets and not enough in others. This means that some parts of the population are overserved while others remain without service. And while radio in theory belongs to the public, the process of acquiring a license to broadcast for profit and the operating of the station has always been pri-marily a business decision. If there are too many stations, the marketplace, the lis-tener, decides which will be successful and which will not. Owners have to constantly modify and change programming strategies in order to survive as a business or sell the station or go off the air. That's the reality of commercial radio. Remember that the decisions directly affecting the programming and production done by a radio station are always tied in with that station's ability to make money from that pro-gramming and the production that supports it. Even noncommercial, educational stations spend more time than ever trying to present programming that will please their listeners so they'll become paying members.

When there were fewer stations, radio did not have to be as competitive in busi-ness terms as it must be today. There was a time when, with a halfway decent sales staff, a local station could always survive just by being on the air. During the 1960s and 1970s, salespeople at some stations became order takers; they could sit in the office and advertisers would always call, even beg, to buy time. Back then, it used to be said about the business of radio that having a station was a license to print money. Many owners got rich. It's not that way anymore. What happened to the business of radio to change that? To answer that question, look at some of the results of the deregulation of broadcasting, the boom economy of the 1980s, and the reces-sion of the 1990s. A new group of business speculators began to buy radio.

Prior to the 1970s, radio stations tended to be owned by older companies that had owned one local or a group of radio properties from the very beginning. In the 1930s, 1940s, and 1950s, companies like NBC, CBS, ABC, Storer, Westinghouse, and others had bought their maximum FCC-allowed allotment of stations, seven AM and seven FM. They were stable and profitable, and beginning in the 1980s, they were all for sale. Like California real estate, almost half of the licensed radio stations changed hands, sometimes more than once, during the 1980s. New group owners, now allowed to own many more stations, took over from the old guard. Because of its perceived profit potential in the 1980s, radio was becoming a business in demand and many new owners wanted in. Some got good deals, but most new owners paid too much. Many have very high monthly payments.

More than any other truth about radio, the debt load that station owners took on in the 1980s is going to affect you as a broadcast professional for the rest of the 1990s. There is good news and bad. The bad news is that there will probably be fewer jobs as station owners "downsize" and reorganize in an attempt to get more work out of fewer personnel. Before the new economic reality, music stations always had a news staff. Under deregulation, many have cut it out entirely. Positions related to programming and production, formerly full-time positions like promotions director, production director, marketing director, and even program director, are being done by someone with several other responsibilities within the station. Fewer people are doing more work. And if you're thinking, "It doesn't affect me, I'm going into TV," think again. All the electronic media have been affected by the new economic reality.

The good news is that radio has been getting stale for a long time and a new transition is probably out there somewhere waiting to happen. This means that if you are a bright, thinking person, radio very much wants you and your new ideas. Now, more than in the past, radio stations and their owners need someone to show them "the next big thing" in programming and production. A way of getting enough people to listen to a station so that advertisers will pay more money for commercials on its air is a way to ensure a good future in the business. And since it is not being done by those currently in control of the stations, the chances are good that someone now sitting in a college radio studio may have the answer. Will you be the one to save radio again?

Programming

The biggest truth about radio programming is that the proliferation of formats has divided the potential audience into increasingly smaller groups, and that translates into smaller potential revenues per station. It hasn't always been this way. At the start of the 1960s, there were only two programming formats used by radio stations: top-40 hit music and everything else. Most of the young people were listening to their music on AM radio while their parents were probably glued to the TV. Programming for high school and college kids could not be found on the tube; no MTV, no Nick at Nite. Eventually those stations playing "everything else" found themselves scrambling either to find a new music format or a nonmusic one like all-talk, all-news, or news-talk. The very largest AM stations tended toward the latter, while the smaller FM stations experimented with different forms of popular music. As always, stations looked for a format that could give them—they used the term deliver—the largest group of listeners with the biggest amount of money to spend.

So out the door went formats like beautiful music, the kind still heard on elevators. The audience for that format was aging and its spending was declining. A big nonformat in the 1960s was called middle-of-the-road because announcers mainly played whatever was left over from the big band era, often mixed in with the most bland from the rock and roll charts. It was a nonformat because station owners and announcers guessed what their audiences liked at a time when the top-40s were doing continuous market research to find out exactly what their audiences would and would not listen to on the air. This nonformat lasted longer than many predicted because of listener and sponsor loyalty. Few remain today. By the 1970s, programming formats that played rock and roll would dominate.

With the possible exception of the major- and large-market classical or jazz station, everyone who wanted a music format that would get a big audience would have to try some variation of the current ratings leader, usually a top-40 station. Some stations tried to compete with that leader by doing top-40 better. Some succeeded, but those that didn't began to experiment with all the permutations of popular music—oldies, adult contemporary, and classic rock, and eventually dozens of subgroups of those formats appeared along with variations of black, Hispanic, and country music. Now, instead of a single format for all-black music, you'll hear on different stations traditional rhythm and blues, soul, and rap, all aimed at a different age and income segment of the black audience. Instead of a single country music format, there will be both traditional and the newer pop version of country. In large Hispanic markets, there is often one station playing the music of old Mexico for adults while another plays music created by and for Mexican-American teens. Combinations of pop and country and rock and black music are also found. What was top-40 or CHR ten years ago is anything but as audiences fragment into smaller and smaller subgroups.

And, due in part to the lower cost of satellite-delivered specialty formats and the number of struggling AM stations looking for programming at the lowest possible cost, new specialty networks are springing up and dying on a daily basis. All-comedy, all-sports, all-game shows, all-shopping, all-Elvis, all-Beatles—practically every possible interest area has been explored. Whatever it is, there is a format that delivers it at a low cost using satellites. Want an all-news station? In the past, the cost of an all-news operation was prohibitive in all but the largest markets. Now with CNN, every station can have high-quality, 24-hour-a-day world and national news at a very low price. With services like Talk Net, even the tiniest station can have New York- or LA-sounding programming. The truth is that there is so much variety in programming and there are so many formats that no single one draws anything near the audience of that legendary AM top-40 powerhouse of the 1960s. Add to commercial radio a tripling of noncommercial licensees since then and it is easy to see how the days of one station "having it all" are gone forever. Like the business side of radio, programming is also going through some interesting changes.

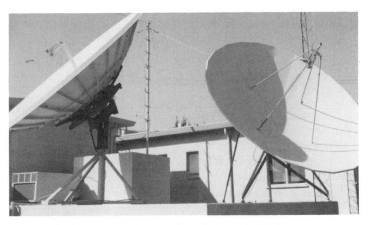

Many radio stations receive programming via satellite.

Technology

Another truth about radio is that it has always been affected by the introduction of new technology. In fact, there is probably no other mass medium that can boast or decry the existence of such diametrically opposed technologies serving the same business. AM radio, around since the 1920s, shares radio's delivery function with satellite-delivered all-digital cable radio. The too old and the too new remain side by side. Inside the station, both production and on-air studios are making a rapid transformation from the traditional analog formats to various digital ones. And it is the technology of mass delivery systems, or "what will replace broadcast FM?" as the main delivery vehicle, that is taking up most of the economic and political discussion time among broadcast owners, independent program providers, government regulators, and manufacturers of equipment.

The technology of the studio and control room is changing faster than anyone would have predicted. First to change was the on-air control room. The quickest has been the near-complete transformation from the vinyl phonograph record to compact disc. Driven mainly by the music and consumer electronic industries, radio stations were forced to play CDs when record manufacturing ended. In the early transition years, many FM stations played CDs for competitive reasons, and some even mentioned it in their promotions. Now all do. Another trend in control room equipment has been the transition from the rotary-pot console to those using vertical sliders. Like the CD, it was a technology influenced from the outside. The use of sliders as volume level control devices started first in the recording studio and slowly made its way into the on-air control room.

Other control room technologies using digital storage/playback devices that replace the reel-to-reel and cart are plentiful but slower to be adopted by broadcasters. There are probably two reasons for the lack of a replacement for the cart: the cart as a playback format is still the overwhelming standard understood by every broad-caster, and there are too many variations of a digital "cart," all by reputable names, but incompatible with each other. A cart is a cart is a cart at every station. When manufacturers standardize on a single format, it will be easier to convert. Stations are still waiting.

And, for at least a decade, many have predicted that in the future, a visitor to an on-air control room would find nothing but a computer with a touch screen. Push the icon and the microphone comes on. Push another to start a commercial. All the electronics would be hidden in a rack. Very good systems are available, but few have caught on. Manufacturers have found that most operators still enjoy touching CDs and carts. Possibly a new generation of DJs used to Sega and WordPerfect will demand the equipmentless studio.

A final category of new control room technology is automation systems. A far cry from early systems using reel-to-reel tape with cue tones to start carts, modern automation is practically invisible. In fact, some of the stations you listen to are so well automated you may not be aware that what you are hearing is being done mostly by a computer. Whether full-time automated programming or just during the over-nights, any station can install a satellite dish on the roof, buy a computer to add local breaks and commercials triggered by the satellite network, and hire a couple of minimum-wage high school kids to baby-sit the whole operation. Of course, local production must still be done, but with currently available automation technology, an owner of a very small station can sell time in the morning and do production in the afternoon with very little time needed to run the station.

An early automation system.

In the production studio, more new technology has caught on as the equipment first developed for the recording studio has been downsized and duplicated for the needs of radio production. The recording studio and the radio production studio are becoming one and the same. Much editing is being done using a digital audio workstation, DAWS, rather than a razor blade and splicing tape. A decision to buy a low-cost production workstation is often made because the production person wants it, rather than for competitive or programming reasons. Older production people still feel more comfortable with reel-to-reel and tape splicing, but as more colleges and their radio stations offer tapeless editing practice for their students, chances are better that a radio station will have one in the future. Compared to cutting and splicing the older magnetic tape, digital systems allow the production person to work faster and more efficiently, with the resulting free time better spent on the creative aspects of a project.

How does recording-studio level production equipment change the type of production done by stations in support of programming? As always, some believe that better equipment allows better productions to be created in less time. And with more stations spending more effort on attracting fewer listeners, stations have to be more competitive. Since most station programming is music produced in the high-tech environment that is today's recording studio, so must its productions and promotions. Programmers know that every audience member has ten preset stations on his or her car radio so there can't be anything on the air that is not great-sounding or audience-grabbing; otherwise the next station push button will be pressed. No one is willing to take a chance on producing or airing a production that is inferior to the music format played or the often high-priced DJ who presents it.

The delivery system, or how the audio gets from studio to home and car, is where much of the technical attention is centered. There has been plenty of political wrangling over current and proposed systems. The original on-air delivery system, AM, died years ago but still refuses to be buried. From the once-dominant source of all radio, AM is still hanging on, successful in major and large markets because of news, sports, and talk programming. The death of AM was probably inevitable as listeners discovered that the audio quality of an FM radio sounded more like their cassettes and CDs than that of AM. Radio manufacturers also helped kill AM by refusing to make a decent radio receiver. It took more than a decade for broadcasters to decide on a technical standard for AM stereo and some improvement in the audio quality of an AM broadcast was required under a recent FCC ruling, but, alas, no makers of radios came forward to build a decent-sounding receiver. Moreover, in some markets, the land used for the AM transmitting antenna is worth more than the station itself. An AM station also requires a lot more electricity, resulting in a higher electric bill, than an FM station that reaches the same size audience. And even if an AM station's signal can be heard in ten states, most of its advertisers will only care about local listeners.

Perhaps the days of FM as the major delivery system for radio programming are numbered. There are many technologies perfected and waiting to be the next radio service. Digital radio, called DAB for Digital Audio Broadcasting, is the most

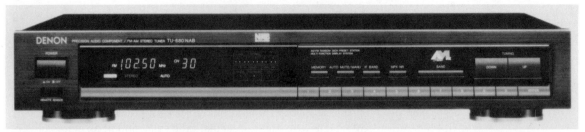

The National Association of Broadcasters had this tuner designed to get the best possible AM and FM sound.
(Courtesy of Denon America, Inc.)

promising and at the same time the most hotly contested replacement for broadcasting. Offering the highest-quality audio and clearest signal, digital broadcasting converts analog audio into a digital stream of 1's and 0's and sends it to the receiver, which converts it back into perfect audio. Who could possibly be against that? Everyone, it seems. Manufacturers will not make receivers until a standard is agreed upon, and current licensees will not give up their positions on FM until they can be guaranteed first choice when any new system is approved. Advertisers will wait until every home and car has one before they spend their money. The most likely scenario, one that would ensure a nod from existing radio station owners, is to go with an "in-band" system, one that allows a station to transmit a digital simulcast version of its programming but hidden in its FM signal, similar to multiplex and SCA, the stereo and subcarrier data that many stations already broadcast.

Cable television providers are already offering one form of "digital radio." DMX, the Digital Music Express, is available in the form of a decoder box that connects to a home stereo system and a remote control. Up to thirty-six channels of announcer-free, commercial-free music can be selected by format. So far, it is a wired system, but companies are already developing ways to send it to special car radios using the low-power technology of the cellular telephone. Will listeners want the new services? Which ones will make it, and which ones will fall by the wayside? Services that use existing technology, like those provided by the local TV cable company, will have a good chance of succeeding since their audience is already wired and the cost of providing the service is small. Those services that require purchase and installation of a special antenna dish and receiver will not be as easy to sell to consumers, and, as always, they will be viewed by existing FM stations as unfair competition. For the near future, local broadcasters will only agree on an in-band compatible digital format and they'll wait for receiver manufacturers to catch up.

Radio has always been in transition. The rules and regulations under which the business of commercial radio has been conducted have changed yearly since the Federal Radio Act of 1927. One year stations are forced to do more local programming, the next year they're encouraged to make more money by signing on with a network. One year stations must do yearly ascertainment of their community of license to decide on programming. Come the next election, they are encouraged to let the marketplace decide. Radio as businesses are free to make a profit, but with the caveat that as license holders they are using a public trust that can be taken away at any time. Programming has also been changing, first as a response to television's popularity, and later as too many stations began to chase a finite number of listeners. But even as more "radio" services are offered that promise no talk and no commercials, radio will always be at its best when it presents programming directed to a local audience in a personal way. The DJ is still a communicator to most, an air salesperson to some, a companion to many. And the technology of production and delivery systems will ultimately determine how the radio station of the future will look and how its programming will get from the studio to the listener.

RADIO AS YOUR CAREER

So why learn about radio, why even consider it as your career if it's boring, repetitive, low-paying, and doomed to be automated? First, that's not a true picture of life in radio. Sure, for some, that first and last job in radio may be a part-time student job minding an automated facility. But there is much, much more to radio than that.

More than any other reason for choosing it as a career, radio can be an intrinsically satisfying experience. It's hard to describe, but there is no better feeling than the inner reward you get from participating in a career in any creative field. It's the feeling you get from completing a production and hearing it on the air for the first time. It's the reaction you get when the people you meet discover that you are in radio. Real or not, this is how those in the performance arts, music, drama, films, TV, and radio are viewed by those they entertain, their audience, and what makes it like no other career. The people you work with and the experiences you have as a radio person are guaranteed to be the most interesting and exciting of your life. The roar of the grease paint.

And while radio will continue to be a satisfying career for many, it's not easy to be a disc jockey or a radio production person. Of course, you're probably thinking, "anybody could do that," and, strictly speaking, you may be correct. Nevertheless, while every person can be taught to push buttons, announce records, and read commercials, the act of communicating in a brief way, the act of sounding interested and informed while personally entertaining an imagined listener, is a real communications challenge. The best disc jockeys and production people are like the best television anchorpeople and talk show hosts, the most popular recording stars, and the best football and basketball players; they earn an unreal amount of money if they succeed in attracting great numbers of listeners to the station. More listeners equals higher ratings equals more advertising revenue. To 90 percent of the radio stations on the air, a skilled DJ is a good investment. And every commercial music-formatted station has a dozen on-air DJs, each one responsible for several hours of daily programming and the off-air production of commercials and other material.

If disc jockeys and production folk are the ones who keep radio on the air, are they all paid well for it? Is it a career worth pursuing? First, some truths about the money. While everyone can cite examples of disc jockeys who make several million yearly, most make far less. In fact, when you drive into the parking lot of your favorite station, look closely at the cars parked there. Notice the Mercedes Benz and the BMW? Those belong to the owner and the sales manager. Acuras? Lexus? Program director, station manager, and most account executives can afford one of these. What about the DJs? See those five-year old Toyota Corollas and Ford Tempos? You guessed it.

While it is possible to find satisfaction in an on-the-air career at least in the short term, many DJs eventually will try other positions within the station. Once in the business as a production person, you will meet a variety of programmers, sales-people, sponsors, and others, and you will soon become aware of new opportunities and new directions for your production skills. Once you are on the inside, the many career paths available to you will be more obvious. From beginning announcer to production director to program director to sales to management, there are a dozen possible ways to succeed in radio. You may find that you are naturally suited for management, music programming, or promotions. An old rule of thumb said that in order to be a station manager, you had to come up through the ranks of the sales department. This is no longer universally true. Some successful managers were successful program directors and, before that, successful DJs. Now, as always, station owners want the largest possible audience of those people with the most money to spend, and for that reason they will always try to select the best people to make it happen. This has not and will not change. It is the foundation of American radio.

Could the disc jockey/production person be an endangered species? At last count, there were more than twelve thousand commercial stations in the United States and 99 percent of them used DJ programming. At an average of six DJs per station, that's still a lot of jobs. But what about automation? What about satellite-delivered programming? Will that replace local production? Again, radio has had automation systems in place for half a century. The older ones were technical abominations, but the new ones are pretty slick, allowing almost seamless transitions from network or taped programming to local announcer and commercials. Too, the delivery of music programming via satellite network is a recent technical innovation, but wired networks have been providing programming since the mid-1920s. The future of the combination radio DJ and production person is probably secure because radio is a local, personal medium, and whenever there is competition, there will be a need for a strong, local communicator. Small stations and dying AMs will continue to use automated satellite networks as they always have.

Finally, unlike no other career, radio gets into your blood. You can't help yourself; you just have to do it. Even former radio professionals who have opted for a different career are found in noncommercial, college, and community stations as volunteer programmers or doing weekend air shifts on the local commercial station. For once you get into radio, it always gets into you. The two of you become inseparable.

Enjoy.

Examples of KSJS Radio Underwriting Spots

Underwriting rules limit your spot only slightly. Otherwise, the more creative you are, the better the spot will be.

Remember: If you need help writing copy for a radio spot, contact any KSJS manager or someone in the production department.

BOX A.1

Here are some examples of BUCs (Basic Underwriting Commercials):

This portion of KSJS is brought to you by <u>FAUX HAIR SALON</u> featuring JoiCo hair products. <u>FAUX</u>'s services are by appointment only. <u>FAUX</u> is located at 378 Campbell Avenue in Campbell and their phone number is 378–9999. That's <u>FAUX HAIR SALON</u> featuring JOI-CO Products.

This portion of KSJS's programming is brought to you by <u>FEDERICO's</u> . . . featuring an authentic Tex-Mex chefs. <u>FEDERICO's</u> is located at 325 South First Street in San Jose. Their phone number is (408)–999–9999. <u>FEDERICO's</u>, another proud sponsor of KSJS programming.

This portion of KSJS's programming is brought to you by <u>DIMENSIONS IN HEALTH</u> specializing in massage therapy. <u>DIMENSIONS IN HEALTH</u> offers a variety of massage therapy ranging from sports to Swedish Massage. <u>DIMENSIONS IN HEALTH</u> is located at 20 South Santa Cruz Avenue in downtown Los Gatos. The staff, directed by Bob Sanchez, can be reached at 408–999–9999 for additional information.

When writing copy, here are some things you should include:

1. **The Sponsor's Name.** Mention the name **at least three times** throughout the spot. Roughly once in the beginning, middle, and end.
2. **Products or Services that the Sponsor Offers.** Again, according to underwriting rules you can't describe them; just creatively list them.
3. **Sponsor's Address and Phone Number.** This should be included in every spot!

A PSA or PROMO :30 or :60 in Length

TREATMENT

A treatment is a written explanation of a radio or television production. It is to justify the concept of the production before the script is written. The treatment can be very detailed or brief. In our case make it brief (one page) as long as you answer the questions below. For this project, convince the station's programming director that your project is worth doing.

1. Is this a PSA or a promotion?
2. What is the format of the station? In the case of KSJS, where the format changes with each public affairs or specialty music program, when will your spot be played?
3. What is the length?
4. Who is your target audience?
5. Will the spot be a hard sell or soft sell?
6. What kind of music will it have?
7. Will you use sound effects (SFX)?
8. What is the format of the spot (single voice, two voice, dialogue copy)?

THE SCRIPT

:30 or :60 PSA or PROMO script must be typed and double spaced. Follow the script format following. All instructions on the script must be in all caps and the dialogue should be normal caps and lowercase letters. Keep in mind when you write your script that it must match your final project <u>perfectly</u>. Consequently, you must make sure it is timed correctly, and you must secure your music and sound effects <u>in advance</u> of writing the script.

BOX B.1 *Example of Radio Script Format*

Client:	The Humane Society	KSJS-FM 90.7
Copy By:	Chan Baran	San Jose, California
Time:	:30	
Start Date:	7-4-93	Kill Date: 7-4-94

SFX   DOGS HOWLING (SINGING) THE BLUES. HOLD BEHIND

ANNCR: We've all heard the expression: It's a dog's life. But if a dog's life is so good, why are all these dogs singing the blues? I'll tell you why. Because these dogs don't have a home and most of them never will. Each week 3,200 dogs and nearly 4,000 cats are put to death by animal control shelters because of overpopulation. It is a problem that can be avoided. Spay or neuter your pets to help stop our animal overpopulation problem. Or adopt a pet by calling your local Humane Society. Let our blues brothers know that we care.

SFX   APPLAUSE AND HAPPY BARKING UP AND UNDER

ANNCR: Help replace the blues with happy sounds! For more information you can call 1–800–555–bark.

THE PROJECT

In producing the :30 or :60 PSA or PROMO you are encouraged to use the reel-to-reel tape deck, the cart machine, and the CD player to help you make this your best project to date. Use a stopwatch (or backtime using the studio clocks) and rehearse before you produce. Don't forget to listen to your project once you have finished to discover any problems before you leave the studio.

C ▼

Simple DJ Assignment

Station ID with introduction of music then segue between two turntables. Recorded live on cassette tape.

How to do it:

<u>MUSIC: TT1 THE LAST :30 OF THE SONG</u>

"Good morning, this is _____ on _____
                                                    your name   call letters, frequ.

bringing you the best this area has to offer. This next song is from _____
                                                                                                                            Group

and it's called _____ ."
                                    Song Title

<u>MUSIC: SEGUE TO TT2 THE FIRST :30 OF THIS SONG THEN FADE OUT</u>.

GLOSSARY

A

ACCENTUATE—To increase the volume of a certain frequency or tone.

ACCOUNT EXECUTIVE—A person in the sales department who maintains contact with clients who advertise on the radio station.

ACTUALITIES—Live or taped news reports broadcast from the scene that contain the voice(s) of the news maker(s) as well as the reporter.

AD-LIB—An unscripted, improvised comment, remark, or speech.

ADULT CONTEMPORARY (AC)—Radio programming music format that emphasizes current popular music while avoiding hard rock.

AFTRA—American Federation of Television and Radio Artists; AFL-CIO labor union of broadcast performers/talent.

AIR MONITOR—A device for checking or regulating performance that is happening over the air.

ALBUM ORIENTED ROCK (AOR)—Radio programming music format that features album music.

ALCOHOL—Used for cleaning tape heads.

ALL NEWS—Radio programming format that features only news and information.

AM (amplitude modulation)—Radio spectrum frequency allocation from 535 to 1605 kHz.

AMERICAN FEDERATION OF TELEVISION AND RADIO ARTISTS (AFTRA)—AFL-CIO labor union of broadcast performers/talent.

AMPLITUDE—The height, peak, or power of a sound or electromagnetic wave.

ANN—Announcer; script notation calling for dialogue by the announcer or talent.

AP—Associated Press.

ASCAP—American Society of Composers, Authors, and Publishers; a music licensing company.

ASCERTAINMENT—Broadcasters are responsible for assessing or "ascertaining" the needs and interests of their listeners.

ATTACK—The way a sound begins.

ATTENUATE—Decrease the energy level of a set of frequencies.

AUDIO—The sound portion of a broadcast.

AUDIO CONSOLE—A desk-type structure equipped with monitoring and other electronic machinery; this device ties all the discrete pieces of production equipment together; also called console, mixing console, mixer, or just a board.

AUDIO CONTROL BOARD—*See* AUDIO CONSOLE.

AUDITION—A function that allows you to preview a sound before it is aired.

AVAILABILITIES (more commonly, AVAILS)—Individual openings for spot announcements in a broadcast.

B

BACK ANNOUNCE—The DJ's recap of the tunes broadcast during the run of music just completed.

BBC—British Broadcasting Company.

BED—The creation of a mood for some content through the addition of background music.

BIAS—A high-frequency signal added to a recording to avoid distortion.

BIDIRECTIONAL MICROPHONE—A microphone with a pickup pattern focusing on two directions, typically the front and back.

BINAURAL EFFECT—Describes the idea that two ears can determine the direction of a sound, but a single ear cannot.

BLOCK PROGRAMMING—Scheduling together content with similar audience appeal.

BMI—Broadcast Music Incorporated; a music licensing company.

BOOST—Amplify.

BROADCAST MUSIC INCORPORATED (BMI)—A music licensing company.

BUSINESS MANAGER—The person responsible for the station's financial matters.

C

CANNED—Prerecorded presentations.

CAPACITOR—A device that stores an electrical charge.

CAPACITOR MICROPHONE—*See* CONDENSER MICROPHONE.

CAPSTAN—The motor that determines the speed at which the tape runs.

CARDIOID MICROPHONE—A microphone with a heart-shaped pickup pattern; unidirectional pickup pattern; narrower versions of this pattern called hypercardioid and supercardioid.

CART—A continuous loop tape cartridge.

CHANNEL—The electronic path from the console to the tape.

CHIEF ENGINEER—The person whose main function is to keep the station physically (electronically) on the air.

CHINA MARKER—A grease pencil for marking tape.

CLOCK—Visual representation of how a broadcast day is programmed; sometimes called format wheel.

COMBO—When one person simultaneously operates equipment and serves as talent.

COMMUNICATIONS ACT OF 1934—Legislation granting federal government the right to license and regulate broadcasting.

COMPACT DISC (CD)—Small disc containing digitally coded music read by a laser.

COMPANDER—A combination compressor and volume expander designed to give you complete control over the dynamic range of your audio.

COMPRESSOR—Volume-controlling devices between console and transmitter that keep all sounds at about the same "real" loudness; also called limiters.

CONDENSER MICROPHONE—An older style microphone that has a diaphragm that moves in response to sound waves and then comes in contact with a metal disk; also called a capacitor microphone.

CONSOLE—*See* AUDIO CONSOLE or AUDIO BOARD.

CONTEMPORARY HIT RADIO (CHR)—Radio programming music format featuring current hits and "top-10" records; formerly known as Top 40.

CONTROL ROOM—Where the director, engineer, and others adjust and/or control the recording or broadcast.

COPY—Written material to be read by talent. *See also* SCRIPT.

COPYWRITERS—Those who produce written copy for productions.

CORPORATION FOR PUBLIC BROADCASTING (CPB)—Government-supported organization created to promote the development of public broadcasting.

COUNTRY—Radio programming music format that emphasizes country and western music.

CPMs—Most advertising is bought in *cost-per-thousands* (Roman numeral for thousand is M).

CROSSFADE—Segueing gracefully from one sound to another.

CUE—A signal to begin the next component of a production; also a function on the audio console that allows you to preview a sound to find the beginning before playing.

CUED UP—Prepared and ready for immediate utilization.

CUE MAT—A slippery piece of paper or felt between the record and the turntable platter.

CUE SHEETS—Listings of the individual cuts or selections on each disk.

CUME—The total accumulated audience for a given broadcast period.

CYCLE—A specific period of broadcast programming; one complete sound wave that must pass through the zero line and end at the beginning point while moving in the same direction.

D

DA—Distribution amplifier.

DAT, R-DAT—Rotary digital audiotape; it is a high-quality digital storage device featuring rapid access and cueing of recorded material as opposed to analog; format on tape.

DAWS—Digital audio workstation; sample analog audio and convert it to the 1's and 0's of computer language and store it on a high-capacity magnetic or optical hard disk.

DAYPARTS—A programming segment of a station's schedule.

DEAD AIR—Silence.

DECAY—The way in which a sound stops.

DECIBELS (dB)—The measure of audio "loudness" or strength.

DEGAUSSER—A bulk tape eraser.

DEMOGRAPHIC—A piece of information or data pertaining to important audience characteristics such as age, gender, etc.

DISC JOCKEY (DJ)—Person who performs live, nonstop production of a recorded music program.

DOLBY NOISE REDUCTION—Circuitry to eliminate the hiss from audiotape recordings.

DRIVE TIME—The two radio dayparts with the largest audiences, morning and evening drive time.

DROPOUT—Loss of audio at a splice.

DUB—Electronically copy or rerecord from one tape to another.

DYNAMIC MICROPHONE—A microphone that functions with an attached coil of wire that moves in a magnetic field; sometimes called a moving coil microphone.

DYNAMIC RANGE—The range between the softest and loudest sounds that an instrument is capable of producing or recording as measured in dB.

E

EASY LISTENING—Radio programming music format consisting mostly of quiet instrumentals with a few soft, slow songs.

EBS—Emergency Broadcast System.

ECHO—Gradual diminishing exact repeats of the audio.

EDIT BLOCK—A cutting or chopping block for editing tape.

EDITING—The process of adding and/or deleting material.

ENVELOPE—Parameters.

ENVIRONMENTAL (OR AMBIENT) SOUND—Background or extraneous sound.

EQUALIZATION (EQ)—The process of altering the frequency of response of an audio signal.

EQUALIZER—A system that normalizes an audio signal by altering the frequency response; it can be used to cut or boost specific frequency ranges making an audio signal lighter or more bassy, for example.

F

FADE-IN—Segueing gradually from silence to a louder sound.

FADE-OUT—Segueing gradually from a louder sound to silence.

FADER (OR SLIDER)—Straight-line, up and down, volume controls on an audio console.

FCC—*See* FEDERAL COMMUNICATIONS COMMISSION.

FEDERAL COMMUNICATIONS COMMISSION (FCC)—The regulatory agency charged with oversight of broadcasting.

FEEDBACK—A loud noise or squeal from a microphone or speaker caused by improper placement, circuit noise, accidental closing of the circuit, or another error or problem.

FILTERS—Devices that screen out particular frequencies.

FLANGING—Mixing two versions of the same signal to create a swooshing effect.

FM—Frequency modulation; radio frequency from 88 to 108 MHz.

FOLEY ARTIST—The person who adds environmental sounds to a tape.

FORFEITURE—A fine; the most common FCC sanction against a station.

FORMAT—The general character of a station's programming.

FRC—Federal Radio Commission.

FREE-FORM—A station without a format.

FREQUENCY—The number of electromagnetic waves that occur during a certain amount of time.

FREQUENCY RESPONSE—The frequency range that a microphone can reproduce.

FUNDAMENTAL PITCH—The lowest frequency that a sound produces.

G

GENERAL MANAGER (GM)—The chief operating officer of a station.

GENERATION LOSS (OR DEGENERATION)—Loss of fidelity with each subsequent duplication of a tape.

GIGAHERTZ (GHz)—One billion Hertz.

GREASE PENCIL—Employed in marking edit points on a tape.

H

HARD SEGUE—Abruptly stopping one sound and instantly beginning another.

HARMONICS—Overtones that are integer multiples of the fundamental frequency.

HARMONIZER—A device for varying pitch, harmonics, and tempo.

HEADLINES—The highlights of the news.

HEADROOM—The difference between the highest level of a signal and the maximum level that can be handled, without noticeable distortion, by the recorder or other audio device.

HEARING—In humans, in terms of frequency, hearing lies between 15 and 20 kHz; in terms of amplitude, hearing lies from 0 dB to 120–140 dB.

HERTZ (Hz)—The frequency of vibrations equal to one cycle per second; named after Heinrich Hertz who discovered electromagnetic waves.

HIGH-PASS FILTERS—Devices that screen out low frequencies.

I

IMPEDANCE—Various levels of resistance the electronic signal encounters as it flows through a circuit as voltage.

INCHES PER SECOND (ips)—The usual measurement of the speed of audiotape.

IN PHASE—Waves that are in phase reinforce each other; also called phase augmentation.

INTERFERENCE—Noise in audio production.

INTERNAL DYNAMICS—Describes changes in volume as it increases, decreases, or sustains.

INVERTED PYRAMID—Newspaper style of reporting news, with most salient information at top of the story and details later.

K

KILL DATE—The last day of broadcast for a specific item.

KILOHERTZ (kHz)—One thousand Hertz.

L

LEADER TAPE—Blank, nonrecording tape placed at beginning of audiotape to allow ease of manipulation in threading.

LEDs—Light emitting diodes.

LEGAL ID—Station identification including call letters, frequency, and location.

LETTER OF ADMONITION—A mild form of FCC sanction against a station; a letter of reprimand.

LICENSE—A governmental grant or authorization to broadcast.

LIMITERS—*See* COMPRESSORS.

LINE LEVEL—The level required in order for the input, or those signals coming in and their source, to be received correctly or "understood" by the console.

LINE MONITOR—A device for checking or regulating performance that is being produced while it is being aired or recorded.

LIVE-ON-TAPE RECORDING—Recording the audio segments in real-time as they happen.

LOW-PASS FILTERS—Devices that screen out high frequencies.

M

MAKE GOODS—Advertising time provided free by the station to compensate a sponsor for a spot that was preempted or broadcast poorly or incorrectly.

MARKET—The area that a station is licensed to serve.

MASTER CONTROL—*See* CONTROL ROOM.

MECHANICAL TAPE EDITING—The act of physically cutting and splicing tape.

MEGAHERTZ (MHZ)—One million Hertz.

MIC LEVEL—The amplitude of signals a microphone is capable of generating.

MICROPHONES—An audio pickup device used for announcers and other talent.

MIDDLE OF THE ROAD (MOR)—The radio format that tries to be everything to everybody; beautiful music and mellow rock.

MIX—Combining two separate sound sources.

MIXER—The unit that controls and blends audio and/or video signals; *see also* AUDIO CONSOLE.

MONITOR—An electronic device for checking or regulating performance while it is being aired or recorded.

MONO—Monaural.

MOVING COIL—*See* DYNAMIC MICROPHONE.

MULTIDIRECTIONAL MICROPHONE—A microphone with a pickup pattern that receives sound from all directions; microphones with changeable pickup patterns.

MULTITRACK RECORDING (multitracking)—A technique of recording sound on sound; if unintentional, called overdubbing.

MUS—Music that is played in the background or as an exclusive part of the program.

MUSIC SWEEPS—The practice of broadcasting several records, tapes, or disks consecutively without interruption.

MUTED—Silenced.

N

NATIONAL PUBLIC RADIO (NPR)—An organization that produces and distributes programs to noncommercial radio stations; funded primarily by member stations, it is based in Washington, D.C.

NEEDLE DROP—The use of a recording in a broadcast or other production; usage fees (called needle down charge) often are based on the number of needle drops in a program.

NEWS DIRECTOR—Supervises the gathering of news, its rewriting, and presentation.

NOISE—Electrical disturbance that interferes with a signal; random sounds that cannot be interpreted or are not useful.

NOTCH FILTERS—Designed to eliminate audio at selected frequencies, not just minimize it like many equalizers do.

O

OMNIDIRECTIONAL MICROPHONE—A microphone that allows sound to enter equally from all sides.

OPEN MICROPHONE—A live microphone; an instruction to turn on or activate a microphone.

OPEN REEL—A tape reel not enclosed in a cassette or cartridge as used on a reel-to-reel recorder or player.

OPERATING LOG—A diary, listing, or record, such as the listing of a station's programs, commercials, and everything else actually broadcast; a running log is a sequential listing, such as the listing of programs by time periods.

OPERATING PRINCIPLES—Microphones are categorized by their physical designs, called operating principles.

OSCILLATES—The vibration of sound or electromagnetic waves.

OUT OF PHASE—When waves are out of phase, they can partially or totally cancel each other out; also called phase cancellation.

OUTPUT—The voltage of the signals going out to their destination.

OUT TAKE—Edited piece of tape.

OVERDUBBING—Unintentional multitracking; a technique of recording sound on sound.

OVERTONES—Weaker sounds generated at a higher frequency than the fundamental pitch; when these overtones are integer multiples of the fundamental pitch they are called harmonics.

P

PACKAGE—A combination of radio programs or commercial spots offered to a sponsor as a unit, usually at a discount.

PATCH BAYS—*See* PATCH PANELS.

PATCH PANELS—A device that ties together several circuits or pieces of apparatus to the console by way of jacks and patch cords; also called patch bays.

PAYOLA—Money or favors given to broadcast producers, or others, to improperly promote a record or other item.

PD—Program director.

PHANTOM POWER—A power supply built into the audio console.

PHASE AUGMENTATION—*See* IN PHASE.

PHASE CANCELLATION—*See* OUT OF PHASE.

PICKUP PATTERN—Microphones are designed to focus on specific locations referred to as the microphone's pick-up pattern.

PICON (PUBLIC INTEREST, CONVENIENCE AND/OR NECESSITY)—The license requirement for broadcasters regulated by the Federal Communications Commission.

PINCH OR PRESSURE ROLLER—A rubber wheel that presses the tape against the capstan (the shaft in the recorder that drives the tape; also called the capstan idler or puck).

PITCH—The psychological interpretation of frequency which determines the highness (high frequency) or lowness (low frequency) of a sound.

PLAYBACK HEADS—A transducer that changes the magnetic pattern on the audiotape into electronic signals.

POSITIONING—When stations engage in marketing to separate themselves from their competition.

POSTPRODUCTION—Referring to the stages after the principal recording; including editing, dubbing, etc.

POTENTIOMETER (more commonly, POT)—An instrument for controlling electrical flow (the potential or flow); also called attenuator, fader, gain control, or mixer. Most commonly used to control sound level in radio receivers and audio systems. To pot-up is to increase the sound level; to pot-down is to decrease the sound level.

PREPRODUCTION—The casting, scripting, and other activities prior to actual production.

PRESSURE GRADIENT MICROPHONE—*See* RIBBON MICROPHONE.

PRESSURE-ZONE MICROPHONE (PZM)—A type of small electrostatic microphone with a flat base plate, in which sound waves are in phase in its pressure zone; PZM is commonly mounted on a wall or other surface near the sound source.

PRODUCER—The manager in charge of finance, personnel, and other non-artistic aspects in the development of a production.

PRODUCTION—The period of the audio work, preceded by pre-production (planning) and followed by postproduction (editing), though the term production often refers to the entire process.

PRODUCTION DIRECTOR—Manager of the production process.

PRODUCTION STUDIO—Production facility.

PROGRAMMING—The overall sound of the station including all programs, music, commercials, etc.

PROMOTION (PROMO)—Refers to the overall activity conducted by a radio station that is designed to help sell a particular product or service; more specifically, the word refers to the preliminary advertisement or announcement of a radio program or station.

PROMOTIONS DIRECTOR—Manager of the promotions department.

PROXIMITY EFFECT—The tendency of some microphones to overexaggerate the bass or low frequencies of a voice when the person speaking is extremely close to the instrument.

PSYCHOACOUSTICS—Concerned with the psychological aspects of sound as mood-setting or as a referent for a particular event or emotion.

PSYCHOGRAPHICS—The study of social class, lifestyle, and personality characteristics of individuals and groups, as compared to demographics (age, income, occupation, education, race, religion, and other more quantifiable data).

PUBLIC AFFAIRS—Programming concerned with community problems and issues; usually consist of interview and discussion programs.

PUBLIC DOMAIN MUSIC—The condition of being free from copyright or patent and thus open to use by anyone; a book, music, or other work whose copyright has expired is in the public domain.

PUBLIC SERVICE ANNOUNCEMENT (PSA or P.S.A.)—A message, usually broadcast free by radio stations; these announcements usually are provided by government agencies and nonprofit organizations and are considered to be in the public interest.

PUNCH IN—A cue to indicate the start of a recording.

PUR—People using radio.

R

RADIO ACT OF 1927—Established licensing provisions and, for the first time, created and empowered a government entity specifically in charge of radio matters.

RAM—Random access memory, the most common type of computer memory, the contents of which can be altered.

RATE CARD—The card or listing issued by a station that contains its advertising rates and requirements.

RATINGS—The unit of analysis to determine the popularity of a program by measuring audience consumption; a percentage of the total households out of all possible radio owners listening to a particular radio station.

RECORDER—A device that receives and retains or preserves audio signals.

RECORD HEAD—A transducer that changes electronic signals to a magnetic field which magnetizes the tape.

RECORD SPINNERS—A protected group of union employees.

REEL-TO-REEL—Tape players utilizing an open reel configuration; sometimes called an open reel.

RELIGIOUS—Radio format with the specific goal: to spread religious ideas to as many people as possible.

REMOTE START SWITCH—A switch located on the console away from the actual device being started which activates the audio source and the motor of the machine.

REVERBERATION (more commonly REVERB)—An audio effect consisting of a reechoing or reflection of sound.

REVOCATION—A reprimand issued by the Federal Communications Commission that revokes a station's broadcasting license.

RIBBON MICROPHONE—A microphone with a thin corrugated foil strip—a ribbon—that vibrates between the magnet poles to which it is attached; also called a pressure gradient or a velocity microphone.

ROTARY DIGITAL AUDIOTAPE (R-DAT or DAT)—*See* DAT.

ROUTING—To choose the path of an audio signal by routing it to a specific channel.

RPM—*R*otations *per* *m*inute, two standard speeds for black vinyl records: 33 1/3 RPM and 45 RPM.

RPU—Remote pickup.

S

SALES MANAGER—In charge of the planning and supervision of all sales operations.

SAMPLERS—*See* DAWS.

SCRIPT—A text of a speech, play, film, commercial, or program or simply a schedule or sequential account; also called copy.

SEGUE—To make a transition from one action, scene, or musical selection directly to another without interruption; pronounced SEG-way.

SFX—*See* SOUND EFFECTS.

SHOTGUN MICROPHONE—A long microphone capable of picking up sound over a great distance, often used in outdoor scenes or large sets.

SHOTGUNS—A scattered or dispersed campaign; in broadcasting, a scatter plan of commercials that are broadcast throughout the day.

SIGNAL—An electrical impulse representing sound.

SIGNAL FLOW—In a sound studio, this is the prescribed patch followed by audio signals.

SIGNAL-TO-NOISE RATIO—The ratio of the power of a desired communications signal to unwanted noise; the higher the signal-to-noise ration, the better the sound.

SLATE—An audio billboard; an identification at the beginning of an audiotape, such as a brief designation of the news event, the reporter, the number of the take, or a countdown such as "three, two, one."

SLIP CUE—A method of starting a record at its proper speed so that the first few seconds are not too slow; the technique, also called slip start, is simply to let the turntable rotate at full speed while the record is held in place and released when needed on cue.

SOFTWARE—Instruction programs and other material used in the operation of computers, as distinguished from the hardware or computer machinery.

SOLO—Used when more than one channel is being mixed to listen to as a single track of a tape or a single audio source without hearing the other channels or interfering with the mix.

SOUND—The sensation of hearing produced by vibratory waves.

SOUND CHAIN—The route that sounds take from their source to their destination and any manipulation (processing) along the way.

SOUND EFFECTS (SE, S.E., SFX, or S.F.X.)—Animal, traffic, weather, and other sound sources other than dialogue and music, produced from an actual source or artificially, for use in broadcast or other production.

SOUND EFFECTS TRUCK—A device with three or four turntables and a mixer for controlling those sounds that were on record and other sounds impossible to create realistically in a studio.

SPLICE FINDER—A device that first erases the entire tape and then stops the erased cart at a point just beyond where the two ends of the continuous tape loop are spliced or joined together.

SPLICING TAPE (pressure sensitive)— Tape used to manually join together tape.

SPOT—Advertising time purchased on an individual basis as compared to a multi-station network or other national purchase; the broadcast announcement itself is called a spot or spot announcement.

STUDIO—The room in which the artist or audio producer works with facilities and other production devices.

SUPPLY REEL—A feed or storage reel on a reel-to-reel tape recorder; also called A-reel or feed reel.

SUSTAINING PROGRAMMING— Nonsponsored broadcast, generally public service.

SYNCHRONIZATION—Simultaneous; having the same period between movements.

T

TAKE-UP REEL—The receiving reel on a reel-to-reel tape player.

TALENT—Performers and other creative people such as writers and directors.

TALKBACK—A communication system within an audio or video studio linking the control room with people in the studio.

TALK-BASED—Radio programming format that dominates AM programming.

TAPE EDITING—The act of physically cutting and splicing the tape.

TAPE TRANSPORT—The system responsible for the tape passing by the head at a steady and standard speed.

TARGET AUDIENCE—The recipient of a communication; the specific, primary, most important group (audience) sought by the communicator.

TEMPO—Speed of the music.

THRESHOLD OF FEELING— Approximately 118 dB.

THRESHOLD OF HEARING—For most people is placed at 0 dB.

THRESHOLD OF PAIN—Near 140 dB.

TIGHT PRODUCTION—The act of transition from one audio source to the next without a pause.

TIMBRE—Quality.

TRACK—A single line of recorded sound; in making a record, each microphone produces a separate track that then is mixed with others; a single cut or piece of music on a record also is called a track.

TRAFFIC DEPARTMENT— Department in an advertising agency or broadcasting station that maintains the daily broadcast log and production schedules to keep work "moving" on schedule.

TRANSCRIPTIONS—A reproduction of a soundtrack on disk or tape.

TRANSDUCERS—A device that transmits energy from one system to another or converts energy from one form to another, such as from acoustic, magnetic, or mechanical energy into electrical energy in a microphone, loudspeaker, or other equipment.

TREATMENT—A prose account of a story outline that precedes the actual script; a proposal that shows how the writer plans to treat the story with the full script.

TRIM POT—A small volume control between the input selector and the fader.

TSL—Transmitter-to-studio link.

TWEETERS—An assembly of two or more loudspeakers or one large speaker for reproducing high frequency sounds.

U

UNDERWRITING—The granting of money to nonprofit, public broadcasting services by companies (underwriters) who receive identification on the programs.

UNIDIRECTIONAL MICROPHONE— Microphone allows sound to mostly enter from the front of the microphone by canceling out some of the sound from the sides and back; the more common of this type is called a cardioid microphone.

URBAN CONTEMPORARY—Radio programming music primarily aimed for black audiences.

V

VELOCITY—The actual speed a wave travels.

VELOCITY MICROPHONE—*See* RIBBON MICROPHONE.

VOLUME—Describes the amplitude or loudness of a sound.

VOLUME UNIT METER (or VU METER)—Provides a visual objective reading of an audio signal's average strength in discrete volume units; this allows the producer to depend on the audio console to indicate when signals are too strong or too weak in order to avoid distortion, overlap, or loss of sound levels.

W

WAVEFORM—A graphic representation of a sound's characteristic shape that is usually displayed on test equipment.

WAVELENGTH—The actual distance between the beginning and end of a cycle.

WIND SCREEN—A piece of metal, sponge foam, or mesh placed over a microphone to muddle the sound of wind in an outdoor location; also used on microphones that will be used close to an announcer's mouth or a woodwind musical instrument; sometimes called a pop or blast filter.

WIRELESS—Telegraphy by radio and without wires; a message sent with electromagnetic waves.

WIRELESS MICROPHONE—Uses a small radio transmitter to replace the connecting cable and thus provides greater mobility.

WIRE SERVICES—A news service, such as The Associated Press or United Press International, that transmits primarily by wire.

WOOFERS—An assembly of two or more loudspeakers or one large speaker for reproducing low frequency sounds.

WRAP AROUND—The introductory and concluding segments of a program or series; the live portion before and after a taped segment.

X

XLR—A three-pronged connector of cables.

Z

ZERO VU—Considered the standard operating level or the reference for proper volume.

I N D E X